Thinking the Unthinkable

Thinking the Unthinkable

THE LIVES OF ROYAL AIR FORCE AND EAST GERMAN FAST-JET PILOTS IN THE COLD WAR

Nigel Walpole

ASTONBRIDGE PUBLISHING

By the same author:

Swift Justice
Seek and Strike
Best of Breed
Voodoo Warriors
Dragon Rampant
Built to Endure
Swift – From the Cockpit

First published in Great Britain in 2012 by Astonbridge Publishing

ISBN 978-0-9537933-2-7

Produced by
The Choir Press, Gloucester

Contents

Acknowledgements and Tributes

This exploration into Cold War heritage would not have seen the light of day without the dedicated help of those who arranged access to new friends in the former German Democratic Republic (GDR), helped carry out detailed research there and acted as interpreters. They included my old friends Oberst Gert Overhoff and Oberst Leutnants Horst Wilhelms, Klaus Kropf and Heribert Mennen, all former officers in NATO's German Air Force (GAF). What follows is a list of the other main contributors to 'Thinking the Unthinkable' – and I apologise for any omissions.

Generalleutnant Klaus-Jürgen Baarß; Hans-J Barakling; Mike Barton; Michael Baumgart; Jörg Behnke; Ben Bennett; Frank Born; Rex Boulton; Air Cdre Dennis Caldwell; Martin Common; Dr Alan Curry; Andreas Dietrich; Dick Doleman; Nigel Eastaway; Tom Eeles; Joachim Faber; Gunter Fichte; Lutz Freunt; Helmut Friz; Hansjorg Goetz; Jürgen Gruhl; David Harrigan; Hans-Joachim Hartwig; Malcolm Hellings; Norbert Hess; Ralf Hinkemeyer; Andreas Hofmann; Rudolf Just; Gunther Kipp; Harald Lares; 'Benny' Luther; Air Marshal Ian Macfadyen; Hannes Mallwitz; Holger Müller; Peter Müller; Rudolf Müller; Air Cdre John Nevill; Erwin Nützmann; Barrie Palmer; 'Gerd P'; Air Cdre Rick Peacock-Edwards; Peter Peil, Andrew Pennington; Air Cdre Graham Pitchfork; Udo Reinsch; Edgar Reuber; Hartwig Richter; Doug Robb; Jim Sawyer; Frank-Helmut Scheder; Frank Scholze; Klaus Schmiedel; Ken Senar; Uwe Senf; Mike Shaw; Dusan Schneider; Frank Schulz; Armin Schulz; Manfred Skeries; Brian Skillicorn; Bob Snare; Gerd Tonnerson-Hoffman; Michael Wegerich; Joachim Went; Maj Gen. Peter Williams and Jerry Wilmot.

Finally, this work owes much to my Dutch wife, Margreet, who followed me faithfully throughout Europe as my secretary and interpreter, scrutinised my use of the English language and saw me through difficult times with equal measures of criticism and encouragement.

To the best of my knowledge, this work contains no material which is subject to copyright.

Tribute

This book is dedicated to Oberst Leutnant Horst Wilhelms, GAF (Ret'd), a typical 'Cold War Warrior' and invaluable member of our research team, who died in January 2012, and to all those on both sides of the 'Iron Curtain' who did their duty during the Cold War.

Glossary

AAA: Anti-Aircraft Artillery
AAFCE: Allied Air Forces Central Europe
AAM: Air-to-Air Missile
AAR: Air-to-Air Refuelling
AB: Air Base
ACB: Airfield Construction Branch
ADIZ: Air Defence Identification Zone
ADR: Airfield Damage Repair
AEW: Airborne Early Warning
AFCENT: Allied Forces Central Europe
AFTS: Advanced Flying Training School
AFV: Armoured Fighting Vehicle
agl/asl: Above Ground/Sea Level
AI: Airborne Interception/Air Interdiction
Air Cdre: Air Commodore (Brigadegeneral)
AM: Air Marshal (Generalleutnant)
ACM: Air Chief Marshal (General)
AOB: Air Order of Battle
APC: Armament Practice Camp
AR: Anti-Radar
ARM: Anti-Radar Missile
ASM: Air-To-Surface Missile/Airfield Survival
    Measures
ATAF: Allied Tactical Air Force
ATOC: Allied Tactical Operations Centre
ATC: Air Traffic Control/Air Training Corps
AVM: Air Vice-Marshal (Generalmajor)
AWACS: Airborne Warning and Control System
BAF: Belgian Air Force
BAFO: British Air Forces of Occupation
BAOR: British Army of the Rhine

BFTS: Basic Flying Training School
BMEWS: Ballistic Missile Warning System
BRIXMIS: British C-in-Chief Mission to Soviet
    Forces in Germany
BVR: Beyond Visual range
C & R: Control & Reporting
CAP: Combat Air Patrol
CAS: Close Air Support
C3I: Command, Control, Communications &
    Intelligence
CBU: Cluster Bomb Unit
CENTAG: Central Army Group
CFS: Central Flying School
CO: Commanding Officer
COC: Combat Operations Centre
CAP: Combat Air Patrol
CPX: Command Post Exercise
CR: Central Region/Combat Ready
CRC: Control and Reporting Centre
DACT: Dissimilar Air Combat Training
DF/GA: Day Fighter/Ground-Attack
DHS: Diensthabendes System (QRA)
DME: Distance Measuring Equipment
ECM: Electronic Counter-Measures
ECCM: Electronic Counter Counter-Measures
EDC: European Defence Community
EGAF: East German Air Force
ETA: Estimated Time of Arrival
EW: Electronic Warfare
FAC: Forward Air Controller
FAF: French Air Force

FAG: Fliegerausbildungsgeschwader (Flying School)

FBW: Fighter-Bomber Wing

FD: Fliegerdivision (Air Division)

FEZ: Fighter Engagement Zone

FG: Fliegergeschwader (Flying Wing)

FGA: Fighter/Ground-Attack

Fg Off: Flying Officer (Oltn)

Flt Lt: Flight Lieutenant (Hptm)

FO-FAFK: Führungsorgan der Front -und Armeefliegerkräfte (Frontal and Army Air Force)

FO-FMTFK: Führungsorgan Front-und Militärtransportfliegerkräfte (Frontal Forces and Transport Command)

FOD: Foreign Object Damage

FOL: Forward Operating Location

FR: Fighter Reconnaissance

FRA: First Run Attack

FRB: Fla-Raketen-Brigade (SAM Brigade)

FRR: Fla-Raketen-Regiment (SAM Regiment)

FRG: Federal Republic of Germany

FR: Fighter Reconnaissance

FTS: Flying Training School

FTX: Field Training Exercise

FuTB: Radar Technical Battalion

FuTK: Radar Technical Kompanie (Radar Company)

GAF: German Air Force (NATO)

GCA: Ground Controlled Approach

GCI: Ground Controlled Interception

GDA: Gun Defended Area

GDR: German Democratic Republic

GFS/GS: Gefechtsstand (Operations Centre)

GLO: Ground Liaison Officer

GSFG: Group of Soviet Forces in Germany

Gp Capt: Group Captain (Oberst)

GSM: General Situation Map

GST: Gesellschaft für Sport und Technik (Pre-military training programme)

HAG: Helicopter Flying Training Wing

HAS: Hardened Aircraft Shelter

HE: High Explosive

HG: Hubschraubergeschwader (Helicopter Wing)

HIMEZ: High Missile Engagement Zone

hp: Horsepower

Hptm: Captain (Flt Lt)

HUD: Head-Up Display

IADS: Integrated Air Defence System

ICBM: Intercontinental Ballistic Missile

IDF: Interceptor Day Fighter

IFF: Identification Friend or Foe

IGB: Inner German Border

ILS: Instrument Landing System

IMC: Instrument Meteorological Conditions

IR: Infra Red

IRE: Instrument Rating Examiner

IRH: Infra-Red Homing

IRT: Instrument Rating Test

IRLS: Infra-Red Linescan

JG: Jagdfliegergeschwader (Fighter Wing)

JAG: Jagdfliegerausbildungsgeschwader (Fighter Training Wing)

JBG: Jagdbombenfliegergeschwader (Fighter-Bomber Wing)

JS: Jagdstaffel (Fighter Squadron)

JLS: Jägerleitstelle (Fighter Control Unit)

KHG: Kampfhubschraubergeschwader (Attack Helicopter Wing)

KVP: Kasernierte Volkspolizei (Police Barracks)

LAA: Light Anti-Aircraft

LABS: Low Angle Bombing System

LARS: Low Altitude Radar System

LaSK: Landstreitkräfte (Army)

LAZUR: Automated Command Guidance System

LCR: Limited Combat Ready

LFA: Low Flying Area

LGB: Laser Guided Bomb

LK: Leistungsklasse (Skills classification)

LLADS: Low Level Air Defence System

LOMEZ: Low Missile Engage Zone

LSK: Luftstreitkräfte (Air Force)

LSZ: Luftschiffzone (Air Weapons Range)

LSK/LV: Luftstreitkräfte/Luftverteidigung (Air Force/Air Defence)

Ltn: Second Lieutenant (Plt Off)

LVD: Luftverteidigungsdivision (Air Division)

MAD: Mutual Assured Destruction

Maj: Major (Sqn Ldr)

MEZ: Missile Engagement Zone

MFG: Marinefliegergeschwader (Naval Wing)

MHG: Marinehubschraubergeschwader (Naval Helicopter Wing)

MFPU: Mobile Field Processing Unit

MOB: Main Operating Base

MPC: Missile Practice Camp

MRS: Mission Restriction Sign

NATO: North Atlantic Treaty Organisation

N/AW: Night/All-Weather

NBC: Nuclear, Biological & Chemical

NDB: Non-Directional Beacon (Nav Aid)

NF: Night Fighter

NCO: Non-Commissioned Officer

NKVD: Soviet Secret Police

NL: Netherlands

NORTHAG: Northern Army Group

NOTAMS: Notes to Airmen

NVA: Nationale Volksarmee

NVG: Night Vision Goggles

OAZ: Operative Ausbildungszentrale (Exercise facility: 'Swimming Pool')

Oberst: Colonel (Gp Capt)

OC: Officer Commanding

OCA: Offensive Counter Air

OCU: Operational Conversion Unit

OHS: Offiziershochschule (Officers' School)

Oltn: First Lieutenant (Fg Off)

OPCON: Operational Control

OSL: Lieutenant Colonel (Wg Cdr)

OTR: Operational Turn Round

PAR: Precision Approach Radar

PBF: Pilot Briefing Facility

PGM: Precision Guided Missile

Plt Off: Pilot Officer (Ltn)

PI: Practice Interception/Photo Interpreter

pps: Pulses Per Second

PR: Photo Reconnaissance

PRA: Permanent Restricted Area

prf: Pulse Recurrence Frequency

PSP: Pierced Steel Planking

PUNCAS: Pre-Positioning of Material Configured in Unit Sets

QFI: Qualified Flying Instructor

QWI: Qualified Weapons Instructor

QRA: Quick Reaction Alert

RAP: Recognised Air Picture

RAF: Royal Air Force

RAFG: RAF Germany

RCAF: Royal Canadian Air Force

RE: Royal Engineers

RN: Royal Navy

RNLAF: Royal Netherlands Air Force

RoE: Rules of Engagement

rpm: revolutions per minute

RRR: Rapid Runway Repair

RWR: Radar Warning Receiver

RSBN/RSDN: Soviet Navigation Aids

RSO: Range Safety Officer

RTB: Return to Base

SAR: Search and Rescue

SARH: Semi-Active Radar Homing

SAM: Surface-to-Air Missile

SACEUR: Supreme Allied Commander Europe

SAU: Systema Awtomaitscheskowo Oprawlenija (Automatic approach aid)

SHORAD: Short Range Air Defence

SATCO: Senior Air Traffic Control Officer

SEA: South East Asia

SEAD: Suppression of Enemy Air Defences

SEATO: South East Asia Treaty Organisation

SED: Sozialistische Einheitspartei Deutschlands (Socialist Party)

SHAPE: Supreme Headquarters Allied Powers Europe

SHORAD: Short Range Air Defence

SIF: Selective Identification Feature (In connection with IFF)

SLAR: Sideways Looking Airborne Radar

SOC: Sector Operations Centre

SOP: Standard Operating Procedure
SOXMIS: Soviet Mission in West Germany
Sqn Ldr: Squadron Leader (Major)
SSM: Surface-to-Surface Missile
SSR: Secondary Surveillance Radar
STOL: Short Take-Off and Landing
SU: Signals Unit
TACAN: Tactical Air Navigation (Aid)
Taceval: Tactical Evaluation
Tac recce: Tactical Reconnaissance
TACS: Tactical Air Control System
TAFS: Taktische Aufklärungsfliegerstaffel
(Tactical Recce Squadron)
TAS: Transportfliegergeschwader (Air Transport
Wing)
TLP: Tactical Leadership Programme
TTW: Transition to War
TWU: Tactical Weapons Unit
UAV: Unmanned Air Vehicle
UK: United Kingdom
UN: United Nations

USAF: United States Air Force
VFR: Visual Flight Rules
VIP: Very Important Person
VMC: Visual Meteorological Conditions
VOPO: East German Police
VPL: Volkspolizei Luft (Air Police)
VSTOL: Vertical and Short Take-Off and
Landing
WEU: Western European Union
Wg Cdr: Wing Commander (Lt Col/OSL)
WO: Warrant Officer
WRAF: Women's Royal Air Force
WW1/WW2: World War One/Two
ZDK: Zieldarstellungskette (Target Towing
Flight)
2TAF: Second Tactical Air Force (RAF)
2ATAF: Second Allied Tactical Air Force
4ATAF: Fourth Allied Tactical Air Force
ZDS: Zieldarstellungsstaffel (Target Towing
Squadron)

Foreword

Oberst a.D Gert Overhoff

I am pleased to add my tribute to the combat pilots at the 'sharp end', on both sides of the Iron Curtain in Germany during the Cold War. 'Thinking the Unthinkable' is unique, in that it looks through their eyes at their lives in the air and on the ground, at work and play, as they faced each other across the Inner German Border. Sheer practicalities limited the scope of this work to two microcosms of the Warsaw Pact and NATO: the East German Air Force and the Royal Air Force in Germany, but they provide good examples of how air power was orchestrated within the two great defence alliances – without losing all national identities. This is not the work of a single author, but an amalgam of personal testimonies from both sides, mixed with historical details obtained from the archives; it does not pretend to be an intellectual discourse on the Cold War.

As a career officer and fast-jet pilot in the West German Luftwaffe throughout the Cold War, I got to know the RAF and the author well within the NATO community. He and I had similar backgrounds, he flying air defence Hunters, fighter reconnaissance Swifts and strike/attack Jaguars on the front line in Germany, while I did likewise in the F-86, F-104 and Tornado. I was also deeply involved in the dissolution of the East German Air Force, and became closely associated with both services again in the production of this book, so I feel able to commend its contribution to our heritage.

Gert Overhoff

Preface

An eerie silence descended over the windswept airfields of Bentwaters and Woodbridge in south-east England on that cold dawn in October 1962, leaden skies adding to the sombre mood of the pilots at cockpit readiness aboard some 48 single-seat, all-weather F-101 Voodoo fighter-bombers, and the crew chiefs sheltering from the chill east wind beneath their aircraft. Each aircraft was loaded with a nuclear bomb – and this was no exercise. The men and women of the USAF's 81st Tactical Fighter Wing, together with thousands of others on both sides of the Iron Curtain who were similarly involved in Cold War deterrence, were left with their own thoughts as they waited quietly and anxiously for Kennedy and Khruschev to end their war of words in the dangerous game of 'brinkmanship' over the Cuban missile crisis. The result was crucial; it would either send the Voodoo warriors deep into Eastern Europe, helping to pitch the whole Continent into war – and probably Armageddon – or allow the crews back to warm coffee bars. What were these pilots thinking, as they sat alone in their cockpits: the mission, the weather, 'the bomb', the return trip (if any), their wives, children ...; perhaps they were doing their best not to 'think the unthinkable' – and were they any different from the nuclear bomber pilots on standby behind the Iron Curtain?

My interest in what was going on, 'on the other side', goes back to my first operational flight in a brand new Hunter F.4 of No.26 (Fighter) Squadron at Royal Air Force (RAF) Oldenburg on 25 November 1954, as I burst through the overcast which covered the North German Plain into the clear blue sky above. There I was greeted by the evocative sight of myriad contrails as jet fighters from several North Atlantic Treaty Organisation (NATO) nations weaved their seemingly illogical patterns above. More would be combatants replaced those who left the fray, either exhilarated or exasperated, depending on their performance; some of the newcomers tracing white 'tramlines' from the US and Canadian bases in south Germany, and from Dutch and Belgium airfields in the west, every man fancying his chances against the other. A complete absence of contrails over the Inner German Border (IGB), which, *inter alia*, defined the 'no go' airspace separating the NATO forces from those of the Warsaw Pact in the east, where the Soviet contrails were also clearly visible to us, as the early MiGs cavorted across the sky. Those on the ground below me could not see what I saw from 45,000 ft (13,600 m) – an early manifestation of the Cold War in North Germany.

My interest in military aviation predates that memorable experience by some 15 years, to 1940 when I watched the Spitfires and Hurricanes launch from nearby RAF North Weald to do battle with the Luftwaffe over London, and saw the results in the air and on the ground. I am sure that it was this which moved me to join the RAF in 1951, to train as a fighter pilot, and while doing so I paid scant regard to the life and ways of our potential adversaries. However, when operational, command and staff responsibilities came along later, it became increasingly important to learn about the military men and women we might face in war – and their war fighting capabilities. One might have expected this interest to cease with the end of the Cold War – but on the contrary.

I had already decided that, in retirement, I would undertake certain heritage projects which would not only pay tribute to those who served in the Cold War, but might also generate small contributions to military charities. This led, over the following twenty years, to the publication of eight books and many articles on military aviation during that era, but all the while I nurtured the idea of bringing together the lives of combat pilots on the two sides of the 'Iron Curtain' – the very men I watched in the sky above Germany back in 1955 (and on many other occasions thereafter). With the end of the Cold War, and the help of friends and colleagues in the (West) German Air Force, I was able to get to know a large number of former combat pilots and their controllers from the 'Luftstreitkräfte' (LSK), the East German Air Force (EGAF), within the Nationale Volksarmee (NVA), also to visit many of their old bases, and those of the Soviet Air Force, once homes for the Group of Soviet Forces in Germany (GSFG), in the now defunct GDR. So it was, that beginning in 1999, 'Thinking the Unthinkable' began to take shape.

For this book, I have drawn predominantly on the personal testimonies of front line pilots, mainly from those in the ranks of colonel (Oberst) and below, highlighting their times in the air and on the ground, at work and play, using the EGAF and the RAF as microcosms of their respective alliances, NATO and the Warsaw Pact. Sheer practicalities precluded the option of drawing on the experiences of what might be called the 'team leaders', the Soviet Air Force (Warsaw Pact) and the United States Air Force (NATO). We saw the Cold War from the front line, arguably from rather narrow perspectives, but I make no excuse for that, nor for indulging myself with a few guarded views of my own on some of the realities which I believe might have been overlooked within the more convenient assumptions which helped shape the way we at the 'sharp end' contributed to 'deterrence'. I must make it very clear that any views expressed or implied in what follows are entirely my own, or those of contributors to this text, and not of any political or military 'establishment'.

Perhaps I started out with the hope of comparing the lives of airmen on the front line within the two groupings, but this naive idea soon succumbed to the reality that the two systems were too dissimilar for sensible comparison. Also, I readily accept that this work is far from comprehensive; it can do no more than touch on a number of salient features of those troubled times in a limited field, and then only in as far as they affected the two air forces. From the outset, I assured all those who were good enough to join me in this task that I would not dwell on the ideologies and politics which were at the very core of the tensions between East and West, although these must be mentioned from time to time, where they impacted on military preparations. Moreover, I have, in the main, avoided the temptation to criticise too overtly some of the strategies, tactics and thus training methods adopted by the two sides, or some of the arguable intelligence assumptions on which they may have been based. I would like to think that I have, for the most part, reported only on the 'facts' as they were given to me, but of course I cannot guarantee the veracity of these 'facts'; typically, figures on aircraft and weapons performance have, in some cases, varied widely between written sources and verbal opinion.

There were those who, for diverse reasons, tried to persuade me not to attempt this tribute to our 'Cold War warriors', fearing that I would not gain full access to the truth in the East, given that vestiges of old ideologies and pride do remain and might obscure some of the facts, that memories have faded with time and that much could be lost in imperfect translations from German to English. Fair comment, but others, on both sides of the Iron Curtain, took the more positive view that, imperfections notwithstanding, this was a part of our heritage which deserved to be recorded, and by those who would have had to bear the brunt of any initial hostilities had deterrence failed, and it was this argument which I found most persuasive. I apologise to all my new friends who spoke only German and Russian throughout the Cold War, for any misunderstandings, misquotes or comments out of context; translation, interpretation and language difficulties having been a perennial problem throughout. I did have the advantage of understanding the mutual, professional language common to all 'fast-jet' pilots. In my 38 years of service as an RAF pilot, I flew air defence fighters, was part of the Fighter Command Tactical Evaluation (Taceval) team, commanded a fighter reconnaissance (FR) squadron, a fighter/ground-attack (FGA) squadron and a maritime strike/attack squadron, and was Wing Commander Operations on the Jaguar Strike Wing. Most of my operational flying was in Germany and in my five years as the Assistant Chief of Staff Operations (Offensive), at NATO's Second Allied Tactical Air Force (2ATAF), I was deeply involved in contingency planning and rehearsing retaliatory operations should they be needed in North Germany. It was then that my interest in the Pact forces, on the ground and in the air, in that region, was at its greatest.

'Thinking the Unthinkable' is no literary gem, nor is it an intellectual polemic on the

Cold War, its political background, causes, aims or objectives; it has no 'axe to grind', and no attempt is made to suggest which pilot or aircraft would have prevailed against another. There are no definitive conclusions – they are left to the reader – in what is merely a word picture of the life and times of two specific, opposing air forces in the Cold War, in a text which seeks only to provide food for thought in a cursory overview of two great defence alliances, seen through the eyes of some who served on the front line in Germany. That said, it is reasonable to postulate that hostilities, once started, could have escalated rapidly through a conventional phase into tactical nuclear warfare, and thence to the use of strategic nuclear weapons – in an all-out war from which there would have been no winners. That peace prevailed is usually attributed to a sensible realisation within the Warsaw Pact and NATO hierarchies, that each side could annihilate the other in a massive exchange of strategic nuclear weapons, in 'Mutually Assured Destruction' (MAD). However, 'deterrence' was made up of many parts – and it is to the airmen of two specific, opposing tactical air forces that this tribute has been written.

It is important to realise that air operations are heavily dependent, directly or indirectly on myriad support agencies, some more obvious and visible than others, often working tirelessly with little recognition or praise. In this context, the air traffic and fighter controllers are recognised in Chapter Five, but limited space precludes more than a mention of the many others, including those within aircraft maintenance, transport, supply, catering, administrative, fire and medical support – and that is a matter of regret.

I knew some of the Voodoo pilots who sat quietly with their thoughts for those long hours during the Cuban Crisis of 1962, because I had served with them on an exchange posting in South Carolina, so I was with them in spirit – thinking the unthinkable.

Chapter One

Tensions

An Iron Curtain has descended across the Continent
Winston S Churchill, 1946

In 1945, with a world tired of war, there was a great deal of well justified admiration for the manner in which the Russians had resisted the all-powerful German army and air force, most spectacularly at Stalingrad. 'Uncle Joe' Stalin was high on the popularity list of Allied leaders, and 'Joe for King' could be seen scrawled across the walls of London. General Eisenhower, the Supreme Allied Commander in Europe (SACEUR), went as far as to suggest that nothing mattered more to post-war Russia than friendship with the USA, and this desire showed signs of being reciprocated. For most, earlier fears of communism appeared to have dissipated, and it was hoped that the Soviet Union would adopt a form of democracy which was not far removed from that practised in the United Kingdom (UK). As if to meet this half way, in the wake of disastrous capitalist policies in the 1930s, the UK seemed to be marching inexorably towards socialism. Promises of a Utopian new world of central planning and state control, coupled with the benefits of a planned economy and a welfare state anticipated, were winning the day, and there was even talk of an Anglo-Soviet Alliance. US President Roosevelt was also optimistic that the relatively good wartime relationships with Russia would persist thereafter, allowing harmonious agreements over the future of post-war Germany. Indeed, he is quoted as saying: 'I think that if I give him (Stalin) everything I possibly can and ask nothing from him in return, *noblesse oblige,* he won't try to annex anything and will work with me for a world of democracy and peace'. Within months, Roosevelt was dead, and would never know how wrong he had been.

Those who yearned for peace and the good times were only too happy to see grounds for optimism following early signs of harmony during the 'Big Three' Conference (Roosevelt, Stalin and Churchill), at Yalta in February 1945, three months before the war ended in Europe. It was there that the foundations were laid for administering a de-nazified and demilitarized Germany, divided into US, Soviet, British and French zones, and Russia would become a member of the United Nations (UN); East European countries would have free elections and the general principles of war reparations were agreed. On the face of it, all seemed set fair for the way ahead, but in the following five months, President Truman replaced Roosevelt, while Prime Minister Attlee took over from Churchill in a landslide victory for the UK Socialist Party over the Conservatives, and it was a very different story when the two new leaders met Stalin at Potsdam in July 1945, to put meat on the bones of the framework agreed at Yalta. Here, there was a noticeable cooling in relationships, with Truman taking a firmer line and angering Stalin by failing to reveal to him (what he already knew) that the US had the atomic bomb. There were acrimonious exchanges over zone boundaries, excessive Soviet demands for war reparations and Russian interference in the internal affairs of its East European neighbours, especially in Poland, where the Russians helped to install a communist government and, unilaterally, enforced changes in its national frontiers. It was now very clear that they were bent on creating an effective buffer between the Soviet Union and Western Europe, in what would be 'master and servant' relationships, while Turkey was subjected to a war of words accompanying Soviet demands that their ships be allowed access to the Mediterranean through the Dardanelles.

A few lone voices in the West continued to spell out the realities of the time. From the opposition benches Winston Churchill remained strident in his claims that the Allies were being lulled into a false sense of security, and that Soviet Russia would take advantage of any political or military weakness among the occupying powers. In a prophetic speech 'Sinews of Peace', at Westminster College, Missouri, on 5 May 1946, Churchill observed, most aptly: 'From Stettin in the Baltic, to Trieste in the Adriatic, an Iron Curtain has descended across the Continent'. As a result, great European nations in the east now lay in the Soviet sphere, all subject to increasing influence from Moscow. Churchill's warnings were barely heard above a clamouring for the fruits of peace, as the Western Allies continued to carry out speedy and massive reductions in their military forces in Europe.

Churchill did have important supporters. The eminent US diplomat George Kennan, who had lived in Moscow since 1933 and was an authority on Russian matters, also warned of an enduring incompatibility between Soviet and Western cultures, thinking and systems of government. Having been invaded from the west in 1812, 1914 and 1941, the Russians had an innate mistrust of European powers, this sense of insecurity prescribing all their words and deeds; indeed, in the aftermath of World War 1 (WW1), Lenin warned that their nation was subject to an 'antagonistic capitalist encirclement'. With this mind set, Kennan argued that, in the long run, there could be no peaceful co-existence, and postulated a separate Anglo-American agreement over Germany, within a Europe partitioned between Russia and the Western partners, with the perhaps naive hope that neither would intrude on the other. He said as much in what became known as his 'Long Telegram' (8,000 words) to Washington on 22 February 1946, entitled 'Sources of

Soviet Conduct', in which his reaction to developments in the Russian psyche were direct and unequivocal. He rationalised that the primary determinant of Russian foreign policy was that long held feeling of insecurity, coupled now with a pathological fear that, if exposed to the rest of the world, its people would become so restless that they would question the very ideology of communism and thereby undermine all its internal and external policies. He claimed that genuine compacts and compromise were not part of Stalin's vocabulary, and that the new creed of overt communism made the traditional Soviet neurosis of insecurity even more dangerous. Every divisive means could now be expected in the Kremlin's expansionist policy and crusade to spread the Kremlin's dogma of communism, no stone left unturned in pitting the capitalist nations against each other, seeking internal unrest, racial and social conflict; there would be no holds barred, with military and civil violence and every destructive means used to promote communism world-wide. This was strong, unpalatable stuff, but what followed seemed to support the central thesis. The Soviet Union reacted with the shorter, but equally disturbing 'Novikov' telegram, which claimed that the US was in the grip of monopoly capitalists, building up a military capability 'to prepare the conditions for winning world supremacy in a new war'. The diplomatic temperature was rising.

There were transient signs of give and take, with the Russians allowing such early concessions as the inclusion of some opposition voices in the governments of Bulgaria and Romania, and agreeing in principle to the creation of a UN body to control atomic energy. Finland escaped the extremes of Soviet influence, being 'allowed' a mixed economy and free institutions while, in a rare mood of conciliation, Russia reduced its efforts to subjugate Iran. However, perceptive analysis might conclude that these were merely tactics with ulterior motives, each a means to an end, in a perpetual game of confrontation and appeasement, opportunism and conciliation, of co-existence, pluralism and totalitarianism, as circumstances and reaction in the West allowed. In the end, each of the East European countries succumbed to the pressures from Moscow, becoming either Soviet Socialist Republics or satellite states. So far, hostilities were limited to a war of words, but Stalin was becoming ever more bellicose, even mooting the possibility of an 'imperialist' war with the capitalist world, thereby racking up international tensions. This was the 'Cold War'.

The term 'Cold War' might be attributed to the British satirist George Orwell, who used it in his work entitled 'You and the Atomic Bomb', published in October 1945 to describe a period of 'peace that is no peace', an ideological confrontation between the Soviet Union on behalf of communism and the largely capitalist West. Being most appropriate, the expression was taken up and used widely, typically by US presidential advisor Bernard Baruch in his 1947 speech in South Carolina 'Let us not be deceived ...', and by columnist Walter Lippmann in his book 'Cold War' (1947).

Some claim that the Cold War had its origins back in the middle of the nineteenth century, as relationships between the Russian Empire and the other nations in Europe deteriorated, or at the end of WWI with the Bolshevik Revolution, when Lenin proclaimed that the Soviet Union was surrounded by hostile capitalist states. However, it is generally accepted that it began in earnest in the immediate wake of WW2, and was in full swing from the late 1940s.

Slowly, the West awoke from its post-war lethargy, with the realisation that the Soviet Union and its satellites could back the spread of communism with a total (conventional) military force three times the size of that of the Allies in Europe, and that this required a very positive response. The implications were clear and unwelcome; a more robust stance would require a massive rearmament programme, with all the attendant expenditure, together with an indefinite US presence world-wide. America accepted that the European nations would need a great deal of help if they were to contribute to the containment of communism, and 'containment' became a central plank of Western policy.

All this coincided with a critical point in the Greek civil war, in which there was now a grave danger that the communists would gain the upper hand just when the UK had finally decided that it could no longer support the legitimate government in Greece financially. With perhaps a similar fate awaiting Turkey, and the stability of the whole region at risk, it was time to put the policy of containment to the test, and

America rose to the occasion. In March 1947 the US Congress approved a $400 million package of aid to Greece and Turkey, within the 'Truman Doctrine', which sought to: 'support free peoples who are resisting attempted subjugation by armed minorities or by outside pressures'. Then, in June 1947, came the 'Marshall Plan', which pledged economic assistance for all European countries which participated, including Russia. The latter declined the offer, probably on the grounds that economic integration with the West might prejudice Soviet control, and even seduce Eastern Bloc nations into the Western camp; it countered by launching the 'Molotov Plan', later to become the 'Comecon' (Council for Mutual Economic Assistance). The Marshall Plan had a huge impact on the European economy, *inter alia* helping to deter pro-communist factions in several countries from ousting their legitimate governments – Greece and Italy being prime examples of its success within the context of the Truman Doctrine. This brought another Soviet response, with the establishment, in September 1947, of the 'Cominform', a version of the Communist International ('Comintern'), which had been dissolved in 1943; this was intended to resurrect the flow of information between the communist parties of the USSR, Bulgaria, Czechoslovakia, Poland, Hungary, Yugoslavia, and (interestingly) France and Italy. Although sometimes likened to NATO, Cominform was little more than another means of promoting ideological orthodoxy in pursuance of Soviet policies. Perhaps it was by this means, among others, that the Soviets sensed Czechoslovakian disaffection with communism in 1948, and pre-empted the 'free' elections there scheduled in May with a *coup d'état* in February. The remaining democratic institutions in the Eastern Bloc were then swept aside, albeit in 'bloodless' coups, about which the Western allies could do little; many of the anti-communist leaders were rounded up and imprisoned or deported.

In 1948, the Western Allies increased their attempts to revive the industry and economy of West Germany, by merging the American and British occupation zones, to come under a federal government, making good use of the Marshall Plan and introducing the *deutschmark* to replace the *reichsmark*. All these measures combined rapidly to produce the desired results, the implications of which did not go unnoticed in the East, perhaps helping to precipitate one of those trials of strength and potential flash points in the Cold War, which could have led to open hostilities. In late 1948, the Soviet Union began obstructing the Allies' right of passage along the overland corridors through Russian occupied East Germany to their sectors of Berlin, and this culminated, in 1948, in a full blockade of all ground routes to Berlin.

In order to break the siege, the Western Allies put together a Combined Allied Task Force (CALTF), a massive armada of predominantly American and British transport aircraft, the British contribution being 'Operation Plainfare'. This was an extraordinarily ambitious plan, not only because of the volume of cargo needed to sustain West Berlin, which included coal and oil, but also because there were few Allied airfields in Berlin or eastern West Germany able to handle the huge number of aircraft which would be needed. Accordingly, the RAF's Airfield Construction Branch (ACB) and American engineers, using local labour, toiled night and day, building or renovating runways and hardstandings, while installing all the necessary support facilities. The ACB comprised a small core of 'old hands' from WW2, a large number of junior officers, recently graduated from universities with degrees in chartered surveying or engineering, and RAF airmen on National Service. Having planned the work on airfields in Schleswig Holstein and close to the IGB (Sylt, Schleswig, Lübeck, Fassberg, Celle, Wunsdorf), these men then supervised a huge German workforce until each project was complete. Of necessity, the ACB was given its head, with very little interference from above, and as a result it achieved more than was asked of it through innovation, improvisation, individual initiatives, drive and collective endeavour, their work often continuing well into the airlift, but with no interruption to the flying programme. Initially, and in great haste, runways were constructed of WW2 Perforated Steel Platform (PSP) strips recovered from disused wartime airfields, often laid double on whatever suitable foundations were available, typically hardcore from Berlin bomb sites, overlaid with tarmac or asphalt. They were just adequate for the heavy transport aircraft, and as a basis for the new tactical aircraft then in the pipeline. The massive airlift underlined the Allies' determination to resist Soviet aggression – in any form, and the blockade was lifted in May 1949, the month in which the Federal Republic of Germany (FRG) was founded in the West, followed on 7 October 1949, by the establishment of the GDR.

Meanwhile, containment was being pursued with great vigour, as a political, economic and military buttress was created in Europe against the threat of communism. Britain, France, Holland, Belgium and Luxemburg had set up the Brussels Treaty in March 1948, making provision for military assistance to any member at risk, and with the addition of the US, Canada, Denmark, Norway, Italy, Portugal and Iceland, this developed, throughout 1949/50, into the fully established NATO. Of its 14 initial Articles, Article 5 was the most significant: 'that an attack on any one or more of the member nations be considered an attack upon them all'. In that event, all possible means, including military, would be brought to bear in order to restore peace in the Atlantic area covered by the treaty. The impoverished, war-torn Western Europe now had the comforting economic and military strength of America behind it, with US forces in place in Europe, and the deterrent protection of its huge nuclear 'umbrella'. NATO's military structure and defensive shield, with its complementary nuclear and conventional components, continued to develop, with Turkey and Greece joining in 1952, followed by the FRG and Italy in 1955.

Alarm bells were also ringing elsewhere in the world. In June 1950, communist armies in North Korea crossed the 38th Parallel into South Korea, in an attempt to unify their country by force. The UN was quick to condemn the action, and muster an international military force, led by the Americans, to counter the invasion. Further south, the Chinese communists, under Mao Tse Tung, had been busy driving the US-backed Chiang Kai-shek's Kuomintang Nationalist forces off the mainland, into exile on the island of Formosa (Taiwan), and tensions in South East Asia (SEA), dating back to 1946, were increasing. All this helped extend the West's policy of containment, world-wide, the Americans joining Japan, Australia, Thailand, the Philippines and New Zealand, in the South East Asia Treaty Organisation (SEATO), thereby providing them with contingency bases for their rapidly increasing air, sea and land forces.

It was the threat from communism and the Soviet Union which had brought the western nations together in cohesive defence alliances which, although wholly defensive in nature, Russia viewed with increasing alarm, and as a significant threat to its ambitions – at a time when the Eastern bloc faced internal turbulence. Stalin died in 1953, his close allies Molotov and Malenkov were marginalised, the head of the NKVD (Soviet Secret Police), Beria, was executed by his political rivals, and the new leader, Nikita Khrushchev, denounced Stalinist policies. Hopes that that there might now be a rapprochement with the West were soon dashed, when Khrushchev famously announced to Western ambassadors in Moscow, in November 1956: 'We will bury you!' To that end, the Russians had been far from idle in the first half of the 1950s; having exploded their first atomic bomb in October 1949, they set about creating a strong nuclear arsenal, while expanding their already huge conventional forces throughout the Eastern Bloc, and assisting materially in covert arrangements to arm the GDR.

Nineteen fifty-five was a particularly significant year in the Cold War. When West Germany became a full member of NATO, the Soviet Union responded with the creation of the Warsaw Pact, in which East Germany, Poland, Hungary, Albania, Romania, Czechoslovakia and Bulgaria joined the USSR in signing a 'Treaty of Friendship, Co-operation and Mutual Assistance'. The European nations, now armed to the teeth, faced each other, East against West, in two fully structured military alliances. At stake were two fundamental and extreme alternatives: peaceful co-existence or Armageddon.

That is the initial politico-military background against which two opposing air forces, the EGAF and RAF, within their respective alliances, began the Cold War in earnest.

Chapter Two

Birth and Evolution

If you are not prepared to use force to defend civilisation, then be prepared to accept barbarism.

Thomas Stowell

In times reminiscent of the 1930s, when Germany flew in the face of the 1918 Treaty of Versailles and laid firm foundations for what was to become the formidable Luftwaffe of WW2, so it was that in the late 1940s East Germany began to offer basic flying experience in gliders and light aircraft, at civilian flying clubs, to those seen to be suitable to be at the core of a new air force in the 1950s. This was known as the 'Gesellschaft für Sport und Techniq' (GST) programme, just one of several sinister vibes then emerging from the Soviet led communist bloc in Europe, which set alarm bells ringing in the West. Great Britain took note, offering its young men the chance to become military pilots – and in 1951 the author was one of many hundreds who answered the call. This chapter traces the birth and evolution of the EGAF, within the Warsaw Pact, from its birth in 1956 to the end of the Cold War, and the simultaneous development of the RAF in Germany within NATO. Set against the larger political and military background, it will concentrate on tactical air power, air defence and offensive forces, including the armed helicopters, and

the all-important command and control organisation, touching only briefly on other support facilities.

GST was open to boys between the ages of 14 and 18, but only to those who showed themselves to be both highly motivated and politically reliable, and who pledged themselves, in principle, to serve as officers and pilots in the air arm of the East German police, the 'Kasernierte Volkspolizei' (KVP), a thinly disguised embryo air force. An application to join the GST programme triggered a detailed investigation into the aspirant's general behaviour, his loyalty to the communist party and that of his parents, other close relations and girl friends, his family background and social conduct. Contacts with West Germany or other non-communist states would be of particular interest. A high school degree or, exceptionally, an equivalent professional qualification was a prerequisite, but no specific standard was required in the Russian language, the basics of which were taught at schools in East Germany and used operationally in the Warsaw Pact. The candidate would then undergo more stringent physical, medical and flying aptitude tests at the Luftfahrtmedizinisches Institut (Aviation Medical Institute) at Königsbrück, near Dresden, returning there on successful completion of GST for more rigorous flying aptitude and medical tests before being accepted for formal flying training. Despite this demanding selection process, subsequent failure rates in training were high, said by some to have been 90% in the early stages, one MiG pilot reporting that only 3 of the 56 applicants in his group achieved operational status. For those who succeeded, strict physical and medical tests would be repeated every year throughout their service. Women were not formally admitted into the air force, as pilots, until the early 1980s, but the author discovered that one, Iris Wittig, did qualify to fly with the KVP in 1953, and was later believed to have served with a fighter squadron at Cottbus, before becoming an instructor pilot at Rothenburg.

Qualification for officer training thus depended primarily on a candidate's 'political pedigree', medical suitability and social background, his chances of selection enhanced if he came from the 'working class' and had been, or was a member of the communist 'Freie Deutsche Jugend' (FDJ) – the Free German Youth, or the 'Sozialistische Einheitspartei Deutschlands' (SED) – the Socialist Unity Party of Germany. Hence came the sardonic suggestion that, within the selection process, political integrity was seen as more important than officer qualities or flying. Thereafter, the successful applicants were required, on a regular basis, to convince

their masters that they remained dedicated and 'obedient' servants to the party, with the inclination and ability to disseminate the prescribed ideology – and promotion depended on evidence of this. Indeed, the whole of the GDR evolved under the watchful eyes of the 'Ministerium für Staatssicherheit' (MfS), the Ministry for State Security, or infamous 'Stasi', whose motto was: 'Shield and Sword of the Party'.

Although some potential RAF pilots were given familiarisation flights within the Combined Cadet Force (CCF) or the Air Training Corps (ATC), with the more promising offered basic flying training at civilian flying clubs or the University Air Squadrons (UAS), these were not prerequisites for entry into the RAF. A volunteer's background would be investigated, perhaps not to the same depth as in the NVA, but any contacts or connections with communist states, parties or individuals could attract special attention. Otherwise, the selection procedures were not unlike those in the EGAF, with similar medical examinations followed by assessments of flying aptitude, leadership and personal qualities.

Back in East Germany, a technical training programme began to develop at Kamenz airfield in 1952, the Russians supplying engineering instructors and five, non-airworthy MiG-15 fighters, while 271 East Germans began flying training, covertly, in Russia. This group, known as 'Lehrgang X' (Course 'X'), left for Zysran, a Russian base on the River Volga, in September 1952, to spend the next year learning to fly the piston-engine, two-seat Yak-18 'Max' and Yak-11 'Moose' basic and advanced piston-engine trainers, again with Russian instructors – and Klaus-Jürgen Baarß was one of the 271. When Klaus returned to Germany in 1953, he was appointed Chief Flying Instructor at No.1 Aeroklub (Aero Club), flying Yak-11s at Flugplatz Cottbus. In a highly successful career which followed, he would fly most variants of the MiG, graduate from the Russian Monino Academy in Moscow and the NVA's 'Friedrich Engels' Military Academy in Dresden, as he progressed rapidly through the ranks to become the Deputy Commander of the EGAF's air defence forces 'Luftstreitkräfte/Luftverteidigung' (LSK/LV), and retire as a Generalleutnant.

The RAF was but one of the Allied air forces facing the Warsaw Pact over the IGB in North Germany during the Cold War, but it exemplified the way the NATO forces might have met the clear threat from the East. In the immediate wake of the Allies' victory in WW2, the British Air Forces of Occupation (BAFO) wound down rapidly, leaving a resident force of 10 RAF piston-engine fighter squadrons to patrol the skies above North Germany, from Denmark south to Kassel, between the IGB and the border with Belgium and Holland, while helping to maintain access to Berlin, through East Germany, along the agreed corridors.

The blockade of Berlin by the Soviets in 1948 (Chapter One) was the first major confrontation between East and West in Germany, and the West's decisive response which lifted the siege in 1949, set a precedent in the Cold War. It was now clear to the Allies that, if armed conflict was to be avoided there, it was necessary to increase

and pool all their military resources within a single, cohesive command structure, and from 1950 all assigned NATO forces in Continental Europe would come under the operational command of SACEUR, exercising his authority through the Supreme Headquarters Allied Powers Europe (SHAPE), in Paris.

At the same time the RAF began increasing its numerical and qualitative capability in Germany, replacing all its piston-driven aircraft there with first generation jet fighters, to 16 squadrons in all by 1952. BAFO was re-named Second Tactical Air Force (2TAF) in 1951, with its HQ at Bad Eilsen, while HQ No.2 Group, at Sundern (Gütersloh) exercised operational control of the RAF squadrons based in North Germany, HQ No.83 Group at Wahn (Köln), those assets in the southern sector of the British Zone. Despite the collective effort of NATO, the West's conventional forces on the Continent were still outnumbered by those in East Europe, and it was clear that more had to be done to redress this inequality, and thus defer the need to use nuclear weapons. Again, Britain played a significant part in this expansion, increasing the number of its squadrons in 2TAF to 31 by the end of 1952, to 50 in 1953 and to 56 in 1954, bringing the total number of RAF combat aircraft to 648 – all assigned to or earmarked for SACEUR. This build up and ever changing inventory of RAF combat aircraft in Germany is dealt with initially in Chapter Three: 'Defence of the Homeland' (for the fighters), and in Chapter Six 'Strike Force' (for the offensive aircraft).

Shortly after the Berlin blockade, the ACB began up-grading the 'Plainfare' airfields and those at Jever, Oldenburg, Gütersloh and Sylt, for the new breed of fast-jets. They then went to work on five big new airfields in the 'Clutch' between the Ruhr and the Dutch border, resulting in RAF Wildenrath, Brüggen, Geilenkirchen, Laarbruch and Nörvenich. They also built RAF hospitals at Wegberg and Rostrop and a huge headquarters complex at Rheindahlen, for 2TAF, the British Army of the Rhine (BAOR), the NATO staffs of Northern Army Group (NORTHAG) and 2ATAF. All these tasks were completed between 1952 and 1955, and mirrored for the American, French and Canadian forces of the Central Army Group (CENTAG) and 4ATAF, in South Germany. The new airfields in 2ATAF were built to a NATO standard, with concrete runways of at least 2,000 yd (1,830 m), where possible parallel taxiways and emergency grass airstrips, and clusters of individual aircraft pans, randomly spaced and protected by concrete, earth covered revetments.

Meanwhile, in East Germany, a new air force was being born. In April 1953, 101 MiG-15s arrived in the GDR, on loan from the Soviet Air Force, for jet training to begin on 'Jagdfliegerregiment 1' (JFR-1), No.1 Fighter Regiment of the KVP, at Cottbus, with Soviet instructors and the East German engineers trained at Kamenz. However, the worsening economic situation and civil unrest which followed, led to the suspension of jet training in the GDR, and the return of all the MiGs to the Soviet Air Force, leaving JFR-1 to continue training on the Yak-18 and Yak-11.

The Russian Yak-18, which first emerged in 1946, began as a 'tail-dragger', but by 1954 it had been modified with a tricycle undercarriage, improving its forward view on the ground and rendering it more suitable for pre-jet training. It was this variant which entered service with the NVA, to be replaced in 1959 by a more powerful version, which could achieve speeds of 254 km/hr (137 knots) at sea level, and climb to 5,000 m (16,500 ft). Successful students then progressed to the higher performance piston-engine Yak-11, which had a maximum speed of 480 km/hr (250 knots) and a service ceiling of 7,000 m (23,000 ft).

In March 1956, shortly after the Western Powers had agreed that the FRG should contribute to NATO's defensive shield in Europe, the GDR announced, with the full backing of the Soviet Union, the formation of the NVA, and the LSK/LV. No.1 Aero Club at Cottbus became Fliegergeschwader-1 (FG-1), with Hauptmann (Hptm) Baarß as its first commander, and he presided over its rapid development into a fighting unit, initially using the Yak-18s and Yak-11s to simulate combat tactics, pending the arrival of the first MiG-15UTI 'Midget' trainers and MiG-15bis 'Faggot' fighters, in late 1956. Jet flying resumed on FG-1 in early 1957, and by November, 21 of its pilots had converted to the MiG. Within a year, all six fighter wings were equipped with a mix of single and two-seat MiG-15s, soon to be replaced by the much improved, single-seat MiG-17 'Fresco', but still supported by MiG-15 trainers because there was no dual version of the Fresco. The NVA had now well and truly entered the jet age.

'They said it would float!' Not everything went according to plan in the construction of RAF Wildenrath in 1952.

ACB

'We just stuck poles in at either end of the proposed runway – and took in from there!'.

Don Hanson

Manpower. Man-driven, one-ton 'Frog' steel rammers were used to compact operating surfaces, before paving the operating surfaces at RAF Brüggen.

Les Rowe

A USAF C-54 on a rapid turn-round at RAF Celle in early 1949, at the height of the Berlin Airlift. Note the Pierced Steel Planking (PSP) Aircraft Servicing Platform (ASP).

ACB

A major ceremony at Kamenz on 8 September 1956 had marked the official inauguration of the EGAF Officers' School, 'Offiziershochschule' (OHS), the event being attended by the head of the air force, Major General Zorn, accompanied by a large party of political and civilian dignitaries. When at steady state, a three or four year course at the OHS would begin with six weeks of basic military training and five months of ground instruction which included community sciences and Russian language tuition, together with a heavy emphasis on physical training and sport. High on the agenda was the subject of 'leadership', the term applied here in its broadest sense to go well beyond the development of inherent human qualities, in dealing extensively with the dissemination of political and military doctrine, planning and organisation, and timely communication of orders to achieve specific objectives. A number of central themes resonate with the 'Principles of War', in British military thinking, typically 'Maintenance of the Aim', 'Concentration of Force', 'Economy of Effort' and, (particularly for the EGAF in the last two decades of the Cold War) 'Offensive Action'. The following chapters will show how these principles were applied in practice within the NVA, with an emphasis on centralised authority, detailed planning and supervision at all levels, seemingly leaving little discretion, for instance, to flight leaders on the ground or in the air. The principle of constant preparedness was reflected in the NVA's high alert states and numbers of personnel retained on duty at all times, while redundancy in equipment,

such as radar cover and communications, was there to ensure the continuous and rapid flow of intelligence and execution of orders. 'Security' was also a major feature of the NVA's leadership training, some might say 'too high', with the culture of 'need to know' practised to excess. One LSK/LV pilot transferring from the MiG-21 to the MiG-29 on JG-3 at Preschen remembers that the colleagues he left behind on the MiG-21 were not allowed to know anything about, or go anywhere near the new aircraft on their shared flight line: 'it was as if a glass wall had been erected between the two squadrons' (Chapter Four: JG-3). Another pilot, flying from JG-8, Marxwalde, found that the USAF F-111 he thought he had intercepted was, in fact, an LSK/LV MiG-23 'Flogger' which had re-equipped JG-9 at nearby Peenemünde many months before – a fact seemingly unknown to at least some front line pilots at Marxwalde (Chapter Four: JG-8). It was also clear, from answers to the author's questions, that many of the LSK pilots knew little about the 'big picture', the Warsaw Pact and NATO strategies generally or the real intentions, capabilities or tactics of their potential adversaries in NATO, perhaps having access only to that information necessary for them to carry out their specific assignments.

RAF flight cadets also attended formal lectures on the Principles of War, but the author recalls only informal discussions on the many facets of leadership at the RAF College, Cranwell, and there was no political indoctrination of any sort. From the start of their careers, and in addition to periodic tests within their own specialisations, officers seeking further promotion were required to take an interest in, and have a broad understanding of all military matters, national and international, and were examined in these subjects before admission to RAF and joint service staff colleges, designed to equip them for higher command. At these institutions, current NATO and Warsaw Pact strategic and tactical thinking was studied in depth, against a backcloth of international politics and economics.

However, the fundamental doctrinal difference between the RAF and the LSK in leadership training, was the latter's dedication to the communist ideology, compared with the absence of political influences (other than the democratically backed policies of the day) on the British military forces. Whereas it was clearly in the interests of those in the NVA who aspired to higher rank, to demonstrate his or her allegiance to the SED, personal politics did not (at least in theory) affect the chances of promotion in the RAF. In the UK, military volunteers swore allegiance to Queen and Country on recruitment, but thereafter this was taken for granted, the question arising again only if the loyalty of an individual, by words, deeds or relationships, gave rise for concern.

The airfields and installations at Kamenz, Bautzen and Rothenburg, remained at the heart of EGAF ground and flying training throughout the Cold War, having begun there in the early 1950s for those destined for the KVP, when stools and broomsticks were used to demonstrate and practise flight manoeuvres. The first flying training

unit 'Fliegerausbildungsgeschwader-1'FAG-1', was established at Kamenz in 1954, which had all the facilities necessary for academic studies and an airfield adequate for the initial training of transport pilots on the single-engine An-2 aircraft. Basic and advanced training for fast-jet pilots took place at the nearby bases of Bautzen and Rothenburg respectively, with ground school for the first formal course at Bautzen beginning in late 1956, followed by flying training on the MiG-15 in March 1957 and the MiG-17 in the early 1960s. Named Jagdfliegerausbildungsgeschwader-11 (JAG-11); in January 1961, the OHS organisation was formalised in July 1963, when it began to convert to the L-29 'Delfin'. Given the name 'Leander Ratz', after a former commander killed in a MiG fighter on a training flight in Poland, JAG-11 became JAG-25 in 1971 – and later FAG-25, the year the OHS was granted the name 'Franz Mehring', and given the status of a university, offering students the chance to earn a degree.

The L-29 had entered service in 1961, the first of these aircraft being powered by a British Viper jet engine, the remainder by Czech M701s. It was a robust and relatively simple aircraft, which could operate from unpaved airstrips, was stable in flight, had manual controls and reliable ejector seats in its tandem cockpits. With assorted weapons or external fuel tanks carried on two wing pylons, the Delfin enabled 'all-through' flying training; it could achieve speeds of 650 km/hr (355 knots) at a height of 500 m (16,000 ft), had a ceiling of 11,000 m (36,000 ft), and a range of 740 km (400 nm) on internal fuel. From 1971 it was supplemented or replaced by the more advanced L-39 'Albatros', effectively a light attack aircraft with a much improved performance and weapons capability. Although developed from the L-29, it bore no resemblance to its predecessor, with a different planform, permanent fuel tanks at its wingtips, a more capacious fuselage, swept tail fin and variable-incidence tailplane, power assisted controls, hydraulically operated tricycle undercarriage, flaps and airbrakes. There was no internal gun in the NVA aircraft, but gun pods, rockets, bombs or infra-red (IR) air-to-air missiles could be carried on two or four wing pylons, depending on the mark of the aircraft, one of which was also used by the NVA for target towing (Chapter Three). The aircraft was said to have been able to achieve 720 km/hr (390 knots) at sea level, and reach a service ceiling of 10,000 m (33,000 ft). The L-39 has often been likened to the Italian MB.339. From 1961, most of the advanced jet fighter training in the LSK/LV took place at Rothenburg, initially on the MiG-15, later on the MiG-17 and from 1964 on several marks of the MiG-21, beginning with the MiG-21F-13. In these conversion programmes, dual instruction and the first solo sorties were carried out in the two-seat MiG-21s, the first solo flight normally taking place after some 20 sorties/10 hours, followed by a succession of consolidation sorties in the single-seat fighter then on strength. The unit was awarded the title of 'Heinz Chapel' in 1970.

With the perennially poor flying weather on the border with Poland between October and April, the ground instruction at the OHS tended to predominate over flying at Bautzen and Rothenburg, the reverse being true during the better weather in the remaining months. The time and number of flying hours allocated to each phase of training varied with the resources available and the demands of the front line, but a snapshot suggests that totals were in the order of 60–70 hours on each of the first two years, and 100 hours in the third and perhaps a fourth year.

Rudolf Müller completed only two years at OHS, from 1958–1960, but thereafter most students would complete three or four year courses. Typically, Hannes Mallwitz, who began GST in the late 1960s, flew a total of 130 flying hours on the Yak-18, Z-327 and Z-42 piston-engine trainers, gaining valuable experience which counted later towards his military qualifications. He completed all his initial jet training in the L-29 on FAG-25 at Bautzen, where he also converted to the MiG-21 while FAG-15 was detached there during runway repairs at Rothenburg. This advanced training began with four months of ground school and flight simulator training, before five hours of dual instruction and his first solo in the two-seat MiG-21U on 19 April 1974. Thereafter, all his solo flying on FAG-15 was carried out in the MiG-21F-13, in which he accumulated 78 hours of flying to gain an insight into fighter tactics, air-to-air and air-to-ground gunnery, by day and night. Hannes graduated from OHS in 1974 – with a posting to JG-3 at Preschen (Chapter Four: JG-3).

A minority of EGAF fast-jet pilots had the first stages of their flight training in the

USSR, and Norbert Hess was one. Having completed his GST on the Z-42 at Neustadt-Glewe, West Pomerania, in 1978, he built up his flying hours on the four-seat Z-43, before joining a group of 30 promising candidates for a year of formal training at Kiev, followed by nine months at Primorsko-Achtarsk, flying 100 hours in the L-29. In 1981 he moved to Krasnodar, where he flew 60 hours in the MiG-21F-13 before an 80 hour conversion to the MiG-23UB and MiG-23MF at Kasachstan. In 1983, he joined JG-9 at Peenemünde (Chapter Four: JG-9). Andreas Dietrich's training followed a similar pattern and in the same timeframe as Norbert, but he was ultimately destined for the MiG-23BN on JBG-37 at Drewitz in 1983 (Chapter Six: JBG-37).

The rapid evolution of the LSK/LV had its price, but a cursory study suggests that the accident rates at Bautzen and Rothenburg were no more than should have been expected for a new, but fast developing air force at the beginning of the jet age. Although committed primarily to air defence, the more advanced training programme included basic familiarisation in the ground-attack and tactical reconnaissance roles. The demands on these pilots, whose flying was limited to three days a week and who might expect to achieve only 10 hours a month in the air were high – but every minute's flying time was made to count. The statistics show that, in 1958 and 1959, the MiG-15UTIs and MiG-15bis at Bautzen suffered seven landing accidents, with an eighth being due to a collision on the ground. Rothenburg suffered its first fatal accident (a MiG-15bis) in July 1960, and

another in September, when both pilots aboard a MiG-15UTI died. A MiG-15UTI collided with a MiG-15bis on the flight line in April 1961; fire accounted for a MiG-15bis in October 1961, and another suffered damage in a landing accident. In May 1962, a MiG-17 exploded inexplicably over Poland, killing the legendary Oberst Leander Ratz. Another MiG-17 was lost two months later when the pilot ejected unsuccessfully from an estimated height of 100–150 m (500 ft), and in April 1963 the pilot also died when he ejected from his MiG-17, at a height of 200 m (700 ft). From then until 1990 the average annual number of accidents on JAG-25/FAG-25 decreased a little, and was probably no greater than might have been expected in a jet training school at that time, while accidents on FAG-15 at Rothenburg remained relatively light.

Less visible, but no less dynamic, was the programme of training for all the support agencies in the EGAF, such as engineering, fighter control, intelligence, air traffic, meteorology *et al*, all these activities, and more, developing rapidly from 1952, again centred on Kamenz. Of all the non-flying specialists, perhaps those most closely connected with the fighter pilots' objectives were the fighter controllers, the training of which was comprehensive. In 1972, a 'Führungsorgan' section was founded within the OHS for the training of fighter controllers, *ab initio* candidates undertaking three years of theoretical instruction, similar to that given on the ground to the pilots they would control. This included meteorology, engineering, tactics, navigation and the military structure in the NVA, before focusing more

Frank Born, after his first solo in the L-39 'Albatros' at Bautzen.
Frank Born Collection

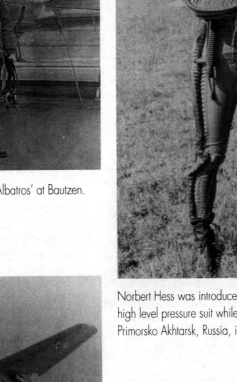

Norbert Hess was introduced to the cumbersome but efficient
high level pressure suit while training on the MiG-21F-13, at
Primorsko Akhtarsk, Russia, in 1982.   *Norbert Hess*

Some pilots earmarked for the NVA's MiG-23 force flew 80 hours
in the Russian MiG-23MS, at Kasachstan, Russia, in 1982/83.
                                                    Norbert Hess

Hannes Mallwitz had his first solo flight in a MiG in the front seat
of this MiG-21U at Bautzen in 1974.

                                                    Hannes Mallwitz

The Yak-11 was much used in the embryo LSK, for advanced flying training and to simulate fighter tactics – pending jet training.   *Rudolf Müller Collection*

Hartwig Richter flew the Yak-18 during his GST.

Hartwig Richter

Rudolf Just graduated as a fighter controller at OHS, Kamenz, in 1978.   *Rudolf Just*

Peter Müller, instructor pilot (no 'bonedome'), with his last batch of students graduating from FAG-15.

Peter Müller

Klaus Schmiedel had flown 83 hours in 220 sorties in the L-29 Delfin on JAG-25 at Bautzen by 1980.   *Klaus Schmiedel*

Zur Erinnerung an den Freiflug auf der MiG-21

Kommandeur *[signature]* **OSL**

Hartwig Richter flew his first solo flight in MiG-21F-13 at OHS in April 1975.
Hartwig Richter

Erwin Nützmann with an L-29 in 1964.
Erwin Nützmann

on air traffic procedures, communications and the fundamentals of fighter control (Chapter Five).

Subject to candidates passing the prescribed tests, there were three RAF pilot training schemes open to them during the early years of the Cold War. The coveted pilot's brevet and a permanent commission in the RAF, with service up to the age of 55, went to those who graduated after two years eight months training at the Royal Air Force College, Cranwell (Lincolnshire). Those seeking to fly during their two years of National Service (which ended in 1960), or preferred short service commissions (eight or twelve years), could be admitted to Basic Flying Training Schools (BFTS), followed by Advanced Flying Training Schools (AFTS). The National Service course of 18 months 'fast-tracked' pilots to serve a short spell on the front line, followed by a requirement for additional service with the Royal Auxiliary Air Force or the RAF Volunteer Reserve on return to civilian life. For simplicity and brevity, this chapter will deal predominantly with pilot training at Cranwell, at a time when this system was perhaps the closest to that which produced military pilots for the NVA.

The author arrived at Cranwell in April 1951, to spend the first two terms (all of which were then three months long), on basic military training. In the following three terms he flew the de Havilland Chipmunk, a simple, tandem-seat 'tail dragger', easy to fly, land and manoeuvre on the ground; 'going solo' after seven hours of dual instruction. At the end of these three terms, in a programme of flying mixed with academic studies, he had flown a total of 125 hours on the Chipmunk (day and night), of which 57 hours were 'solo'.

Advanced flying began on the veteran, well tried and proven WW2 North American, tandem-seat T-6 'Harvard'. Despite its greater size and power (with its Pratt and Witney 550 hp radial engine), transition from the Chipmunk to the Harvard presented no great problem, although the author was among many who experienced the embarrassing if innocuous 'ground loop' after landing. He flew solo for the first time in the average time of five hours, and completed 42 hours on type before the College was re-equipped with the Bolton Paul Balliol.

At first sight the cockpit of the Balliol, with its side-by-side seating, was impressive, but any early apprehension was soon allayed when the instrument presentation was found to be logical and the controls came easily to hand. Again, there was a quantum increase in power and performance, with a 1,100 hp Merlin engine, similar to that which powered the Spitfire, driving a huge (to the students) three-blade propeller. Although the aircraft could operate quite satisfactorily from grass, most of the Balliol training was carried out from the paved runways at RAF Barkston Heath, a satellite airfield south of Cranwell. For this final year, the programme continued to be split between flying, academics and advanced service training.

Some graduates would come to say that, in their career, they found the Balliol the most difficult aircraft to fly accurately, with variations in power settings and torque requiring continuous attention to the turn and slip indicator, and the use of the aircraft's effective rudder to maintain balanced flight. The aircraft was fully aerobatic, with rolls executed at 180 knots (330 km/hr), loops at 250 knots (460 km/hr) and climbing rolls at 270 knots (500 km/hr) plus. The maximum speed was 320 knots (560 km/hr). Spinning, practised regularly, would begin steeply and could become erratic, with unpleasant yawing moments; a maximum of four turns was permitted before initiating the recovery. The recovery procedure of opposite rudder and stick fully forward was usually effective after 1–2 turns and a 2,500 ft (760 m) loss in height, but it was sometimes necessary to use both hands to get the stick well forward and the rudder had to be centralised immediately the rotation ceased. Landing in the normal, engine-assisted, flaps-down configuration, the Balliol should cross the runway threshold at 90 knots (170 km/hr), with care needed when landing in a strong cross-wind. Students were allowed great discretion when tasked to carry out general handling, low flying, spinning and aerobatics solo, and indeed were required to develop their own aerobatic sequences in preparation for the competition between them for the Entry's prestigious aerobatic trophy. Also, few could resist the great temptation to 'play' with any other student they found in the same space of sky, and while this would not have been authorised, many had their first taste of simulated combat at this stage.

The accident rate in the RAF during the 1950s, at the training schools and on the front line, was unacceptably high as the service underwent its massive expansion and pilots at all levels became accustomed to the new jet aircraft. As with other flying schools at the time, Cranwell suffered its fair share of accidents, particularly with the Balliol, in a mix of pilot error, unexplained incidents and technical failures, both the author and fellow student Bob Snare suffering technical defects in the aircraft. In the author's case it occurred at the end of a solo flight, when the port undercarriage leg collapsed on landing, sending the aircraft careering across the airfield, narrowly missing two petrol tankers waiting to refuel a line of Balliols. The aircraft eventually came to rest without great damage and no injury to the pilot – the fault quickly diagnosed by the engineers and the pilot exonerated from any blame. Bob's accident was more dramatic. On that afternoon in June 1954, when Bob took off from Barkston Heath in a Balliol with his instructor for his Intermediate Handling Test, the weather was fine, with a cloud base of 2,500 ft (800 m), good visibility and a surface wind of 20 knots from the west. All went well until Bob opened the throttle after a rapid, spiral descent through a gap in the cloud, to carry out a practice forced landing, at which point 'the engine exploded with an enormous bang' – and stopped completely. The Balliol was no glider, but Bob's gliding experience and quick thinking now helped to avoid a disaster; with no engine and little height or airspeed to play with, he selected flap down, knocked off the fuel cock and the engine master switches, and landed straight ahead in 'one of the biggest pea fields in Lincolnshire'. It had all happened in about 20 seconds, with no chance to transmit a 'MAYDAY', and the two pilots lost no time vacating the aircraft with its hissing, steaming engine. They were not the only lucky survivors; several farm workers labouring very close by believed that the pilot had deliberately steered clear of them. Such is an aviator's luck. This was the first Balliol to be recovered in a state which enabled the cause of similar engine failures to be diagnosed; it transpired that the camshafts of the de-rated Merlins had failed, with the result that all the cylinders fired at once, causing a massive explosion and the total destruction in some of these engines.

At the end of the eight term programme at the RAF College, successful cadets were given a choice of roles (day, night or ground-attack fighters, tactical or heavy bombers, maritime or reconnaissance) and, subject to their suitability, they usually got their first choice. The author chose the day fighter role when he passed out from Cranwell in December 1954, with a total of 279 flying hours on all the training aircraft, and a flying assessment of 'Proficient'. Shortly after his departure, the Balliol was replaced at Cranwell by obsolescent de Havilland Vampire jets, and in the decades which followed, to the end of the Cold War, the flying and ground training syllabi at Cranwell and the Flying Training Schools (FTS) underwent further changes with new aircraft, requirements and circumstances.

Next stop for the author was No.8 FTS at RAF Driffield, Yorkshire, to convert to the twin-jet, two-seat trainer and the single-seat versions of the Meteor fighter, later versions of which were capable of speeds in excess of 500 knots (900 km/hr), had pressurised cockpits and could reach heights of 40,000 ft (12,000 m). In these aircraft, pilots learned the rudiments of jet flying, with an emphasis on the problems of asymmetric flight (the aircraft's engines were spaced well out on each wing), instrument and night flying, low and high level navigation, and close formation, but no battle formation, combat or weapons training at this stage. All this was subject to frequent progress checks by supervisors. In his five months at No.8 FTS, the author flew 38 hour dual and 37 hours solo in the two-seat Meteor T.7 and single-seat Meteor F.4, to pass on to the next stage with an 'Average' flying assessment.

In the mid-1950s, the pilots selected for the day fighter role went on to the Hunter Operational Conversion Unit (OCU) at RAF Chivenor (Devon), those for the night fighter/all-weather (N/AW) force to the Meteor NF.11 at RAF North Luffenham (Rutland), while the pilots destined for FGA went on to Venoms at RAF Pembray (SouthWales). Later, all those selected for the fast-jet force would route through the Hunter OCU, renamed the Tactical Weapons Unit (TWU) in 1975, based at Chivenor and later RAF Brawdy (South Wales), where the Hunters were replaced by the Hawk, two-seat tactical weapons trainer. Instructor pilots for the OCUs and the TWUs were carefully selected for their experience and the expertise they had shown on their respective front line squadrons; they were invariably classified as 'Above Average' pilots, and were both ideal mentors for the fast-jet pilots of the future and for the additional war roles assigned to the TWU and all OCU units. For instance, No.229 OCU at Chivenor became No.234(R), War Reserve Squadron, its Hunters and Hawks both armed with cannon, while the Hawks could also carry 'Sidewinder' air-to-air missiles (AAM), when required to reinforce Fighter Command's defensive screen of the UK over the North Sea.

TWU graduates, according to their particular talents, then went to the OCU optimised for each front line aircraft and its role, to be converted to the type and given a basic grounding in the tactics and weapons delivery techniques they would use operationally. The TWU and OCU syllabi would change, as would the course flying hours, as each new aircraft replaced the old on the front line. Taking account of the number and diversity of these roles and the aircraft employed, no attempt is made here to outline the stepped approach to training for each. Rather, three 'snapshots' are offered as illustrations.

The author joined No. 229 (Hunter) OCU at Chivenor in August 1955, having flown a total of 378 hours, at a time when the brand new Hunter F.1 was having many teething troubles; it was not yet cleared to fire its guns, its engine tended to surge, and the aircraft suffered generally from very poor serviceability. So it was that the author's initial role training had to be carried out in the Vampire, a twin-boom, tricycle undercarriage jet, which flew first in 1943. The OCU was equipped with the T.11 trainer, with side-by-side seating, and the FB.5 single-seat fighter-bomber; both had a service ceiling of 40,000 ft (12,000 m) and

could reach speeds in the order of 470 knots (870 km/hr). After 30 hours in the Vampires and 16 hours of basic familiarisation in the Hunter F.1, the author left Chivenor, with an 'Average' assessment, to join No.26 Interceptor Day Fighter (IDF) Squadron, at RAF Oldenburg, Germany, to fly the Hunter F.4. Those who followed him through the OCU/TWU would fly many more training hours in a succession of much improved Hunter variants: the single-seat F.4, F.6, FGA.9 and FR.10, and the two-seat Hunter T.7, before these were replaced by the Hawk.

A decade later, Tom Eeles also completed eight terms at Cranwell, with broadly the same pattern of ground training, but with a very different flying syllabus, reduced to a total of 180 hours on a single aircraft. The relatively simple Jet Provost, a two-seat (side-by-side) trainer powered by a single Viper jet engine developing 2,700 lb of thrust, could fulfil all the basic training requirements. Tom's advanced training was carried out at RAF Valley, in the Folland Gnat, a two-seat version of the diminutive Midge fighter, capable of supersonic speeds, in which he flew 70 hours before going on to No. 231 OCU, RAF Bassingbourn, Hertfordshire, destined for the Canberra tactical bomber and reconnaissance force. Although not a fast-jet, the RAF Canberras are included in this text because in Germany they performed the same ground-attack and reconnaissance roles as the fast-jets. At 231 OCU, Tom flew 83 hours in various marks of the aircraft, in a basic conversion course which dwelled heavily on asymmetric training (although engine

In the 1950s, many RAF pilots began their flight training on the de Havilland Chipmunk. *David Parsons*

The author had his advanced flying training on the North American T-6 Harvard and the Boulton Paul Balliol at the RAF College, Cranwell in the early 1950s. *David Parsons*

In the 1950s, and beyond, the two-seat de Havilland Vampire T11 jet trainer, shown here in front of an F-86 Sabre, was used extensively by the RAF. *Dennis Caldwell*

These Hawker Hunter F.6 fighters of 229 OCU were used for the operational training of fast-jet pilots at RAF Chivenor in 1965.   *Jerry Saye*

Show Time. Hunters and Meteors of 229 OCU carried out a mass flypast of training aircraft at an RAF Chivenor Open Day in the 1970s.
                                                                              Tim Thorn

The Hawk two-seat fighter trainer, armed here with AIM 9 missiles, took over the operational training role from the Hunter in 1974.   *Geoff Lee/BAe*

failures were rare), with one demonstration sortie only to show that this bomber was capable of carrying out the Low Altitude Bombing System (LABS) manoeuvre, and a single visit to a weapons range to deliver practice bombs. Tom was then posted to No.16 Canberra Strike/Attack Squadron at RAF Laarbruch, Germany, with a flying assessment of 'High Average'.

Rob Sargent's training was different again; it began when he was granted a flying scholarship and flew 30 flying hours in light piston-engine aircraft, to earn a Private Pilot's Licence (PPL) in 1965. After joining the RAF, a basic training course of 171 hours in the Jet Provost was followed by 75 hours of advanced flying in the Gnat at RAF Valley, after which Rob was specially selected to train as a flying instructor at the prestigious Central Flying School (CFS). There he became a Qualified Flying Instructor (QFI), and completed his instructor's tour on the BFTS at RAF Linton-on-Ouse, flying 740 hours there in two years, to bring his total flying to 1,154 hours. Rob's next posting took him first to the OCU at Chivenor, for a course of 68 hours in the latest marks of Hunter, after which he was well equipped for the next stage of his training at No.228 OCU, RAF Coningsby (Lincolnshire), to fly the Phantom FGR.2, primarily in the ground-attack role. He was then posted to No.31 Strike/Attack Squadron at RAF Brüggen, to fly the Phantom FGR.2.

Both the RAF and the NVA placed much emphasis on formal staff training for those officers identified for higher command and staff appointments. Officers who aspired to full careers in the RAF, and had passed the examinations necessary for promotion to the middle ranks, became eligible to compete for places at a number of staff colleges. The primary option for RAF officers during the Cold War was the RAF Staff College at Bracknell, open to flight lieutenants and squadron leaders, but places were also available at the British Army, Royal Navy and NATO colleges. Further promotion in the RAF required satisfactory completion of a staff college course at one of these venues, but there were exceptions, the author attending the National Defence College (NDC) at Latimer as a wing commander. Those who showed the potential for the highest ranks might then be selected for the Royal College of Defence Studies (RCDS) in London, where they would undertake an in-depth study of international political and military matters.

This general requirement for staff training may not have received the same priority in the lower and middle ranks of the NVA, other than for a cadre of 'politically sound' majors and lieutenant colonels with the right potential, who could hope to spend three years at the Friedrich Engels Academy in Dresden, or four years at the Monino Academy in Moscow. Oberst Manfred Skeries, Maj Hannes Mallwitz and Maj Frank Born received this deeper insight into politics, the management of military flying and the employment of air power in the land/air/sea operations – at the higher levels of command. The NVA academy had the additional function of evaluating and teaching new concepts, tactics and use of air power generally, Manfred Skeries recalling that, in 1989, JG-3 offered the academy its ideas for the best employment of its new MiG-29s, and that they then worked together to evaluate these concepts, before passing on their recommendations to a higher authority. However, most of the operational pilots in the EGAF concentrated solely on their professional work on the flight line, with little expectation of securing top jobs in the LSK.

The nuclear arms race was well underway in the 1950s, causing increased tensions, periods of nuclear stalemate and the possibility of Armageddon which stretched into the 1980s. NATO became only too well aware that a pre-emptive nuclear strike or early use of nuclear weapons by the Warsaw Pact would give little or no time for it to bring forward to the front line essential reinforcements, and as a partial solution adopted the doctrine of 'flexible response'. This required each member nation to increase its conventional weapons contribution to the collective effort, in an attempt to defer the need to resort to the use of tactical nuclear weapons, and Britain was in the vanguard. Having cut its fighter force in Germany severely in 1957, its attack and strike capability was increased with the introduction into service there of the long range Canberra BI-6/BI-8 (See Chapter Six: Strike Force). Soon after these aircraft arrived in Germany, any thought of using the Canberra at high level succumbed to the reality that, at height, it would be very vulnerable to much improved Soviet radars, SAM, AAA and fighter aircraft, and the force began intensive training at low level.

Following the Cuban crisis in 1962, when alert states for many military units in NATO and the Warsaw Pact were raised to unprecedented levels, there was a period of relative calm. However, the invasion of Czechoslovakia by five members of the Warsaw Pact in 1968 was mounted with such surprise and rapidity that alarm bells began ringing once more throughout Europe. Although not perceived as an immediate or direct threat to the West, NATO aircraft were again brought to higher states of readiness, and more thought was given to improving the Allies' conventional assets, in another effort to stave off the nuclear options. Britain's response was to transfer its strategic nuclear deterrent responsibilities from Bomber Command to the Royal Navy's Polaris-equipped submarines, and place its 'V' Force, thus released, at the disposal of SACEUR in the conventional role. Some of the nuclear capable RAF Canberras, and all the 'V' bombers, would be based in the UK, to reduce running costs, while affording them greater security, but they still had enough range to attack their targets within greater Germany and beyond – and the RAF would still retain a major presence in Germany.

Back in the GDR, the MiG-15s, MiG-17s and MiG-19s in the LSK/LV were all replaced in the mid-1960s by variants of the MiG-21, which remained the backbone of the LSK/LV until the end of the Cold War, albeit reinforced in the 1980s by one wing of MiG-23MF/ML 'Flogger' fighters on JG-9 at Peenemünde and two squadrons of MiG-29s on JG-3 at Preschen (Chapter Four).

Accepting the premise that offence can contribute significantly to the defence of the homeland, the EGAF began raising a strike/attack force in the 1970s, with the MiG-17Fs of JBG-31/37 at Drewitz, these fighter-bombers being replaced in 1979 by MiG-23BN 'Floggers' (Chapter Six: JBG-31/37). This offensive force was strengthened further in 1984 with the formation of two wings of Sukhoi Su-22 'Fitters' (Chapter Six). Sometimes forgotten is the effect the NVA's transport and armed helicopters could have had on a fast-moving ground battle in Northern Germany. Several variants of the Mi-8 'Hound' and the very formidable Mi-24 'Hind' would have been operated by the Soviet forces and the NVA in support of their ground forces, assets the like of which did not exist in NATO's northern part of Germany in the Cold War. The evolution of the NVA's attack helicopter force is also outlined in Chapter Six.

After completing their flying training on the fast-jets, the fledgling fighter pilots in both the EGAF and the RAF joined their first squadrons for consolidation training and the development of their operational skills, under the tutelage of experienced front line pilots. All the combat pilots who contributed to this text went on to serve their respective air forces well, and their stories are now taken up in the chapters which follow.

Chapter Three

Defence of the Homeland

Man has two supreme loyalties – to country and to family ... So long as their families are safe, they will defend their country, believing that by their sacrifice they are safeguarding their families also.

B H Liddle Hart

Throughout the Cold War, the primary role of the EGAF was air defence of the homeland. This chapter will deal with the overarching air defence organisation and the four main components of that defensive shield: the fighter aircraft and operational training, surface-to-air missiles (SAM), anti-aircraft artillery (AAA) and passive defence measures.

Organisation

LSK/LV. In 1956, the LSK/LV was formed with two divisions:'Fliegerdivision'(FD), each with three flying wings 'Fliegergeschwader' (FG). With its headquarters at Cottbus, 1.FD consisted of FG-1 at Cottbus, FG-2 at Rothenburg, and FG-3 at Preschen, while 3.FD had its headquarters collocated with FG-7 and FG-9 at Drewitz, and included FG-8 at Preschen. Reorganised and renamed in 1961, the divisions became Luftverteidigungsdivision (LVD), the wings Jagdfliegergeschwader (JG). HQ 1.LVD at Cottbus now commanded four fighter wings: JG-1 at Cottbus/Holzdorf, JG-7 at Drewitz, JG-8 at Marxwalde and JG-3 at

Preschen, while HQ 3.LVD was established at Neubrandenburg/Trollenhagen, to command JG-2 at Trollenhagen and JG-9 at Peenemünde. Most of the air bases were located down the East German border with Poland, from Peenemünde in the north to Czechoslovakia in the south, far from the IGB and beyond the useful range of the majority of NATO's fighter-bombers, leaving the Soviet Air Force in the west of the GDR to bear the brunt of any NATO air offensive. As they matured, both LSK/LV air divisions were allocated AAA and SAM regiments, together with the necessary support forces.

As a general rule, an EGAF wing was made up of three flying squadrons (Jagdstaffel 'JS'), with 1.JS manned by the most experienced pilots on the wing and 2.JS by well-qualified operational pilots. 3.JS was responsible primarily for the operational training of newly qualified pilots, their mentors being experienced flight leaders (Oberflieger or Kettenkommandeur) and instructor pilots from the squadron. An LSK/LV squadron in the Cold War would normally consist of three or four flights

(Ketten), each of four aircraft and four pilots, commanded by a flight commander. The squadron commander was in overall charge, selected primarily for his political credentials, his command attributes and capabilities in the air, and as such could hold the rank of lieutenant colonel (OSL), major (Maj) or even a captain (Hptm), often with non-executive OSLs under command. He would have ample support from his immediate deputy, a 'Politstellvertreter' a political/admin. officer, who might or might not be a pilot, a 'chief of staff', other flying deputies, and an engineering officer (also a pilot), all of whom were likely to be either lieutenant colonels or majors.

RAF in Germany

The evolution of RAFG, previously BAFO and 2TAF, with their Group structures, is dealt with in Chapter Two. On their operational stations, the squadrons, typically of 16 Hunter F.4s and 20–24 pilots in the 1950s and 1960s, was commanded by a squadron leader (Sqn Ldr), assisted by two or three flight commanders in the rank of flight lieutenant (Flt Lt) – all of whom were operational pilots. With no specialist, commissioned engineering officer in support at that time, one of these flight commanders would share this responsibility with a warrant officer (WO), in overseeing all engineering work and caring for as many as 100 non-commissioned officers (NCOs) and other ranks on the squadron's strength. The author had this role on his first squadron. All of the other operational pilots on the squadron would have

additional duties (instrument flying, tactical or weapons instructors, adjutant, welfare, ceremonial, sport, social etc). There was no 'political officer'. The structure would undergo continuous changes throughout the Cold War, with the command of all operational fast-jet squadrons passing to wing commanders (Wg Cdrs), who would be supported by five or more squadron leaders, one of whom would have been a professional (non-flying) engineer.

Air Defence Fighters

LSK/LV

Throughout the early years of the Cold War, Russian air defence, and consequently that of the LSK/LV, evolved around a progression of fast-jet Mikoyan-Gurevich (MiG) fighters, this evolution reaching a defining point when the MiG-29 arrived on the scene. While the fighters did have a secondary, ground-attack capability against targets over land and sea, very few flying hours were devoted to this purpose, and it was not until late in the Cold War that politics and military expediency led to the formation of a dedicated offensive force (Chapter Six). Many volumes have been written on the birth and development of each of these fighters, and this information needs no reiteration in this work. However, some basic details on each of the LSK/LV single-seat fighters are given below, while Chapter Four adds specific operational features of the MiGs flown by the six wings. Although the two-seat MiG-15s, MiG-21s, MiG-23s and MiG-29s performed invaluable service as operational trainers, and had war roles, their details are not included here.

MiG-15

Disregarding the MiG-15s which had a very short stay in the GDR in 1963 (Chapter Two), the first MiG-15bis 'Faggot' fighters arrived for the NVA in 1956, accompanied by two-seat MiG-15UTI 'Midgets'. The MiG-15bis incorporated many modifications found necessary in their predecessor and it is believed to have had the power, with a modified Kimov VK-1 engine, to achieve supersonic speeds in the dive. However, recovery from the dive, without an all-flying tail, was very difficult, so a general limit of M0.92 prevailed throughout its service life in the LSK/LV. Maximum speed at sea level has been given as 1,075 km/hr (580 knots), and the aircraft had a service ceiling of 15,500 m (51,000 feet). Without an all-weather capability or guided missiles, this was essentially a 'day only', clear air mass fighter, but it was heavily armed with one N-37D, 37 mm and two NR-23, 23 mm cannon, and could carry additional fuel tanks, unguided rockets or free-fall bombs externally, up to a total weight of 500 kg (1,100 lb). The MiG-15 was a useful stepping-stone to the more advanced MiG-17F, large numbers of which began arriving in 1957, to equip all six wings.

MiG-17

The MiG-17F 'Fresco C' was the main version of the MiG-17 family to be allocated to the LSK/LV, quickly proving to be a significant improvement on the MiG-15 in performance and handling qualities. With its VK-1F engine generating 3,300 kg (7,500 lb) of thrust in reheat and 2,600 kg (6,000 lb) 'dry', it was said to have been able to manoeuver well up to 13,700 m (45,000 ft), climb to heights of 16,600 m (54,500 ft) and achieve speeds of 1,100 km/hr (600 knots) at sea level; it could reach supersonic speeds in a dive and was cleared to M1.03. Notably steady in flight within its normal operating flight envelope, it was a good gun platform for its two 23 mm NR-23 and a single 37mm N-37D cannon. Although designed primarily as an air defence fighter, the aircraft also had a useful ground-attack capability, in being able to carry a maximum of two 250 kg (550 lb) bombs, four 190 mm or two 212 mm air-to-surface rockets, UB-16 or UB-32 pods of S-5, 57 mm unguided rockets, or a variety of external fuel tanks on two wing hardpoints. The MiG-17F was more of a 'bomber destroyer' than an air combat fighter, as was proved when its North Vietnamese pilots battled against formidable USAF opposition during the war in South East Asia (SEA), allegedly losing 100 of the aircraft against 71 'kills' claimed, and it had very limited success there in ground-attack operations. However, with its relative simplicity, the aircraft remained very serviceable, operational turn-round times were good and progressive modifications to the first generation ejection seat enhanced pilot survivability.

Next to arrive, in 1959, was the radar equipped MiG-17PF 'Fresco D', with its day/night, limited all-weather capability. The aircraft had the same engine as the MiG-17F, giving a similar performance but with a slight decrease in climb rate and increase in radius of turn; it was equipped with RP-1 Izumrud radar-ranging (some models retro-fitted later with the RP-5), an early radar warning receiver (Sirena 2) and a ground position indicator (Ni-50B), while the fixed armament consisted of three 23 mm NR-23 cannon. The pilots liked the reliable, robust MiG-17, their main criticism being the heavy fuel consumption in reheat, and its limited use due to overheating. The aircraft arrived in Germany in their natural metal finish, but later their upper surfaces were given a dark green/dark earth camouflage. The MiG-17 was followed by the MiG-19.

MiG-19

The single-seat MiG-19, the first fighter in the LSK/LV to achieve supersonic speeds in level flight, featured a thin, highly swept wing, a re-designed tail assembly and two powerful Tumanskii RD-9B axial-flow jet engines. With reheat, each engine produced 3,250 kg (7,165 lb) of thrust, giving the 'clean' MiG-19S a top speed of 1,452 km/hr (780 knots) at 10,000 m (33,000 ft), and a service ceiling of 17,500 m (57,400 ft). The 'S' was fitted with three 30–mm NR-30 cannon and had four underwing pylons for the carriage of UB-16 or UB-32 rocket pods, but no AAMs, while the 'PM', with its night/limited all-weather capability, was armed with four RS-2US AAMs only – no cannon or other underwing weapons. A little heavier than the 'S', it had a similar per-formance – but with a slightly lower top speed. With most pilots having little difficulty con-verting to the aircraft from the earlier MiGs, the two-seat MiG-19 trainer was cancelled, dual instruction and flight checks continuing to be carried out on the MiG-15UTI.

Gun-armed MiG-19s, in the hands of North Vietnamese pilots, saw action against USAF bombers and their F-4 escorts, over North Vietnam during Exercise 'Linebacker', but with strict orders to engage their adver-saries only on favourable terms and with minimum exposure to the enemy fighters. Be that as it may, the MiG-19 pilots recorded their first success on 8 May 1972, when a pair, led by Nguyen Ngoc Tiep, jettisoned their external tanks and headed straight for a pair of Phantoms to initiate a complicated dogfight. Chasing in and out of cloud bet-ween 1,500–2,000 m (5,000 – 6,500 ft), and protected by his wingman, Tiep finally got the better of his quarry, and both MiG-19s returned safely to Yen Bai. A second pair of MiG-19s also scored a 'kill' that day, but it would not always be that way. Constant vigilance and instant action was required of the Vietnamese pilots to avoid the USAF's AAMs, some of which found their mark, and the MiG-19 was not a good gun platform in high-'G' combat. Also, the more experienced and better trained American pilots, with strength in numbers, had developed and employed tactics to suit every contingency, whereas the Vietnamese were learning on the job, and some of the MiGs ran out of fuel while recovering to base. However, the MiG-19 proved to be more manoeuvrable than the F-105s and F-101s, the 30 mm cannon quickly showed its worth in close combat – and the Vietnamese pilots learned fast.

MiG-21

The first of some 11 versions of the MiG-21 (including the 'trainers') to join the LSK/LV was the MiG-21F-13 'Fishbed C', which arrived in the GDR in 1962. Powered by a single Tumansky R11F-300 engine, which produced 8,380 lb of thrust 'dry', and 12,650 lb in reheat, it had a maximum speed of M2.05 or 2,125 km/hr (1,150 knots), and a ceiling of 19,000 m (62,335 ft). It was armed with a single 30 mm cannon and could carry two R-3S IR missiles – or two 500 kg (1,100 lb) 'dumb' bombs; it had radar ranging but no missile guidance radar. There followed a succession of variants: MiG-21PF 'Fishbed D'; MiG-21PFM/SPS 'Fishbed F'; MiG-21M 'Fishbed H'; MiG-21MF 'Fishbed J' and MiG-21bisA/B 'Fishbed L/N'.

The MiG-21PF, a descendant of the MiG-21F-13, had the more powerful R-11F2–300 engine, generating 6,120 kg (13,500 lb) in reheat and 3,950 kg (8,700 lb) 'dry'. Performance figures vary, but it is believed to have been capable of speeds in the order of M2.05, 1,300 km/hr (700 knots) at sea level, and a service ceiling of 19,500 m (64,000 ft). The nose cone was increased in size to accommodate the RP-21 'Spin-Span' radar, and was no longer restricted to three positions but varied automatically with the aircraft's speed. The diameter of the intake was also increased, to admit the necessarily greater airflow for the new engine. Having evolved at a time when both Warsaw Pact and NATO hierarchies believed that the new supersonic jet fighters and high performance AAMs rendered close quarters air combat with the gun irrelevant, the 'PF' and basic 'PFM/SPS' MiG-21s were armed with missiles only, such as the beam-riding RS-2US, the R-3S or R-60 IR AAMs. Bombs or UB pods of unguided rockets were available for the ground-attack role. The MiG-21PF had

no brake parachute and remained equipped with the unpopular SK-1 ejection seat, which had the canopy hinged at the front and the pilot protected from wind blast in a capsule or 'cocoon' during ejection, with severe limits to its safe use at low level.

The MiG-21PFM/SPS had the same engine as the 'PF', with only slight modifications which had little effect on performance and, initially, the SK-1 seat, but later models incorporated the much improved KM-1 escape system, with the canopy hinged to the starboard wall of the cockpit, clearing ejections from ground level to 25,000 m (82,000 ft), at speeds above 130 km/hr (70 knots). The chord of their fins was increased to improve yaw stability, as was the size of the fin itself, and a brake parachute was fitted in a container at the base of the fin; there was also provision under the fuselage for the SPRD auxiliary rockets to significantly shorten take-off runs. Landing speeds were in the order of 250 km/h (135 knots) and low speed control was enhanced by the incorporation of blown flaps, this being achieved by passing air bled from the engine compressor over the upper surfaces of the flaps.

The 'PFM/SPS' was the 'lightweight sports car' of the MiG-21 family, fast, agile and simple; it was a firm favourite with most pilots, but as a fighter it lacked the range, the radar performance and especially an internal cannon, a weapon found to be necessary during the air war in SEA. So it was that the Soviets adopted the immediate expedient of retrofitting the MiG-21SPS with a single, twin-barrel GSch-23 cannon in a GP-9 'Gondel' under the fuselage – the fighter then becoming the MiG-21SPS/K.

The controversial MiG-21M 'Fishbed H' was powered by a R-11F2S-300 engine, with a maximum thrust of 3,900 kg (8,600 lb)'dry' and 5,700 kg (12,500 lb) in reheat, giving the aircraft a maximum speed of M2.1 and 1,300 km/hr (700 knots) at sea level. Officially, the 'M' had a service ceiling of 17,300 m (57,000 ft), but one pilot reported that he had 'topped out' at a height of 21,000 m (70,000 feet), albeit at a very low airspeed and with no manoeuvrability, having 'snapped-up' from a speed of M1.8. The RP-21MA radar, already obsolescent, provided missile guidance, and once again internal guns had found favour, this aircraft being equipped with 250 rounds for its GSch-23 twin-barrel, semi-internal cannon, thus leaving the fuselage centreline pylon free to carry a 800 litre or 500 litre fuel tank. Four wing pylons were also available, typically for two beam-riding RS-2US and two R-3S IR missiles, pods of unguided rockets, a variety of bombs or additional fuel tanks. Towards the end of the Cold War, double carriers were fitted for the carriage of four R-60M IRH missiles and three auxiliary fuel tanks, significantly increasing the aircraft's operational capability. However, with the 'M' being heavier than the 'SPS', and its performance less impressive overall, it was probably the least popular MiG-21 variant.

The penultimate MiG-21MF 'Fishbed J' did much to overcome the criticisms of its predecessor, the heavy and underpowered MiG-21M. With the more powerful Tumansky R-13–300 turbojet, giving 6,600 kg (14,500 lbs) of thrust in reheat, 4,000 kg (8,800 lb 'dry') the aircraft could reach speeds of M2.1, and a ceiling of 17,000 m (58,000 ft); it was equipped with an advanced RP-22 radar, with a much improved autopilot and avionics fit. Weapons included a GSch-23, 23 mm cannon, and each of the single fuselage and four wing pylons could carry a 500 litre or 800 litre tank, RS-2US beam riding, R-3S, R-13M or R-60M IRH AAMs, UB pods of unguided rockets or free-fall bombs.

The last MiG-21s to join the LSK/LV inventory were the formidable MiG-21bis-A 'Fishbed L' and the MiG-21bis-B 'Fishbed N'. An almost complete internal refit included new R-25–300 engines which produced 7,200 kg (16,000 lb) of thrust in reheat, 4,100 kg (9,000 lb) 'dry', enabled these fighters to reach speeds of 2,230 km/hr (1,200 knots) at 11,000 m (36,000 ft) and 1,150 km/hr (620 knots) at sea level – with a ceiling of 22,000 m (72,000 ft). Their combat capability was also greatly enhanced by the incorporation of advanced avionics and the RP-22 monopulse radar, which offered better discrimination and a limited 'look-down/shoot-down' capability, for a range of AAMs, including the R-60 IR missile. The small, lightweight, highly manoeuvrable R-60 entered service with the Warsaw Pact in the mid-1970s, and was upgraded later to R-60M and R-60MK; it had a theoretical maximum range of 10 km (5.4 nm), but some operational pilots claimed that its practical range was more in the order of 6–8 km (3.3–5 nm). This 'launch and leave' AAM incorporated an optical and/or active radar proximity fusing system, to trigger a lethal expanding rod, high-explosive fragmentation warhead within a few yards of the target. Moreover, the sensitive seeker head could, depending on the degree of heat emitted, acquire a target in a head-on attack. The 'bis' was fitted with the improved GSch-23L cannon, and could carry an 800 litre (180 gall) tank or an ECM pod on its centreline pylon. The MiG-21bis-A incorporated the automated command guidance system 'LAZUR', which enabled a fighter controller to data-link encoded headings, heights and speeds required for an interception, direct to a fighter's cockpit instruments, setting markers to which the pilot (or auto pilot) would fly; LAZUR equipped MiG-21s could be identified by a small, three prong antenna below the nose intake. The MiG-21bis-B had the 'Systema Awtomatitscheskowo Uprawlenija (SAU), automatic flight control system which, when coupled to the auto-pilot, facilitated landings in very poor weather conditions. SAU would take over from the 'WOSRAT' recovery system at 20 km (11 nm) on the approach, at a height of 600 m (2,000 ft), then keep the aircraft on the runway centre-line and glide path down to an authorised 40 m (130 ft) and 800 m (880 yd), with flap, speed brake and undercarriage selections demanded by lights in the cockpit. LAZUR and SAU enabled 'silent' operations, and they were said to be highly resistant to contemporary ECM.

MiG-23

The first MiG-23MF 'Flogger B', all-weather air defence fighters, supported by MiG-23UB 'Flogger C', two-seat operational trainers, began to arrive in the GDR in 1978,

while the more advanced and operationally capable MiG-23ML 'Flogger G' followed in 1982, all three variants remaining on strength until the demise of the LSK/LV in 1990. With the 'ML' some 1,500 kg (3,300 lb) lighter, and the R-35–300 which replaced the R-29–300 giving significant additional thrust, the 'ML' had a marked edge in performance over its predecessor. Although the figures vary depending on the source, the MiG-23ML was generally credited with a maximum speed of M2.35, 1,250 km/hr (680 knots) at sea level, and a service ceiling of 18,500 m (61,000 ft). Landing at speeds between 200 and 250 km/hr (110–135 knots), depending on the aircraft's weight, with the brake parachute deployed, could result in a ground roll in the order of 700 m (770 yd).

Pending the availability of a fully proven RP-23 'High Lark' radar, with a performance far in advance of earlier models, the first MiG-23MFs may have been fitted with older RP-22 'Jay Bird', and up to four R-3S or R-3R AAMs, but with the 'High Lark' or Sapfir L radar and tandem hard points retrofitted to the fuselage centreline pylon, the later aircraft could carry a maximum of eight advanced AAMs. This might comprise six R-60/R-60M close combat weapons, plus two medium/long range R-23R/R-24R SARH, or two short range R-23T/R-24T IRH missiles. Alternatively, two more 23 mm cannon could be attached to the tandem hard points, adding to the single GSch-23L carried internally. The 'MLs' were also equipped with an SO-69 ECM jammer and a BVP-30–26M chaff and flare dispenser, the on-board systems giving the 'ML' a 'look down/shoot down' capability, and thus increasing the threat to low flying NATO aircraft.

MiG-29

In 1988, the arrival in the GDR of the MiG-29 'Fulcrum'(or'Tochka Opori' in Russian) offered the LSK/LV a quantum leap forward in air-fighting capability, its protagonists claiming then that in some ways it equalled, if not exceeded, the performance of the American F-15C – but this is debatable. The aircraft had an integrated fuselage, engine compartment and highly swept, fixed delta wing, which gave it outstanding lift over a wide range of angles of attack; it was cleared to 9G. The two massive Klimov RD-33 turbofans engines, each developing 5,100 kg (11,240 lb) 'dry' or 8,200 kg (18,000 lb) in reheat, were slung below the fuselage and wings, their independent air intakes blanked off at speeds below 200 km/hr (110 knots), to avoid Foreign Object Damage (FOD) on take-off and landing – during which time air was sucked through louvres in the upper wing roots. Reports on performance vary, but it seems likely that the aircraft could achieve M2.3 and a service ceiling of 18,400 m (60,000 ft). Landing speed could be as low 250 km/hr (135 knots). The MiG-29 had an integral GSch-30–1 gun, a centreline pylon for a 1,500 liter (330 gall) fuel tank and six wing pylons could carry a maximum weapon load of 4,000 kg (8,800 lb). The RP-29E pulse-Doppler radar was able, theoretically, to detect a small target at a distance of 100 km (62 miles) and track ten targets simultaneously, its semi-active missiles being effective

out to 70 km (43 miles), but the MiG-29 pilots interviewed believed that these claims were very optimistic. For air defence duties, a typical weapons fit might be two radar-guided R-27R missiles on the two inner pylons and four R-60 or R-73 IRH missiles on the outer pylons. For ground-attack, each pylon could accommodate a pod of S-8s or a single S-24, 240 mm unguided rocket, free-fall bombs up to 500 kg (1,100 lb) or ZAB-500 napalm canisters on multi-shackle racks. The aircraft incorporated up-to-date passive ECM, chaff and flare dispensers, and provision could be made for the carriage and delivery of nuclear stores. The Soviet and LSK/LV MiG-29s were believed to have had a sophisticated Identification Friend or Foe (IFF) system which not only differentiated between hostile and friendly radar returns, but had a system which inhibited the firing of beyond visual range (BVR) AAMs against friendly aircraft. CO-69 passive radar warning sensors were wrapped around the fuselage, while in the space below the twin fins, above the two engines, lay clam-shell airbrakes, enclosing the brake parachute. A forward-facing periscope assisted rear seat occupants of the 'UB' in take-offs and landings. The MiG-29 pilots also welcomed the KM-1 ejection seat.

Royal Air Force Germany (RAFG)

The RAF's special responsibilities for the integrity of West German airspace, agreed after WW2 and exercised through NATO's integrated air defence network, remained in force throughout the Cold War, and these

All wings within the LSK/LV operated the MiG-17F.
Rudolf Müller

One of the first of many MiG-15s to equip the LSK/LV from its formation in 1956.
Rudolf Müller

Night flying with the MiG-19 was high on JG-3's training agenda.
Rudolf Müller Collection

A MiG-23ML of JG-9, Peenemünde, off the Baltic coast.
Norbert Hess

This early variant MiG-21PFM was equipped with AAMs only (no cannon), and the unpopular SK-1 ejection seat. *Author*

(Right) This MiG-23UB, which shows the aircraft's tail-down attitude on the ground, served with both JG-9 at Peenemünde and JBG-37 at Drewitz. *Author/Cottbus Museum*

(Left) MiG-21bisSAU, No.848, was one within the last batch of MiG-21s to equip the LSK/LV. This aircraft, which carries a SPS-141 electronic jammer, two external fuel tanks and two AAMs outboard was fitted with the latest KM-1 ejection seat and SAU automatic landing aid. The author's chief Luftwaffe assistant, Oberst Gert Overhoff, is inspecting the cockpit.

Author/Cottbus Museum

(Right) With all five weapons pylons occupied by external tanks, the MiG-21MF could stay airborne for more than two hours. *Erwin Nützmann*

(Left) The formidable MiG-29 began to arrive at Preschen, to equip two squadrons of JG-3, in 1988. *Rudolf Müller*

are touched on in Chapter Five: Command, Control, Communications and Intelligence (C3I). The RAF contribution began with a small force of obsolescent piston-engine fighters and fighter-bombers, replaced by the Vampire FB.5 fighter-bombers, Meteor night fighter and reconnaissance jets by the early 1950s; the Vampires then gave way to Venom FB.1 and FB.4 fighter-bombers. Although the British aviation industry had been one of the main leaders in jet engine and aircraft technology in the last years of WW2, with the Meteor and Vampire aircraft, the impetus in this field had been lost in the post-war years, but the firms responded well to events in Europe and Korea, with Supermarine and Hawker competing for the next interceptor day fighter. In the trials which followed, the Hawker Hunter beat off competition from the Supermarine Swift, to become the RAF's first choice, but pending its delivery to the front line, 427 Canadian-built F-86E Sabre fighters, of the type proven in Korea, were leased to the RAF from 1952, in the Mutual Defence Aid Programme (MDAP), primarily for service in North Germany. Within the next four years, these were replaced by Hunter F.4s and F.6s on 13 squadrons, each of 16 aircraft, split between RAF Oldenburg, Jever, Brüggen and Geilenkirchen, where they served until 1957. Two Meteor NF.11 night fighter squadrons were based at RAF Ahlhorn (North Germany), and two at Wahn (Köln), while the Swift was relegated to the low level, fighter reconnaissance (FR) role, two squadrons of 16 aircraft serving effectively at Jever and Gütersloh from 1956 to 1961. In March 1955, the RAF contributed an assort-

ment of 540 aircraft to NATO in North Germany, but in 1957 the British Air Ministry decided, quite wrongly, that missiles would soon take over from manned aircraft, and by March 1958 this number had dwindled to 205 aircraft. All nine Venom ground-attack squadrons were disbanded and the number of Hunter IDF squadrons was reduced dramatically to four, all based first at Ahlhorn and later Gütersloh. Javelin N/AW squadrons, based at Brüggen and Geilenkirchen took over from the Meteor NF.11s. Meanwhile, thoughts were now turning more to the need for air defence through offensive action, aiming to reduce the impact of Warsaw Pact air power on the West, and this was reflected in the major increases in the RAF's nuclear strike, conventional attack and reconnaissance contribution to 2ATAF (Chapter Six).

On his first tour in RAFG in 1953, Rex Boulton flew the single-seat Vampire fighter-bombers in the Day Fighter/Ground Attack (DF/GA) role, on No.93 squadron at RAF Jever, before being posted later that year to No.130 Squadron at the new airfield of Brüggen, again flying the Vampire, before converting to the F.86 Sabre and finally the Hunter F.4 – again on DF/GA duties.

A second tour of duty in Germany took him to RAF Geilenkirchen in 1962, to join No.5 Squadron, recently equipped with 15 N/AW Javelin Mk.9s, supported by one T.3 dual control trainer and manned by 22 crews. The Javelin was a twin-engine 'delta-wing' interceptor, armed with four 'Fireflash' IR missiles and two 30 mm Aden cannon, each loaded with 250 rounds of ammunition, giving a rate of fire of 1200 rds/min. With a crew of two, the navigator sat behind the pilot operating the AI Mk.17 intercept radar and navigation systems. The aircraft could achieve Mach 1 in a vertical dive, but its normal operating speed was M.82–M.92, and it had a service ceiling of 55,000 ft (16,720 m).

No.5 Squadron comprised 'A' and 'B' Flights, each flying by day or night on alternate weeks, while maintaining four fully-armed aircraft and crews on Quick Reaction Alert (QRA) at all times, with two aircraft at two minutes and two at 15 minutes readiness, a commitment shared with a second RAF N/AW squadron in Germany – all subject to regular practice 'scrambles' to test the system. Connected by landline, the two aircraft at two minutes cockpit readiness were in continuous communication with a Ground Control Interception (GCI) station. With QRA, many extraneous duties on the squadron and the station, plus courses, sporting commitments, sickness and six weeks' leave per year, flying hours for each crew averaged 18 hours per month. Theoretically, Wednesday afternoons were 'sports afternoons', but flying and other duties often took precedence.

Most of the operational flying training, day and night, consisted of practice inter-ceptions (PI's), carried out with pairs of aircraft from the same squadron, each pilot taking it in turn to act as target; they chose their own height, usually 1,000 ft–5,000 ft (300 m –1500 m) above or below the known fixed height of the interceptor, thus ensuring a safe vertical separation. The GCI controller would continue passing vectors after the fighter's crew reported 'Contact', until their radar 'locked on' to the target and they transmitted the code-word 'Judy' – at which point the target aircraft would switch off its navigation lights and commence evasive action. Thereafter, the GCI would cease giving instructions and revert to a monitoring role. The first visual contact with another Javelin was invariably with its jet pipes. The training missiles were inert, having a fully active infra-red sensing head, but no motor or warhead. The training included low level interceptions, but over land ground returns on the radar tended to obscure the target and reduce the contact range, therefore it was better to approach from below the target height. Over the sea, however, using the very accurate radio altimeter to fly safely at the lowest per-mitted height, much better results could be achieved. The Javelin could not claim to have a realistic 'look-down-shoot-down' capability, and the missile was also liable to lock on to extraneous heat sources.

Despite the inherent difficulties of coun-tering the low-level threat it was taken seriously, and Javelins flown at minimum 'safety height' on north-south search patterns across likely hostile penetration routes proved remarkably successful at night. The training schedule also included day fighter battle formation tactics involving up to eight aircraft and two v two combat, ending in a rapid recovery to base using the procedure best suited to the weather conditions.

As with all Allied squadrons, No.5 Squadron enjoyed regular detachments to other NATO bases, from the Mediterranean countries to the north of Norway in summer and winter thus giving their air and ground crews the experience of operating under adverse weather conditions in the north, revelling in some good Mediterranean weather in the south and socialising with their NATO colleagues. At home, all officers not on duty had to attend formal Dining-In Nights (in full 'Mess Dress' uniform), usually on one Friday evening every month; there were regular Summer and Winter Balls on all RAF bases and periodic cocktail parties – all paid for by mess members. Accommodation for all ranks was also very good, on and off-base, while subsidised fuel coupons helped offset the high cost of petrol. Most ranks managed to buy a car, which they were allowed to import into the UK tax free at the end of their tour of duty. The Javelin fighters were replaced by higher performance N/AW Lightnings.

No.19 Squadron, one of the two squadrons of Lightning Mk.2/2A fighters to replace the Javelins, arrived at RAF Gütersloh in September 1965, to add a powerful new dimension to the RAF Germany force. No.92 Squadron followed four months later, to be based temporarily in the rear area at RAF Geilenkirchen but with regular detachments to Gütersloh to share the 'Battle Flight' (QRA) commitment, until moving forward to join 19 Squadron there in January 1968. Lightnings on Battle Flight were held at five minutes readiness, and were subject to many practice scrambles, not only to test their reaction but also that of their opposing force on the other side of the Iron Curtain, and it was quite usual for the pilots of Lightnings and

MiGs to 'eyeball' each other across the IGB, at height. To the west of the IGB, an Air Defence Identification Zone (ADIZ) and a 'buffer zone', into which military aircraft could only fly with special permission and under positive radar control, minimised the chance of Allied aircraft straying into the GDR. In exercises (and war), if a base was considered to be at immediate and serious risk, some or all of its aircraft might be 'scrambled for survival', in accordance with that base's published procedures.

Unlike many of its contemporaries, the single-seat, twin-engine Mach 2 Lightning was highly manoeuvrable at all levels, and could achieve supersonic speeds at low level. While the Airspeed Indicator (ASI), 'stopped' at 700 knots, and a training limit of 650 knots was imposed to preserve the aircraft's structural life, these speeds could easily be exceeded, albeit with some directional instability in the case of the Mk.2 (partially remedied in the Mk.2A by its larger fin). Both versions were equipped with a Ferranti AI-23/23B, I-band radar, which had a night/limited all-weather capability, and were armed with two 30 mm Aden cannon, together with two de Havilland Firestreak AAMs, an additional pair of 30 mm Aden cannon or 48 2-inch unguided rockets in an interchangeable weapons pack. The Mach 3 Firestreak was a pursuit-course missile, with IR guidance and a 50 lb annular blast fragmentation warhead (see 'Air Weapons Training', below). The main deficiency of the Mk.2 Lightning, in the light of an increasing low level threat from the East, was shortage of fuel, but this had been foreseen, and a 'return-to-works' programme began in 1966, with the introduction of a new ventral tank, containing 610 gallons, to replace the original 250 gall tank, together with an enlarged fin and cambered wing leading edge to improve low speed handling. Sortie lengths could also be increased with air-to-air refuelling (AAR), at that time using Victor tankers which often landed at Gütersloh after a refuelling exercise – usually carrying a barrel of good English beer from its home base at RAF Marham. The Lightning was a complex aircraft, and the two Germany squadrons could not claim to maintain a good serviceability rate for its 12–14 aircraft (including one or two dual T.4 aircraft), but when needed, the squadrons' groundcrew always rose to the occasion. The Lightning pilots expected to be tasked predominantly at low level, hoping for visual acquisition of targets, with little help from their AI-23B radar and usually below the effective height of the NATO area defence radars. Flying Combat Air Patrols (CAPs) on Low Level Search Patterns (LLSPs), the Lightning's very impressive acceleration, manoeuvrability and cannon armament, proved invaluable in exercises against contemporary NATO fighter-bombers.

Flight Lieutenant Ian Macfadyen was typical of the young men who flew their first operational tour on the front line in Germany. He passed out from the RAF College, Cranwell, in 1963 and joined No.19 Squadron to fly the Lightning, initially at RAF Leconfield, before the squadron moved to RAF Gütersloh in September 1965. He remembers that demands on the pilot in his cramped cockpit were high, especially on low level interceptions at night in an Electronic Counter-Measures (ECM) environment, but the RAFG air defence squadrons treated the low level threat very seriously in their training. The fuel consumption at low level was very high, but sortie lengths were increased from 1967 with the introduction of a larger ventral tank on the Lightning Mk.2A. Ian found the aircraft a sheer delight to fly and very forgiving, with an outstanding performance at all levels, but he recalled that it needed careful handling in tight turns near the stall. NATO Taceval teams gave the two Lightning squadrons in Germany consistently high marks in the annual operational evaluations.

In the mid-1970s, the RAFG Lightnings were replaced by the Phantom FGR.2, a British version of the US Navy's F-4J Phantom. The FGR.2 was equipped with British avionics and two Rolls Royce Spey 202 engines, each producing 20,500 lb thrust in reheat and 12,250 lb 'dry'. In its air defence role, it could exceed Mach 2 at 40,000 ft (12,000 m), had an impressive initial climb rate of 32.000 ft/min and a ceiling of 57,200 ft (17,400 m). The RAFG Phantoms could be armed with four Raytheon AIM 7 'Sparrow' or the British 'Skyflash' semi-active, radar guided missiles, plus four AIM-9L, all-aspect IRH missiles, or a Suu-23, 20 mm Vulcan six-barrelled Gatling gun on the centreline pylon. The FGR.2 would see out the Cold War in Germany.

Sabres of No.112 Squadron, at RAF Brüggen in 1953.

RAF Brüggen

No.26 Squadron airborne in Hunter F.4s from RAF Oldenburg in 1957, on a Saturday morning 'wing-ding'.

RAF Oldenburg

A pair of Hunter F.6s of No. 26 Squadron, climb out of RAF Ahlhorn in 1958.

John Merry

No.11 Squadron Javelin N/AW.4s, scramble from RAF Geilenkirchen in 1961.

Author's Collection

Javelin N/AW.1s replaced the Meteor NF.11s of 87 Squadron, RAF Brüggen, in 1957.

Dick Carrey

No. 26 Squadron pilots gather around one of their Hunter F.4 day fighters, in 1957. *Author*

Supersonic Lightning fighters of Nos 19 and 92 Squadrons were based at RAF Gütersloh from the second half of the 1950s, this pair being led by a Hunter FR.10 over the Mohne Dam in 1967. *Author's Collection*

Squadron Leader Dennis Caldwell, with Flight Lieutenant Dave Cutting (right) arrive with 19 Squadron at RAF Gütersloh in August 1965, to add to the forward defence of the FRG with their Lightning Mk.2 supersonic fighters. *Dennis Caldwell*

A IV Squadron Hunter taxies past a visiting Javelin N/AW squadron (bottom, right), behind a flight line of Hunters of 14 Squadron and Lightnings of 92 Sqn at RAF Gütersloh in 1967. *Tony Buttler*

Air Defence Readiness Postures

LSK/LV The great concern within the NVA, that NATO would deliver a surprise attack on the GDR, called for high alert states within all its air defence forces. To that end, LSK/LV documents published early in 1989 required both air division and fighter wing operations centres to be manned continuously at all times, and for every fighter wing of 36 aircraft to observe three permanent readiness levels:

Level 3: Twelve fighters, fully fuelled and armed, with pilots and support personnel readily available for a first take-off in three hours – with the squadron operations cell manned ten minutes before that time.

Level 2: Requirements as for Level 3, but for a first take-off in one hour.

Level 1: Requirements as for Level 2 and 3, but for a first take-off in 30 min (MiG-29: one hour).

All remaining personnel, except those on leave outside the GDR, had to be combat ready in 24 hours. In addition, the following five readiness states brought specified numbers of fully operational fighters and pilots to stand-by, with all the necessary operational facilities functioning correctly and the support personnel in place:

Readiness State 3: First take off in 15 min.

Readiness State 2: First take-off in 6–8 min (MiG-29: 11 min).

Readiness State 1: First take-off in 4 min (MiG-29: 7 min).

Readiness State 'Engine Running': First take-off in 2 min.

Readiness State 'Airborne': Aircraft airborne and ready for commitment.

Also, each wing maintained two fully operational fighters (plus a spare), with pilots, at immediate readiness on 'Diensthabendes' (DHS), the equivalent of NATO's QRA force. The number of fighters brought to the various levels of standby depended on perceptions of the threat at the time, the number increasing, for instance, during the Cuban crisis of 1962, and in the late 1970s when the USAF declared its intention to replace the Pershing I nuclear Surface-to-Surface Missiles (SSMs) with the longer range Pershing II, and to introduce some 100 cruise missiles into NATO's European arsenal. There was a tense time again in the 1980s, when one NATO nation failed in its protocol to advise the Warsaw Pact that it was bringing forward a major exercise close to the IGB by 24 hours.

The LSK/LV pilots appeared to have had no problem reacting fully to a surprise alert, their rules on manning requirements and availability being so strictly observed, and their pilots expected to be abstemious in their habits whatever their stand-by commitments; indeed, their personal discipline in this again seemed second to none. No NVA pilot interviewed was able to recall any accident or incident occurring during alert exercises.

RAFG

NATO units had similar readiness requirements, with squadron executives wholly responsible for ensuring that they had enough resources and manpower available to meet their specific commitments when an alert was called – and very elaborate arrangements were in place for that purpose. Because so many of the RAF's personnel were spread widely around each base in Germany, a duplicated 'snowball' call-out system would be triggered, sometimes involving the local German police, and the author is not aware of any occasion on which this failed to achieve the desired effect when the station was exercised.

The progressive proliferation of nuclear weapons and increase in Warsaw Pact conventional forces in Germany brought the ever greater risk of a surprise attack and threats to high value targets such as the permanent air bases on both sides of the IGB. This prompted the two sides to intensify their efforts to get their aircraft off the ground as soon as possible, either to 'hold' in the air or disperse to other airstrips, according to local procedures (See 'Passive Defence', below). An allegedly authoritative LSK/LV document lists ten different warning signals, using sirens, horns and loudspeakers for each type of alert, ranging from an initial recall of personnel to their place of duty, to changes in alert states, chemical, fire, disaster and other contingencies – and finally for a mass launch of aircraft for survival. Concerned that the use of too many automatic means for this purpose was open to human error, the RAF tended to rely more on 'tannoy' or loudspeaker messages, but this was not foolproof, especially when coded messages were deemed to be necessary – as one story from JG-8 at Marxwalde proved (Chapter Four: JG-8).

Every RAFG wing practised its rapid reaction procedures regularly, with survival scrambles called at any time, usually without warning and often outside working hours.

The author was involved in many of these alerts in Germany, and witnessed a veritable torrent of pilots and groundcrew, in various states of dress, rushing to the flight line, using any means of transport available, or simply by foot, competing with each other to help get the maximum number of their squadron's aircraft 'on state' before their rivals on the base. He recalls that in the late 1950s many pilots kept their flying kit in their rooms at night, and that the fully serviceable, combat-ready fighters of the four big squadrons at RAF Gütersloh were lined up outside the hangars, cockpit ladders already in position, aircraft documentation and the pilots' authorisation sheets ready to sign. On reaching the flight line, each pilot would carry out a quick external check of his aircraft, climb into the cockpit, call for any groundcrew present to pull the ejector seat pins and remove the ladder, before triggering the starter cartridge and ordering the wheel chocks to be removed. In peacetime, take-offs were authorised only if the weather and other factors were considered acceptable; otherwise the pilots were ordered to 'taxi through', down the runway and on to a holding area, where they might remain for their planned airborne times before returning to their dispersals. The times at which each aircraft reached the runway threshold were logged in Air Traffic Control (ATC) for the record, as they would be for take offs. By this means a very large number of fighters could be launched in a very few minutes from the 'scramble' signal, for them to proceed thereafter to their prescribed targets or holding areas at the heights assigned. Of course, things did not always go to plan, as was the case on one such exercise at Gütersloh in 1958, when pilots were 'scrambled' directly from their beds without warning at 0300 hrs on a winter's night and soon had every serviceable fighter on four squadrons taxiing. ATC, its equip-ment always on standby and controllers readily available, ordered a 'taxi-through', but for reasons unknown, one pilot from No.26 Squadron could not communicate with the 'tower' on the ground. Thinking that he might be in a temporary 'blind spot', and refusing to be left behind, he joined the stream of taxiing aircraft, lined up with the rest of the wing and began his take-off run as the aircraft ahead of him disappeared into the night fog. Only then, as he reached take-off speed and had to 'leap-frog' over the aircraft ahead of him on the runway, did he realise that this was a 'taxi-through' exercise. Having got airborne safely, he finally established communication with the ground, to be told that all the airfields in West Germany, Holland and Belgium were 'Red' (below weather minima), and that he was alone in the air. However, he now had every radar service in the area at his disposal and eventually got back on to the ground safely – having earned the name: 'Press on Fred'. Authority to launch aircraft (as opposed to having them taxi-through) had to be approved by a senior flier. As for their fitness to fly, a few pilots may have volunteered to remain on the ground, for diverse reasons, but there always seemed to be enough of their colleagues fit and willing to replace them. The risks inherent in scrambling pilots from their beds and launching them

into the night, with abbreviated flight preparation, were recognised and accepted as necessary in the early days of the Cold War, but with aircraft systems then relatively simple and standard procedures well rehearsed, no accidents were known to result. Later, the rules changed, but rapid reaction was still an imperative and very impressive scramble times continued to be achieved in NATO.

In peacetime, the primary task for the LSK/LV and RAF fighter pilots on DHS and QRA duties was to intercept and visually identify 'unknowns' appearing on radar within their area of responsibility, and to take such further action as might be ordered. Normally, such an operation would be strictly controlled from the ground, but if communications failed a pilot might have to defer to the published rules of engagement (RoE) and react accordingly. 'Unknowns' usually fell into one of three categories: 'friendly' aircraft (military and civilian) which had suffered radio failure, were lost or had simply strayed unintentionally into 'hostile' airspace; those which were deliberately probing air defence systems or carrying out reconnaissance tasks, and defectors seeking sanctuary 'on the other side'. In 1956, an off-duty RAF fighter controller spotted a Russian Il-28 flying at low level over Borgentreicht, probably taking photographs of the radar site at Auenhausen; it turned back into the GDR before he could reach a telephone and raise the alert. In the same year, the author himself committed an unforgivable navigation error and crossed into the East in a Venom from RAF Celle, but he too got back across the border safely, at very low level and very high speed! On 18 August 1962, the pilot of a Sea Hawk F1 (RB-364) of the German Navy, belonging to the Marinefliegergeschwader-1 (MFG-1), at Schleswig-Jagel, also had a lucky escape. After taking part in an exercise with the aircraft carrier 'Saratoga' in the Atlantic, he had taken off from Gibraltar carrying three fuel tanks and a reconnaissance pod externally, and was flying at a height of 11,000 m (36,000 ft), when he entered the GDR by accident in the area of Eisenach, was intercepted by a Soviet MiG-21 and severely damaged by cannon fire. He turned west at once, declared an emergency, and succeeded in reaching the FRG safely. There, having decided that his aircraft was still airworthy, he flew on to Bremen, where Focke-Wulf (the maintenance company for the Sea Hawk), was based, but on his final approach there found that his undercarriage had been damaged and would not lower hydraulically, electrically or manually. Rather than have this busy civil airport brought to a standstill with an aircraft immobilised on the runway, he was ordered to carry out a 'belly landing' at the nearby Luftwaffe base of Ahlhorn. This went well, the aircraft being recovered quickly and transported to Bremen by road, where it was broken up – but not before it was thoroughly inspected by some 'very important people'. The recce pod was taken away separately. Others were not so lucky, both the RAF and USAF having aircraft shot down by Soviet fighters. No record can be found of any Warsaw Pact aircraft suffering a similar fate at the hands of NATO, but one

Soviet pilot did defect to the West, crash-landing his MiG in southern Germany. In Chapters Four and Five, LSK/LV controllers and pilots tell of some experiences when their MiGs were launched from DHS but, being in the rear areas of the GDR it is thought that none engaged a NATO aircraft; that was left to the Soviet Air Force, deployed in strength between them and the IGB. The all-important air traffic and fighter control of the EGAF and RAFG air defence aircraft is dealt with fully in Chapter Five.

Operational Training

The fledgling EGAF and RAF fighter pilots were familiarised with tactical flying and air weapons at their respective fast-jet training schools, but they still had much to learn on the front line before they could be considered 'operational'. Accordingly, each pilot would be subjected to a rigorous programme of follow-on operational training, run by the squadron supervisors.

LSK/LV

This training on the LSK/LV wings was governed by strict guidance from divisional level, interpreted by wing staff before dissemination to the squadrons for implementation at the hands of a squadron's deputy commanders and flight commanders. Central programming and rigid control appeared evident at every level, with sorties planned to make good use of every minute in the air that their fuel allowed, and to maximise the use of the three days a week allocated to the NVA in the very congested and restricted airspace which it had to share with the Soviet Air Force in East Germany. Added to this, there were frequent shortages of aviation fuel and of operational pilots in the LSK/LV to fulfil all the readiness requirements, the supervisory roles and extraneous tasks – all of which sometimes made it difficult to provide every pilot with the flying he needed to retain his licence, and to upgrade him to the next recognised level of proficiency. Pilots were upgraded in status on satisfactory completion of specific exercises in a range of target interceptions, simulated combat and weapons deliveries, at high and low levels by day and by night, in different weather conditions and with increasing numbers of aircraft involved. The annual flying syllabi, followed religiously on the LSK/LV wings, ensured that all these essentials were covered, with every sortie completed satisfactorily before a pilot progressed to the next step on the training agenda. By this means the EGAF aimed to generate operational pilots in the shortest possible timeframe, each aspiring to three increasingly demanding levels of proficiency, 'Leistungsklasse' (LK). Each stage required the completion of a specified number of flying hours (including GST training), the syllabus of training prescribed for that level and satisfactory results in progressively more difficult technical examinations – the latter including political issues and aspects of leadership. The first of these classifications, LK.III, could be awarded after 350 hours flying, enabling the recipient to carry out interceptions by day and in clear weather; the second, LK.II, after 500 hours, allowing interceptions by day in Instrument Meteorological Conditions

(IMC), and the third, LK.I, after 600 hours, permitting interceptions by day and night in all weather conditions. Each award earned the appropriate uniform insignia. Thereafter, the ultimate aim of every LSK/LV pilot was to qualify for 'free play' rather than 'canned' combat manoeuvring – but this was hard to achieve.

In meeting these demands, with all the constraints upon them, it would be easy to accept that flight supervisors were left with very little discretion in the management of the flying programmes, but several of those given this task were at pains to assure the author's team that there remained some ways of 'managing' the published syllabus to take account of a new pilot's personal progress. Jörg Behnke, a MiG-21 pilot on JG-7 was one; he had earned his LK.I classification and become a 'four-ship' (Kette) leader and flight instructor, before being chosen as one of the wing's 'Plannungs-offiziere' (planning officers). He and other well qualified pilots from the squadrons and the wing staff were responsible for drawing up the wing's flying programme for each of the three flying days in the week. They would be guided first by the standard requirements published at wing and divisional levels, before taking account of a newly arrived pilot's performance and progress and applying a modicum of lateral thinking to add value to a sortie. For instance (given sufficient fuel) a high level intercept task might be followed by a visual reconnaissance of a military target at low level and a simulated airfield attack on the home base, thus achieving three tasks in a typical MiG-21 sortie of 40 min.

Klaus Schmiedel, a senior pilot on JG-3, was not so sanguine; he claimed that the inherent inflexibility of the system could pose great problems for supervisors attempting to balance operational imperatives with the currency requirements and progressive training of their pilots. He recalls that the planning officers had some two hours to outline three flying options for the following day: one for clear weather, the second for a mixed weather situation and the third for full instrument conditions, for some 40 pilots who should normally be available to fly some 20 single-seat and four two-seat MiGs. The pilots then had to carry out their individual planning for whatever tasks they were assigned in the 'master plan' (formation, combat, general handling etc), and have the plans checked/approved by a senior pilot before they were authorised to fly. Within the fighter squadrons of the LSK/LV, on-going instruction in pure flying, instrument flying, tactics, combat and weapons was given by those pilots judged to have both the experience and expertise for the purpose; there were no specific schools or formal courses to qualify them for these roles, but their more experienced pilots did take part in special air combat exercises to improve their skills.

Jörg Behnke described the standard two-day training cycle which was common to all the fighter squadrons in the LSK/LV, recalling that his wing usually flew on Tuesday, Thursday and Saturday (until 1200 hrs), with each preceding day being devoted to debriefings, flight preparation for the following day and extraneous activities. The few exceptions to this schedule included specific exercises or the need for special dispensation to make up for a deficit of flying caused by bad weather or other factors. A two-day work schedule might comprise:

Day 1: 0740–0815. De-briefing the previous day's flying, analysis of results, updating records.

0815–0900. Physical training

0915–1000. Commander's briefing (intelligence, met, general orders etc).

1000–1030. Coffee break

1030–1115. Issue of tasks and map preparation for the next flying day (3/4 options).

1115–1200. Study/up-date of flying orders and regulations, etc.

1200–1245. Wing lunch.

1245–1530. Flight briefings/ sortie preparation/ authorisation.

1615. Final briefing.

Day 2: Normally, a flying day would entail two six-hour shifts; 0600–1200 hrs and 1400–2000 hrs, but these periods were flexible to meet such special requirements as exercises, air-to-air or air-to-ground gunnery, missile firings or night flying. The following timings relate to planned take-off (TO) times:

TO-3 hrs. Breakfast and medicals. A communal breakfast would consist of food considered suitable for those flying, but contrary to some rumours, what the pilots had to eat, and how much of it, was not supervised. However, those due to fly were required to have some form of sustenance several times a day, and this might be recorded by a flight surgeon, who would also give each pilot a brief medical, recording blood pressure, pulse rate and body temperature – perhaps repeating this again on days when multiple combat sorties were scheduled. Collect any classified material and personal weapons.

> TO-2 hr.15 min. Short wing/squadron briefing
> TO-2 hr. Weather check airborne
> TO-1 hr. 15 min Commander's briefing (met, ATC, ops, flight safety).
> TO-45 min. Pre-flight checks, start-up etc.

RAF Germany

NATO and national headquarters established criteria and broad guidelines for operational training on the front line, to encourage standardisation within the six air forces (RAF, GAF, USAF, Royal Canadian Air Force (RCAF), Royal Netherlands Air Force (RNLAF) and Belgian Air Force (BAF), which frequently operated together in Germany for most of the Cold War, but each nation had its rules and procedures for conducting this training. Although the degree of discretion handed down to lower levels of command varied, many of the flight line supervisors, including those in the RAF, enjoyed a great deal of freedom on how, and at what pace, they brought their pilots up to the standards required by NATO and national headquarters, while maintaining

the proficiency of their operational pilots. Often, squadron commanders would appoint a fully operational pilot as mentor to a newcomer, to monitor his briefings, debriefings and progress, fight his corner with the sortie schedulers and, if necessary, pass him on to a qualified specialist in a particular phase of his training (tactics, combat, low flying, weapons etc). At various stages in this training, the mentor might hand over his charge to an executive for a second opinion particularly when considering upgrading a pilot to Limited Combat Ready (LCR) and Combat Ready (CR). NATO squadrons had the advantage over those in the EGAF, in being able to fly five days a week, at high and low level, over much of the FRG and Western Europe. Moreover, they often had more fuel to play with, giving them the opportunity to fly to less familiar territory and accomplish more aspects of their training in each sortie. From their early days on a squadron, RAF pilots enjoyed a large measure of freedom in planning their own sorties on the ground, adapting to unexpected circumstances in the air and developing their individual skills, but with every sortie vetted and initialled by a qualified 'authorising officer' before flight – and with a full debriefing after the flight. Given the very poor European weather in which these fighter pilots would be expected to fly in combat, great emphasis was placed on instrument flying in the RAF, newly qualified pilots having to undergo an initial Instrument Rating Test (IRT), consisting of a technical examination on the ground and an airborne assessment – and thereafter to repeat this annually with a qualified Instrument Rating Examiner (IRE). Depending also on the number of hours flown in simulated and actual instrument conditions, and the total number of flying hours achieved to date, one of three 'instrument cards' ('White', 'Green' or 'Master Green') could be issued, each entitling the holder to fly in progressively poorer weather. Street-wise RAF pilots trying to launch from another NATO base, but frustrated by the stricter national weather limits there, were known to produce the impressive Master Green card, claiming that this authorised them to take off in any weather they considered acceptable for their skills – and to be released into the gloom while others on that base remained on the ground! In addition, every RAF pilot could expect periodic ground and flying tests within his role, either by specially qualified 'pure' flying examiners from the Central Flying School (CFS) – known as 'trappers' – or by visiting specialists in the role. By these means the proficiency and standardisation of all pilots in the RAF, including those serving on the front line in RAFG, was assured.

The relatively high degree of discretion enjoyed by RAF executives/supervisors at the lower levels of command, and the relative freedom they had when conducting 'on the job' training, should not suggest that NATO pilots as a whole were authorised to do what they liked in the air, to 'bounce' another nation's aircraft or engage in unbriefed mock combat, but it is true that in the 1950s and 1960s, authorised or not, there was much *ad hoc* 'free play' in the skies above North Germany. Indeed, it was not uncommon for large numbers of different types of fighter aircraft, from several nations, to engage in mass combat from 50,000 ft down to low level. Perhaps there was a tacit acceptance among some commanders then that this very hard school, with its steep learning curves, was in itself a natural selection process, bringing out the best in those who would become the future flight leaders and identifying others who might be better employed elsewhere. Although the RAF had the benefit of continuity since WW2, with some pilots from that era, and others with jet fighter experience flying combat in Korea, to act as mentors, the vast influx of new men into the flying schools in the early 1950s gave the RAF and other NATO air forces similar, if lesser problems than those faced by the fledgling EGAF. Some squadron commanders in RAFG had no alternative but to promote pilots into supervisory appointments, arguably before their time – but often to good effect. The author, one of these 'new boys', became a four-ship leader and flight commander towards the end of his first two-year tour on the front line, simply because he was 'next in line'; such an early qualification and appointment would become unheard of in later years.

This combination of lack of experience and expertise, exacerbated by the introduction of the new, high performance jet aircraft (the F-86 Sabre and Hunter), did result in a high incident rate in the 1950s, but in the 1960s, as more experienced flight leaders, better qualified specialists and executives became available, the RAF fast-jet accident rate fell sharply. Those on the front line in Germany were then better able to respond to the more demanding challenges of their role. On the author's FR squadron, for instance, every pilot was at least on his second flying tour, and could react very positively when 'bounced' at low level *en route* to or from his targets, testing his 'lookout', immediate reaction and evasive combat skills – all within published rules. The 1960s brought quantum jumps in operational capabilities, on both sides of the Iron Curtain.

In the RAF, in addition to those pilots who became IREs and QFIs at CFS, others went to the Day Fighter Combat School (DFCS), to become flight leaders, tactical instructors and Qualified Weapons Instructors (QWI) – post-graduate training passed on later to the OCUs and optimised for the aircraft they were flying. These instructors helped to maintain high standards on the front line, pass on the latest doctrines and again ensure standardisation. Late in the Cold War, flight leaders and everyone involved benefited from such mass exercises as NATO's Tactical Leadership Programme (TLP), Tactical Fighter Meets (TFM), Red Flag in the USA and Maple Flag in Canada. These highly competitive exercises brought NATO pilots together with their tactical aircraft employed in their dedicated roles, for a cross-fertilisation of ideas, in planning and flying 'mixed force packages', perhaps 60–100 aircraft strong, combining strike/attack elements, escort fighters, recce and ECM aircraft etc, thereby enhancing their individual and collective capabilities. It is believed that some collaborative exercises of this sort took place within the Warsaw

Pact in these latter days, but rarely in such large numbers of multi-national aircraft. A separate section later in this chapter deals with air weapons training, in NATO and the Warsaw Pact.

Flying Hours

Throughout the Cold War, NATO observers were inclined to comment on the great disparity in the number of fast-jet hours flown by EGAF pilots, and perhaps some in other Warsaw Pact air forces, compared with those in NATO. Whereas LSK/LV pilots could expect to fly between 90–120 hours a year, depending on their status and other duties, their opposite numbers in NATO were consistently logging some 200 hours, but it would be rash to suggest that, in flying twice the number of hours, NATO pilots must be 'twice as good' as those in the EGAF; other factors should be taken into consideration. Much has already been made (above), of efforts by the EGAF to extract value from every minute of fast-jet flying, with the meticulous, sometimes innovative planning of three weather options, and an inspection of old authorisation sheets retrieved from four of the six LSK/LV wings shows that very few of the sorties planned were aborted on the ground or in the air. In most NATO air forces, a squadron or wing's proficiency was judged, in large part, by the number of flying hours it achieved, against criteria published for each (weather factored) month, and the year as a whole, and some NATO executives may have given the hours targets too high a priority *vis-à-vis* realistic operational training. While there is some training value in all flying, and the RAF prided itself with attempting to achieve the hours task regardless of other factors, 'weather aborts' were not infrequent, whereas in the EGAF, with three pre-planned options to choose from, depending on the prevailing weather, there was a greater chance of achieving the objectives and minimising these aborts. On a similar theme, the author's Log Book for the winter months of 1971/72, revealed that about half of the 20 plus hours recorded came from relatively unproductive, high level transits to weapon ranges, flying straight and level above the weather, for a maximum of 10 minutes at low level to drop four practice bombs on ranges in Scotland. Other sorties, such as night cross-countries at high level, carrying the maximum number of external fuel tanks, and morale raising weekend cross-country flights, again at high level from Germany to North Norway or south to North Africa, had little if any operational training value. The recording of flight times was also different in the two camps, the EGAF logging take-off and landing times to the minute whereas, at least in some NATO air forces, it was left to aircraft captains to enter their flight times, as they recalled them, perhaps rounding them up to the nearest five minutes, in a system which was clearly open to error. Flying competitions also featured heavily in NATO, some of value but others merely consuming a large number of flying hours, often to the benefit of the best at the expense of the many, while liable to generate counter-productive 'gamesmanship' and non-operational practices. For these reasons alone they should not be used, *per se*, to

measure operational effectiveness. Others have criticised the number of hours spent by the numerous formation aerobatic teams which sprung up on many RAF fighter squadrons in the 1950s, again favouring a mere handful of the best pilots (usually only five or six for each team). In their defence, however, much of their training was carried out at the end of a training sortie, with light fuel loads, and the value to local morale and international public relations when teams displayed across West Europe, was unarguable. In the EGAF these questions did not seem to arise; none of its fast-jet squadrons is known to have raised a formation aerobatic team during the Cold War. It was also relatively rare for the NVA jets to be involved in mass flypasts, whereas they were frequent, time and resource consuming events for the RAF in Germany during the Cold War, but at least in this case many more aircrew were involved in useful planning and precision flying, again with co-lateral value in local morale and public relations.

The case for committing the maximum available flying hours to the primary purpose of fully operational training, at the expense of extraneous activities, is of course only valid if that training is related directly to the actual threat, and carried out realistically. Research has shown that the LSK/LV concentrated its training on what they believed to be the main threats, but crucial questions arise as to the Warsaw Pact's perception of these threats. Every NVA fighter pilot interviewed spoke with pride of his ability to engage intruders in the middle and upper airspace, at supersonic speeds, but this potential was largely irrelevant; it was almost inconceivable that, from the early 1960s onwards, any NATO aircraft (other than special reconnaissance assets) would have entered GDR airspace at that height or speed. The Warsaw Pact could not have failed to appreciate the full implications of NATO's change in policy from high level to low level operations at that time, so it was interesting to find that relatively little realistic training was carried out by the LSK/LV fighters against low level intruders, at least until the introduction of the MiG-23 and the MiG-29.

While no-one would deny the difficulty of intercepting fast-jets at low level, the author recalls that, in the 1950s, he flew CAPs across likely low level penetration routes into the FRG, albeit at great expense in aircraft utilisation, and attempted to protect crucial targets (eg. airfields) in what were known as 'Rat and Terrier' exercises. Given Visual Meteorological Conditions (VMC), one aircraft would fly at very low level, hoping to silhouette incoming bombers visually against the skyline, the second at about 1,000 ft (330 m), to relay any random plots available from ground-based radars or visual observers, for the two fighter pilots to attempt to predict an intruder's track and plan an interception. Continuous practice brought some success, measured at best by a 'kill', or at least by distracting their quarries sufficiently for them to execute evasive manoeuvres, causing them to jettison their weapons or miss their targets.

As for the LSK/LV's progressive air combat training, this was developed mainly from 'canned' manoeuvres (Chapter Four: JG-1), which were useful in themselves as

handling exercises and in getting to know an aircraft's strengths and limitations, but may not have contributed directly to countering the true, low level threat from NATO aircraft. The author was not aware that any NATO fighters in 2ATAF were earmarked to escort strike/attack aircraft into the GDR, the pilots of which, while well trained in evasive air combat, would have tried hard to avoid any engagements with the Warsaw Pact fighters in order to complete their assigned tasks – and return to base safely.

Several LSK/LV pilots spoke of plans to intercept NATO Airborne Warning And Control System (AWACS) E3As, with large numbers of their MiGs crossing the IGB at high speed and very low level (a hole having been punched through the Hawk SAM belt by other forces), before pulling up in reheat to engage their target (See Chapter Four: JG-3). The EGAF was also believed to have carried out some training against the big, mixed force packages which NATO was known to be practising in the 1980s, but with the likely paucity of aircraft and other limiting factors such as bad weather and poor communications, large NATO packages would surely have been a rare sight over East Germany.

Air Weapons Training

A warplane's performance in its role is, of course, crucial, but its total war fighting capability is also only as good as the operational weapons it has to carry out its duties – and the ability of its pilot/crew to use them to best effect. The EGAF had only those weapons offered by the Russians: the cannon, unguided rockets, beam-riding/ semi-active and IRH AAMs for the fighters and fighter-bombers, SAM and AAA for ground-based defences – but these were reported to have been 'fit for purpose' – and seemingly plentiful. More details on the aircraft weapons are given below, in Chapter Four (for air defence) and Chapter Six (for strike/attack); Both EGAF and NATO relied heavily on cockpit camera recordings to access performance, but both carried out live air-to-air gunnery and missile firings against a variety of targets.

The fundamental need for these training facilities was recognised by the LSK/LV in early 1959, when Yak-11s and MiG-17s of 1.LVD were used to tow airborne targets from Cottbus. They were quickly replaced, in June of that year, by thirteen ex-Soviet Air Force Il-28 ('Beagle') light bombers, one of which was equipped for training, ten converted to target tugs and two to the tac recce role. Initial crew training for the Il-28 pilots, navigators and wireless operators was carried out by Soviet instructors from the 11th Independent Reconnaissance Regiment of the 16th Air Army, at Welzow. With its first commander, Major Hellwig, the EGAF target facilities squadron led a nomadic life; beginning at Cottbus, it carried out many of its sorties during the following two years from Trollenhagen, before moving to Drewitz in November 1961, with a detachment to Preschen from 1963–1965. It returned to Trollenhagen temporarily in 1971 before settling finally at Peenemünde in 1972, under the command of 3.LVD but remaining available to all units in the LSK/LV. In these early days the aircraft themselves acted as targets for the AAA crews and fighter pilots, who used cine cameras only to record their attacks, but within a year the Beagles had been adapted to tow 'Luftsacs' (banners), to enable live gunnery training to take place in a designated area off the Baltic coast at Zingst, west of Rügen Island.

Peter Peil joined the Il-28 squadron at Drewitz; he had completed his GST at Chemnitz and entered OHS in 1959, flying the Yak-18A before attending the air transport training school at Dessau. There he flew 150 sorties in 40 hours on the An-2, in a course which terminated with a mass drop of parachute troops, before progressing to the Il-14 transport, in which he flew 120 sorties in 45 hours. In 1962, he was posted to an Il-14 squadron at Dessau, as an aircraft captain, converting to the Il-28 and joining the target facilities squadron at Drewitz later that year. He recalls that their main work there was to act as targets for AAA units, land based and ship borne, towing Luftsacs for the radar laid ZSU-23-2/4 'Shilka' cannon, on 'racetrack' patterns at various heights off the Baltic coast at Zingst. Peter was fascinated by the sight of rounds emerging from an overcast to burst above, and soon found that if his turn at the end of a racetrack was tighter than recommended, with a tow line of 2,000 m (6,500 ft), he would meet his flag head on (albeit offset). All the guns fired safely out to sea, but with those of a heavy calibre aiming at mirror images of their targets provided by an ingenious system which allowed the aircraft to fly over land. The results were analysed by computers. For LAA practice against low flying aircraft, An-2 transports dropped 'panels', free-fall , from c. 600 m (2,000 ft); whether this was for cine cameras only or live firing is not known. Most exercises involved radar-laid guns, the radar known on some occasions to be 'distracted' or overridden – once with near disastrous results – but no accidents are recorded. The archives show that the unit's Il-28s had other roles, Peter remembering that he was involved in parachute trials on behalf of manufacturers at Seifhennersdorf, with dummies dropped from the bomb bays of the Beagle at 400–600 km/hr (220–320 knots) at heights down to 150 m (500 ft), to assess the stresses sustained.

It was during a detachment to Preschen, while work was being carried out on the runway at Drewitz, that the unit suffered its only major accident in its service with the LSK/LV. On 12 October 1963, Il-28 No.204, crashed just over the border in Poland as it made an Automatic Direction Finding (ADF) approach to land at Preschen. The pilot had suffered spatial disorientation in heavy turbulence, in IMC, and stalled the aircraft too low to effect a recovery. He and his navigator parachuted safely, but their rear gunner/radio operator was slightly injured.

Unlike many of the LSK/LV fighter pilots, Peter recalls that the men of the target force did have sporadic contact with the Soviet Air Force at Welzow, where they had been trained, perhaps because their commander had developed some personal relationships with Russian comrades during his training with them as part of the initial batch of East German airmen on Lehrgang X (Chapter

Two). There may also have been an understanding that, whenever the NVA's Il-28 serviceability was poor, the pilots were given some flying continuity on the Russian Beagles. In 1966, the year in which the unit was granted the name Zieldarstellungsstaffel-21 (ZDS-21) Peter Peil, now a captain, left fixed-wing flying to begin a new career in military helicopters (Chapter Six).

By 1979, the days were numbered for the old Il-28 target tugs in the LSK/LV, as the first pilots and groundcrew began training on their replacement, the L-39 'Albatros', at Bautzen. Two versions of this aircraft began arriving at Peenemünde in 1980: two single-seat L-39Vs, with the rear seat removed to install a winch for towing the KT-04 glider target, and five L-39ZO which had two weapons pylons on each wing for a secondary, ground-attack role. The L-39s reduced the number of aircrew required on the squadron, offered better serviceability with simple, modern technology, greater target speeds and commonality with the training aircraft in use at Bautzen and Rothenburg. The Il-28s were then retired progressively, after 22 years useful service, the last of these venerable aircraft (No.208) flying from Peenemünde to Bautzen on 13 October 1982, where an appreciative audience at the OHS paid proper tribute to this aircraft's illustrious past and also to the squadron's commander, OSL Gerhard Oswald. No.'208' was then honoured further with a prestigious resting place in Berlin's aviation museum at Gatow. In 1981, now reduced to a flight of five L-39s, supported by some 13 officers and 28 NCOs/other ranks, the unit was renamed

Zieldarstellungskette-33 (ZDK-33), and ended its days in October 1990. The five L-39s were flown to Bautzen, where three were handed over to the Bundeswehr, while the remaining two were sold to Hungary.

Especially in the early years of the Cold War, the primary air-to-air weapon for the MiG fighters was the cannon, with live firing training carried out against towed Luftsac and later KT-04 targets. The reusable KT-04 was towed into the air from a wheeled 'dolly', which remained on the ground after take-off, the line between the tug (predominantly an L.39) then extended in flight to 1,700 m (1,900 yd). Those surviving a gunnery exercise were winched in and parachuted back to earth – an airbag cushioning their landings. A miniature aircraft, the KT-04 was hard to see in the air, and harder to attack, the fighter pilots looking first for the brightly coloured L-39 'tugs', flying at 220–270 knots, then attempting to obtain a firing solution with a minimum approach speed of 600 km/hr (330 knots) in a 40–20 deg cone from either side of the target's flight path. This was not a popular exercise. Although it was possible to use the S-5, 57 mm unguided rocket (primarily an air-to-ground weapon) against airborne targets, by changing the sight picture, the general opinion was that this would have been a very inefficient 'weapon of last resort' – needing a very large number of these rockets to achieve a 'kill'.

With the introduction of AAMs in the 1960s, air warfare entered a new era, and new targets were needed. To this end, the LSK/LV fielded the M-6/M6T 'Leuchtbombe' or 'Airborne Small Size Target', which incor-

porated reflectors to return an aircraft's radar pulses, a suitable target for the MiG-21's standard RS-2US 'Atoll' beam-riding missile, and a heat source which burned for five minutes to attract IRH missiles, such as the R-3S or R-13M. The M-6 could be dropped from a variety of aircraft, from heights of 12,000 m (30,000 ft) down to 4,000 m (12,000 ft), descending by parachute at a rate of 7–14 m/sec (23–42 ft/sec), depending on release height, for the short missile firing phase – but it was hardly representative of an aircraft or cruise missile. More realistic, in terms of speed, was an RM-3V 'raketa-mishen' (target missile), modified to reduce its speed and increase its IR 'plume'. A MiG-21 would launch an RM-3V from the port wing pylon as a target for an R-3S fired from the starboard pylon. Live firing exercises with the Luftsac, KT-04, M-6/M6T and RM-3V were carried out regularly over the Baltic in 'Luftschießzone II' (LSZ-II), east of Rügen. While LSZ-II was within range of the LSK/LV fighter bases, some wings detached to Peenemünder or Garz (Herringsdorf) airfields for their live firing exercises. For training with the more advanced, longer range AAMs, it was necessary for the German pilots to deploy to the Russian airfield of Astrachan, Belarus, in the early days flying Soviet MiGs there, but latterly taking their own aircraft with them. There, they had the opportunity to test their skills against the radio-controlled Russian La-17, a small, high speed, unmanned air vehicle (UAV), powered by a turbojet. Initially, the La-17 was air-launched, but this was found to be too expensive and a boosted version (La-17M) was developed, to be launched off the ground from a four-wheel, towed 'dolly'. The

La-17M could fly for a useful 60 min, and at the end of its sortie, given its survival in the air, it was flown back on to the ground for a 'belly landing'. In the summer of 1986, Maj Michael Wegerich led a group of pilots from 2.JS/JG-1 to Astrachan with 12 MiG-21SPS and a two-seat MiG-21U for live missile firings against the La-17 – for what was to be a very successful detachment (Chapter Four: JG-1). Hannes Mallwitz (Chapter Four: JG-1), was also fortunate to have fired live AAMs at Astrachan, and to score a direct hit on an M6 in LSZ-II, but things did not always go to plan for other MiG pilots, with mechanical failures, human errors and incidental factors sometimes intruding. It is said that the EGAF suffered one such embarrassing incident when a MiG-21 pilot fired a rocket into the stern of a harmless fishing trawler in the Baltic – instead of his semi-submerged ship target, leaving a splinter of wood in a sailor's leg. The unit commander was sent forthwith to apologise for the ship's captain, his reception there described later as 'just as bad as a hanging'.

Similar facilities and training were available to RAFG pilots. Live gunnery training in Vampire, Meteor, Sabre and Hunter fighters, in the 1950s and 1960s, was carried out over sea ranges in regular detachments to Sylt, on the border between Germany and Denmark, off the Friesland Islands in Holland and over UK waters. The target was invariably a banner, 6 ft (2 m) in depth and 30 ft (10 m) in length, towed behind an aircraft on a 1,000 ft (300 m) cable, but at Sylt, some pilots had the opportunity to pit their skills against towed gliders. The scoring system against the banners was very precise, with all the rounds fired (20 mm and 30 mm) colour-coded to identify the pilots when the holes were counted on white, Hessian banners, or 'flags', towed behind modified Tempest or Meteor fighters. Gunnery practice for the Javelin squadrons also took place at least twice a year, usually on ranges off the north coast of Holland. This enabled the gun harmonisation, radar ranging and gun stoppage rates to be checked while giving the armourers, photographic section and the rest of the ground crew practice in rapid turn-round of aircraft. Scores with the wing-mounted cannon were invariably low, but few rounds of 30 mm, high explosive ammunition would have been needed to severely damage if not destroy the potential adversaries of the day.

The RAF did not have anything similar to the LSK/LV's M6/M6T parachute targets, or the RM-3V missile for their AAMs, but live firing facilities were available for the British 'Firestreak' and 'Skyflash', the American AIM-7 'Sparrow' and AIM-9 'Sidewinder' AAMs, carried by the Javelins, Lightnings and Phantoms, on ranges over the Irish Sea off the coast of Wales. To this end the RAF acquired 283 of the highly successful Jindivik drones, manufactured in Australia, which towed flares to simulate hostile aircraft or cruise missiles. The first of these, which proved able to remain airborne at 40,000 ft for 15 minutes, achieve speeds of 490 knots and heights of 57,000 ft, arrived in the UK in 1960.

With no facilities available to them for live air-to-air gunnery training in Germany, the early RAFG Lightning pilots recorded all their practice interceptions with the Aden cannon on film, firing their guns into open airspace simply to prove the system and feel their effects – while providing practice for the armourers on the ground. Quite often the effects in the air were more than expected, with various warning captions illuminating due to the vibration of the cannons, which were very close to the cockpit. Likewise, simulated missile firings were recorded on film, but during their tour most pilots had the opportunity to fire at least one missile against a towed target. Ian Macfadyen remembers a detachment from RAF Gütersloh to RAF Valley, North Wales, in which he fired a Firestreak from a two-seat Lightning Mk.4 against a flare towed some 200 ft (60 m) behind a Jindivik in the Aberporth Range off the coast of Wales. The missile, with a live warhead, actually hit the flare with some spectacular results, and in all the excitement neither pilot noticed an alarm warning going off temporarily in the cockpit, almost certainly due to the vibration associated with the missile launch!

Live SAM firings were carried out by RAF (and British Army) units off the coast of north-west Scotland.

Survival Equipment And Training

The NVA paid scrupulous attention to their pilots' personal survival equipment and training. MiG pilots were all required to wear pressure suits above 14,300 m (47,000 ft), the uncomfortable 'suiting-up' taking up to an hour and terminating in rigorous checks of the whole system when pressurised, as the pilot breathed in pure oxygen. Be they more or less fortunate, the RAF Hunter pilots of the 1950s, the author

among them, were flying with a partial-pressure breathing system, in pressurised cockpits but without pressure suits, up to 50,000 ft (15,200 m). Escape, evasion and survival exercises were also high on the agenda in the NVA, usually arranged by the wings locally, with sea survival training, including helicopter retrieval, typically carried out on a lake at Tollensee south of Neubrandenburg. Initially in RAF Germany, realistic training in sea survival and recovery required the aircrew to drop, 'free-fall', from a helicopter hovering some 20 feet above the North Sea off the island of Sylt, to weather the elements in their normal flying kit, with life jackets and in dinghies, until the staff decided they had learned enough. Immersion suits were not in common use until the 1960s. RAFG pilots and navigators also attended a thoroughly uncomfortable winter survival school at Bad Kohlgrub in southern Germany, those caught by German paratroops or police during their final escape and evasion phase in the Bavarian Alps being subjected to undignified and very stressful interrogation procedures – which would be an anathema to civil liberty groups and British health and safety authorities today.

The speed and height at which the Cold War fast-jets operated required innovative systems to enable the crew to escape from their aircraft safely – namely 'ejection seats'. For British combat aircraft, this field was dominated by the firm of Martin Baker (MB). The author began his jet flying on variants of the Vampire and Meteor without ejection seats, and it was a great comfort to progress to the Hunters, which were

Hannes Mallwitz at Astrachan, about to fly
a MiG-21MF of the Soviet Air Force,
accompanied by a second MiG-21
carrying an RM-3 target missile.
Hannes Mallwitz Collection

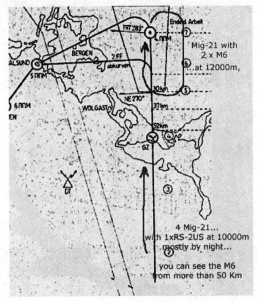

Hannes Mallwitz, JG-1, had the good fortune to be tasked
against a KT-04 at night in LSZ-II – and scored a 'hit'.
Hannes Mallwitz

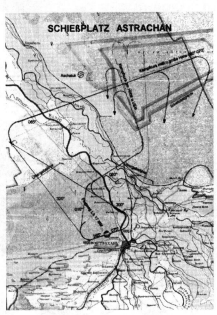

Some LSK/LV pilots fired AAMs against Russian La-17 targets
on the range at Astrachan; with German fighter controllers
assisting them on these APCs. *Rudy Just*

Those KT-04Rs which survived a gunnery exercise, were
parachuted back to earth, an air bag cushioning their fall.
Author's Collection

Adapted from the Il-28 ('Beagle') light bomber, thirteen of
these aircraft were used for a variety of target towing and
reconnaissance tasks from 1959–1980. *Peter Peil*

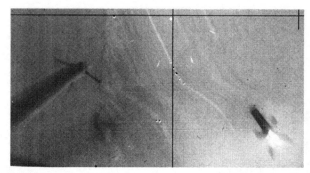

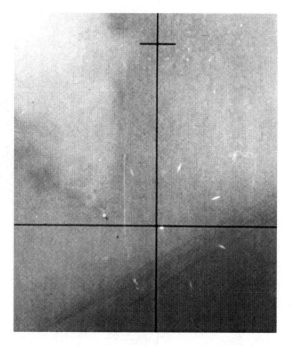

Above and right: In this weapons exercise over LSZ-II, an RM-3 target missile is fired from a pylon on the starboard wing of a MiG-21MF of JG-3, to provide an IR source for a R-3S AAM, launched from a port wing pylon. *Hannes Mallwitz*

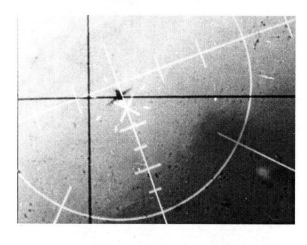

Left: A JG-1 pilot 'captures' another MiG-21 in his gunsight, on a cine training exercise. *Jurgen Gruhl*

A number of EGAF L-39 training aircraft were adapted to tow targets for air-to-air gunnery, taking over from the Il-28s in 1980. The vehicle below is a KT-04 towed target. *Author's Collection*

This head-on view of MiG-17F shows the heavy firepower of its single 37 mm and two 23 mm cannon. *Author's*

The 1,650 km route from Holzdorf to Astrachan involved four fuel stops.
Michael Wegerich

Maj Michael Wegerich, commander 3.JS/JG-1, arrives at Astrachan in his MiG-21SPS.
Michael Wegerich

'One-Man Band. An engineering officer from 3.JS/JG-1, conducted business at Astrachan with minimum equipment.
Michael Wegerich

Memento of a job well done at Astrachan.
Michael Wegerich

'Vodka on the Wolga'. The German 'anti-icing fluid' came in very useful at an unofficial celebration of a successful JG-1 detachment to Astrachan, enjoyed by Soviet and German pilots and ground-crew alike – without the presence of a flight surgeon!
Michael Wegerich

The high-scoring RAFG Hunter gunnery team in1959; L to R: Flt Lts Jock McVie, Philip Alston, Wg Cdr Peter Thorne, Flt Lts Mike Davis, Bill Boult and Ron Stuart-Paul.

Phil Alston

The 37 mm round used by the early MiG fighters, compared with the 30 mm ammunition used by the RAFG Hunters and Swifts, and the 20 mm rounds of the earlier Vampires and Meteors. *Author*

In 1953, Fg Off Dennis Caldwell scored an unbeaten 82% in his F-86 Sabre, at an APC on the German Island of Sylt.

Dennis Caldwell

A Firestreak IR missile, fired by Ian Macfadyen from a Lightning Mk.4, scores a direct hit on the flare towed by a Jindivik drone over the Aberporth Range, in 1967.

Ian Macfadyen

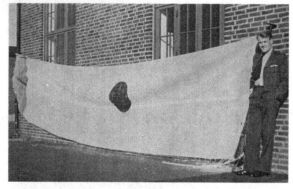

Fixed armament for the MiG fighters comprised 37 mm, 30 mm and 23 mm cannon. *Author*

equipped with MB2 seats. True, separation from these early seats had to be carried out manually after ejection but, by the mid-1950s, barometric pressure control units (BPCs) provided automatic separation at the height pre-set on the ground. Even then, all the early seats had worrying height and speed restrictions, below which safe ejection could not be guaranteed, these only reduced to 'zero/zero' with the introduction of rocket seats. The Soviet aircraft industry, and hence the EGAF, followed suit, but the MiG-15s and MiG-17s had minimum restrictions of 400 km/hr (220 knots) and heights of 150 m (500 ft), despite some successful ejections down to speeds of 200 km/hr. The 'SK' seats fitted to the first MiG-21F-13/PFM/U were designed for speeds up to M2.0 at high altitude, with the canopy hinged at the front and blown free from the aircraft, via a complicated arrangement of hinges and locks. During the ejection the pilot was protected from the wind blast in a 'cocoon', christened the 'white coffin', but the sequence was too slow to use safely at low level and was dispensed with in later models of the seat. The recommended limits then depended on height, speed and the aircraft's attitude when the ejection was triggered, but could be as low as 150 m (500 ft) and 170 km/hr (90 knots). With these seats and limits, the pilots remained at great risk during take-offs and landing, when emergencies were most likely (vide. Maj Liebert's fatal ejection from a MiG-21PFM, on take-off from Trollenhagen 6 May, 1988, using an SK seat (Chapter Four: JG-2)), so the race was on to secure real improvements. These came with the KM-1 seat,

fitted to the MiG-21SPS/M/MF/bis/US/UM, from which safe ejections were possible on the ground at a minimum of 130 km/hr (70 knots), and up to a maximum of 700 km/hr (380 knots) unless there was added protection for the pilot. Then came the K-36 DM, with which the Su-22 and MiG-29 were equipped, which enabled ejections on the ground down to speeds of 75 km/hr (40 knots), and up to a maximum of 950 km/hr (520 knots). Fast-jet pilots in the EGAF, underwent 'live' parachute descent training, annually, from the start of their careers, whereas RAF pilots merely practised landing techniques.

Surface-To-Air Weapons

NVA SAM. It is worth repeating that the Cold War fighter force should not be treated in isolation of other Warsaw Pact or NATO air defence systems, especially SAM and AAA, but space precludes more than a brief mention of them here. In addition to the vast armoury of SAM deployed by the NVA Army (LaSK) and Soviet forces in the GDR, the LSK/LV fielded a formidable force of its own. SA-2B 'Guideline 1', SA-2D 'Guideline 3/5', SA-3C 'Goa' and SA-5 'Gammon' provided area defence, while SA-7 'Grail', SA-6 'Gimlet' and SA-18 'Grouse', were deployed at wing level for local airfield defence. 1.LVD commanded 51.Fla-Raketen-brigade (51.FRB) and 41.FRB (each equivalent to a NATO SAM wing), together with Fla-Raketen-Regiment 31 (FRR-31), in the centre of the GDR, while in the north, 3.LVD had 43. FRB, FRR-23 and FRR-13. At the 'sharp end', Fla-Raketenabteilung (FRA)

A typical ejection sequence from a MiG-21F-13, using an SK seat, which included a 'cocoon' designed to protect the pilot on ejection, but it had undesirable height and speed minimums. *Armin Schulz*

The author began his operational flying in the Hunter with the Martin Baker (MB) Mk.2 seat with minimums of 100ft (30m) and 120 knots (220km/hr) and ended on the Jaguar with the MB Mk.9B 'zero/zero' seat. *Author's Collection*

EGAF pilots practising sea survival and recovery procedures, typically in the Tollensee lake, south of Neubrandenburg. *Author's Collection*

All MiG pilots underwent ejection seat and parachute training in the NVA. *Norbert Hess*

Hartwig Richter, JG-1 'suiting up' for a high level flight. *Hartwig Richter*

SAM units were scattered throughout the GDR, each with its specific area of responsibility. Technical support was provided by collocated Funktechnische Bataillone (FuTB).

The author is indebted to 'Gerd P', a professional SAM officer from the NVA, for his insight into that part of the NVA SAM screen attributed solely to the LSK/LV. Gerd graduated from OHS at Kamenz in 1984 and from then until 1989 he served first with FRA-4124 at Beetz, near the Soviet air base of Oranienburg, north of Berlin, and later at FRA-4122, Proetzel, close to the NVA HQ at Strausberg, both within 41.FRB,1.LVD, and both equipped with the SA-2. While at Beetz, Gerd fired a live SA-2 on the range in Kasachstan. As a platoon leader on both units, he was responsible for the missiles and the launching procedures within his section, part of a force within an FRA of 45 missiles: six ready to fire within 3½ minutes, six 'ready to fire' on trucks for an immediate re-load, and 33 held in a bunker, to be assembled as required. The SA-2, of which there were several variants, is a command guidance missile with solid fuel boosters, a liquid fuel upper stage and electronic counter-counter-measures (ECCM), the latter enhanced progressively throughout its lifetime. The SA-2 was introduced into the EGAF in 1964 as the main weapon within its SAM force, remaining in service until the end of the Cold War. Performance figures vary with their source, and with the variant, but in optimum conditions the SA-2 is believed to have been able to carry out successful interceptions up to a maximum height of 23,000 m (75,000 ft), and down to

100 m (330 ft). The SA-2 gained prominence in 1960, when a high flying American U-2 reconnaissance aircraft was destroyed by the missile over Russia (although it was said that 14 rounds had to be fired against it to achieve the 'kill'), and another U-2 was shot down by the missile over Cuba in 1962. In 1967, the SA-2 also had some success against the Israelis in the Six Day War in the Middle East, and throughout that decade against US aircraft in SEA.

The SA-3C Goa, which served from the 1970s, was reputed to have been successful against targets from 100 m (330 ft) to 20,000 m (65,000 ft), while the SA-5 Gammon, which joined the front line in the 1980s, could reach targets up to a height of 40,000 m (130,000 ft) but down to a minimum height of only 300 m (1,000 ft). Meanwhile, the LaSK was operating huge numbers of mobile SA-9 Strela 'Gaskin' and SA-13 Strela 'Gopher' missiles. The NVA SAM threat to any aircraft flying in the middle or upper airspace was very real, but its true effectiveness against targets 'in the weeds' during the Cold War remains a matter of conjecture.

Overall command and control of the LSK/LV SAM force was exercised from the central command bunker at Fürstenwalde, from where authority was delegated as required to the divisional bunkers at Kolkwitz (1.LVD) and Colpine (3.LVD), specific tasks then allocated to wings (Chapter Five). At each level, SAM and AAA liaison officers were collocated with the respective wing commanders and their fighter controllers, this being essential for the de-confliction of the three primary weapons systems. For optimum performance, the SAM units were located throughout their areas of responsibility on prepared bases, but most had a mobile capability. Depending on their specific purposes and circumstances, they made use of a variety of radars for target acquisition and tracking, for example the NATO named: 'Spoon Rest', 'Fan Song', 'Flat Face' and 'Side Net' (Chapter Five).

In 1989, Gerd was promoted to Battery Chief, on Fla-Raketenabteilungs Gruppe 511 (FRAG-511) at Eckolstadt/Apolda, near Erfurt, which was equipped with the SA-5 'Gammon', and he remained there until the end of the Cold War. After reunification, he was tasked with the disposal of 1,000 redundant SA-2s, held in storage with 51.FRB, nearby Sprötau, and in 1991 was accepted into the Bundeswehr, for continued employment in his specialist role. To this end, he re-trained on the American Hawk SAM and became a Tactical Control Officer (TCO) at Erding, near Munich, before qualifying as a Tactical Director (TD) and SAM Allocator, first at the Control and Reporting Centre (CRC) at Freising in1999, then at CRC Meßstetten from 2002. His expertise in the LSK/LV had been put to good use.

NVA AAA. In addition to SAM, the LSK/LV had a large number of light and medium calibre Anti-Aircraft Artillery (AAA), cannon and heavy machine guns to protect their airfields. They included the towed ZPU-14.5 and ZU-23/2, and the fully mobile ZSU-57/2, ZSU-23/2 and ZSU-23/4, all three of the latter mounted on armoured fighting vehicles (AFV). The Russian ZSU-23/4 'Shilka', a four-barrel, 23 mm gun, produced between 1957–1962, was subsequently modified to be fully mobile with a crew of four (commander, driver, gunner and radar operator). Computerised, with a RPK 2 'Tobol' 'J'-band radar, it was very accurate, had a range of 20 km (11 nm), and performed satisfactorily in most weather and poor light conditions. Having a stabilised system, the gun could shoot on the move, with each of four barrels firing up to 1,000 rds/min, giving a combined firepower of up to 4,000 rds/min – from an on-board total of 2,000 rds. With an integrated Nuclear Biological and Chemical (NBC) suite, which included an air filtration unit and fire protection equipment, the AFV could operate in a nuclear fall-out environment. Despite this impressive capability, the ZSU-23/4 had serious deficiencies when it attempted to engage aircraft flying at very low level and high speeds. It had no laser range finder and its short (weather dependent) detection range made automatic tracking difficult at high angular target speeds within 7 km (4 nm), thus calling for high skill levels from the operators. The radar also suffered from heavy ground clutter at target heights below 60 m (200 ft), and with a maximum of 15 mm of armour, the tracked vehicle was highly vulnerable to anti-tank missiles, cannon and heavy machine guns. Moreover, if the guns overheated after prolonged firing bursts (eg.15 secs), they tended to jam or even break up – at great risk to the crew. All that said, this was a gun which the Cold War NATO pilots feared.

RAFG SAM. Following the adoption by NATO of a 'flexible response' defence policy, and the Soviet invasion of Czechoslovakia in 1968, the RAF deployed Bloodhound and Rapier SAM units to Germany to protect its airfields. Three flights, each of eight Bloodhound Mk.2 launchers were sited on the 'Clutch' airfields, with the HQ unit and 'A' Flight at RAF Brüggen, 'B' Flight at RAF Wildenrath and 'C' Flight at RAF Laarbruch, each with its dedicated Tp.86 radar for missile guidance. In June 1970, 'C' Flight was the first of the three sites to become operational, the others following in 1971. Although dating back to the 1940s, the Tp.86 radar, mounted as high as practicable to minimise clutter from local buildings and trees, could illuminate fighter-size targets at high and low level, and begin engagements at a range of more than 70 miles (110 km), but minimum engagement ranges were said to be 2½ miles (4 km), owing to the 2½ sec in which the missile accelerated. The radar returns were Doppler analysed, so targets could be tracked approaching or departing, as was proven when the system was put to the test by USAF 'Wild Weasels' ECM aircraft; they turned away from their approach to 'break lock', but were immediately acquired again as they turned inbound in an effort to continue an attack. The Tp.86 was also found to have some resistance to ECM. Sqn Ldr John Gale commanded 'B' Flight; he had been an operational fighter pilot and was well known to the author for his professional approach to his duties; John remembers that their annual live firings at Jindervik targets flying at 500 ft (150 m), over the sea ranges off the coast of Wales, were consistently successful. However, in common with others in his specialisation, he was uneasy over shortcomings in the system's capability to discriminate between friend and foe, with the consequent need for procedural deconfliction with flying operations. That said, Bloodhound compared well with other contemporary SAM, and with the whole system benefiting from in-service experience with its predecessor, the Mk.1, the squadron's serviceability rates were very high. While many of the missile controllers were redundant aircrew, who found their working routines on the static Bloodhound units rather mundane, they excelled when it came to the very challenging exercises against live targets, and NATO teams gave 25 Squadron excellent marks on all counts in periodic Tacevals. The RAF Bloodhound units in Germany remained at a high state of readiness, manned and on watch at all times, until the mid-1980s, when local airfield protection was left solely to Rapier SAM units.

The Rapier mobile SAM system was optimised for short range, low level operation. Early versions, which entered service in 1971, comprised a wheeled launcher carrying four missiles, an optical tracker, generator unit and stores trailer, all delivered by two Landrovers. A third Landrover was needed to tow the 'Blindfire' radar unit, added later to give the system (already incorporating IFF) an all-weather capability. Other developments followed, progressively enhancing Rapier's overall effectiveness. Four RAF Regiment Low Level Air Defence (LLAD) squadrons, each equipped with eight fire units, were sited on all the RAF flying stations in Germany. The first of these, No. 63 Squadron, RAF Regiment, became operational at the most forward of these bases, RAF Gütersloh, in 1974.

RAFG AAA. At the beginning of the Cold War, RAF airfields in Germany were protected by L40/70, 40 mm AAA, a Swedish gun which originated in the 1920s and proved valuable to the Allies in WW2. With the introduction of the faster jet aircraft, the L40/70 was given a larger but lighter projectile, fired from a single barrel at a high muzzle velocity of 1,030 m/sec (3,380 ft/sec) and a rate of fire of 240 rounds/minute; it was 'laid' by power from an integral generator, and later models would have radar. At RAF Oldenburg, in the 1950s, an RAF Regiment L40/70 squadron was attached to each of the three flying squadrons, the pilots (including the author) revelling in attempts to track their peers as they approached the airfield at high speed and low level to break and land. Analysis showed that their success rates were somewhat less than those of the professional gunners! When the L40/70s were withdrawn from Germany, there was a period when RAF airfield defence depen-ded on the British Army, but short range RAF air defence (SHORAD) resumed again in earnest with the arrival of the Rapier squadrons. In addition, a 'Tigercat' SAM squadron was held at readiness in the UK, to be deployed to Germany, if required.

Dispersal & Passive Defence

While this tribute focuses primarily on the 'teeth arms' of the EGAF and the RAFG fighters, fighter-bombers, armed helicopters and anti-aircraft weapons, it would be wrong to neglect the passive survival measures adopted increasingly on both sides of the Iron Curtain, which gave these forces some security from hostile action. On the Main Operating Bases (MOBs), these covered a wide range of concealment, protection and recovery measures, aimed at prolonging their operational effectiveness, without hindering on-going operations. These included natural and man-made camouflage, decoy targets, redundancy in take-off and landing strips, on and off-base dispersal, 'hardened' shelters for aircraft, munitions and personnel, some of the latter air-filtered and with decontamination facilities in anticipation of NBC operations. These and other measures evolved con-tinuously with every development in counter-air operations – in both NATO and the Warsaw Pact.

The need to protect or disperse certain operational assets was underlined forcefully during the Six Day War of 1967 in the Middle East, when the Israeli fighter-bombers all but wiped out the Egyptian Air Force, the largest in the Arab world. That they were able to do so was because their targets were easy to acquire from the air, unprotected and often lined up neatly on the flight lines, offering ideal targets for the fighter-bombers. The lessons were not lost on the Warsaw Pact or NATO and led to much debate on the relative merits of protection and dispersal. Prioritising protection, all the

The SA-2 'Wolchow' was reputed to have had a height range of 100 m (330 ft) up to 35,000 m (115,000 ft).

Rudolf Müller Collection

Bloodhound 2 SAM protected RAF bases in Germany in the 1970s/1980s.

Author's Collection

Rapier SAM replaced L40/70, 40 mm LAA for the RAF's Short Range Air Defence (SHORAD) in Germany in the last two decades of the Cold War.

RAF Brüggen

SA-5 'Wega'

Rudolf Müller

The formidable ZSU-23/4, 23 mm LAA cannon, used extensively throughout the Warsaw Pact.

Author

One of the patterns flown by the Il-28s and their targets, over the Baltic coast, for ground-based live gunnery training.

Peter Peil

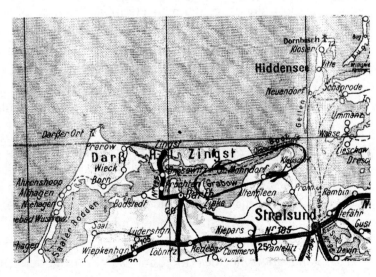

RAF Germany stations, and progressively every NATO MOB in the Central Region of Europe, began huge Airfield Survival Measures (ASM) construction programmes in the early 1970s.

Taking RAF Brüggen as an example, 60 concrete and earth-covered Hardened Aircraft Shelters (HAS), each expected to withstand a direct hit from a 250 kg (550 lb), or a near miss by a 500 kg (1,100 lb) bomb, were built within existing revetments in the four squadron dispersal areas. A further site, close to the runway threshold at the west end of the airfield, accommodated up to six fighter-bombers on QRA, while similar concrete protection was given to the aircrafts' weapons. Underground storage below each HAS was seriously considered and may have been adopted by the USAF, to minimise vulnerable movement on an airfield, enhancing security and expediting complex loading procedures. In addition, hardened and filtered Pilot Briefing Facilities (PBFs) and Hardened Personnel Shelters (HPS) were built within each of the four squadron sites, together with a Combat Operations Centre (COC) within the domestic site, perhaps with the hope of making it more difficult to locate in a single pass from the air. The RAFG COCs were manned at all times in peace and occupied in exercise and war by the Force Commander (the Station Commander) and his primary battle management staff. Once all these facilities were complete, all Cold War flying in RAF Germany was conducted from the COC and PBFs, each with independent auxiliary power units, air filtration systems, decontamination facilities, food and water

storage and sleeping accommodation, while the aircraft were dispersed in their HAS. The southern taxiway at Brüggen, acting as an alternative runway, was brought into use periodically, without incident. As an option of last resort, the station's aircraft could have accessed the straight, if narrow and tree-lined road beside the camp from Elmpt village to Roermond town. Later, all the airfield facilities, including the runway and taxiways, were coated with a drab green preparation, in a 'tone down' programme to make them harder to recognise quickly from the air. Also, the necessary materials (aggregate and steel matting) and heavy plant were pre-positioned on the airfield to make good any of the paved surfaces damaged in an air attack. To this end, every operational RAF base in Germany hosted a squadron of the British Army's Royal Engineers (RE), the 'Sappers', they being responsible for Rapid Runway Repair (RRR) or Airfield Damage Repair (ADR), and they proved their worth during every station exercise. Indeed, it was not unusual, in the middle of a NATO Taceval, even during an intensive period of flying, for a hole to be blown in a taxiway to test ADR and note the time taken to render that taxiway useable again with a paved surface. This whole process could take as little as 30 minutes to fill a crater made by a 1,100 lb (500 kg) bomb.

Meanwhile, very similar work on survival measures was being carried out by the NVA in the GDR, the results of which remained very evident to the author's team when it visited the now long defunct airfields there. In general, they found that the standard

HAS, albeit smaller and perhaps less well built than its NATO equivalent, should have served its purpose, Likewise, the operational facilities, including the divisional, wing and DHS bunkers, while entirely functional were less lavish than those in the West. Notwithstanding the effort put into the Warsaw Pact's version of NATO's ASM programme, the EGAF placed great emphasis on local airstrip redundancy and aircraft dispersal. The wings ensured that all their pilots remained current in operations from the grass runways provided on all its LSK/LV airfields and reserve airstrips, including their use at night, with or without the assistance of the SPRD rockets (which could reduce a MiG-21's take-off run to as little as 400 m (440 yd). Chapter Four contains personal stories from the LSK/LV wings, of these dispersal exercises.

In the 1950s, RAF tactical squadrons based in north-west Germany were equipped with vehicles to give them a truly mobile capability, and suitable airfields in Holland, such as Beek, Deelen, Venray. Valkenburg and Woensdrecht, were prepared to receive NATO aircraft in the event of a fall-back of Allied forces. Those pilots unfit or otherwise not required to fill a cockpit would drive one of these support vehicles, the author remembering one deployment from Oldenburg to Sylt, in which he drove a Magirus three-ton truck carrying a Hunter gun-pack, escorted closely by the German police, at break-neck speed through the centre of Hamburg. By the mid-1960s, this organic transport had been withdrawn, but regular 'Round Robin' exercises kept most of NATO's operational bases well practised in 'turning round' (and sometimes re-arming) visiting aircraft. At that time there were no plans to use highway strips in the FRG, but by the 1970s provision was made on some new autobahns for fast-jet operations, and Jaguars from RAF Brüggen were among the first 2ATAF fast-jets to evaluate the use of one such strip near Hamburg. It is probable that the GAF, and perhaps other NATO air forces, had contingency plans for the use of these strips, but the author was not aware of any co-ordinated plan for their general use within 2ATAF during his time, and there were no regular rehearsals of the concept in the RAF. Although some of the RAF's tactical aircraft were supposed to have the capability to operate of suitable grass airstrips, none, other than the Vertical and Short Take-Off and Landing (VSTOL) Harriers, were known to practise this operationally in Germany.

Being far from the IGB, and with many higher priority targets for NATO in the west of the GDR, early attacks by tactical bombers on the EGAF fast-jet bases on the border with Poland, were unlikely. It was, therefore, understandable that day-to-day training in the EGAF continued, more conveniently, from the traditional flight lines adjacent to 'soft' hangars and operational facilities, the aircraft only dispersed to assigned war sites, on or off-base, with the necessary support, during exercises or in war. This could be accomplished very rapidly, as was well-proven in many Cold War exercises. Indeed, it was standard practice in these exercises for one of the three squadrons on a wing to deploy, at very short notice, to its dedicated war reserve airstrip (eg. Alteno for JG-1, Klein Koris for JG-7). The author flew over both these airstrips (now long dormant) with an ex-MiG pilot, and visited them on the ground – and was impressed by their basic suitability for the purpose. There were no give-away concrete runways or operational buildings easily visible from the air or on the ground, and wooded areas on at least one side of the long, grass airstrips served to hide the minimum buildings necessary and support vehicles – and the fighters after they had landed.

Mission Evaluation

The overall operational effectiveness of NATO's air forces within the Allied Air Forces Central Europe (AAFCE) was measured best by the AAFCE Taceval organisation, based at Ramstein Air Base (AB), West Germany, and national teams, the author being a member of the Fighter Command team from 1967–69. Patterns for NATO and national Tacevals varied over the years, and what follows is but one sample. While flying hours and the results of national weapons scores were taken into account, they were recognised as imperfect yardsticks of a unit's true and total operational capability, and there was no substitute in Germany for regular visits to operational units by the multinational Taceval teams. These teams, of up to 100 highly experienced specialists in every operational activity in which a unit was likely to be involved, would begin their comprehensive evaluation by arriving at a base, without warning, to carry out the first of two phases

of the exercise, the 'surprise' phase being followed, immediately or after a warning period, by a longer phase which simulated every event likely to occur in war. The first phase tested the unit's alert and readiness posture, its ability to recall a high percentage of its manpower within a specified timeframe and prepare a given number of aircraft (with war loads) – perhaps launching them against 'equivalent' targets. The second phase would be set in a realistic war scenario, invariably requiring all personnel to wear full NBC protective clothing, while reacting correctly and expeditiously to every incident within the team's pre-planned programme. This could include defecting aircraft, Spetsnaz intruders, sabotage, unexploded bombs, damage to aircraft operating areas and runways, with key personnel being 'killed' or 'wounded', to see how their deputies coped – often with several of these incidents coinciding. At RAF Brüggen, tin helmets and gas masks were donned throughout every air raid, even in hardened and filtered facilities – on the grounds that these could be breached in the attack – and if anyone was spotted taking more than nine seconds to fit his or her gas mask, they were invited to spend a short spell in the station's gas chamber. The RAF in Germany put much effort into NBC protection, and in the late 1970s many of the aircrew were provided with additional breathing equipment to allow them to move through contaminated air from their filtered accommodation to their aircraft, there to transfer to the aircraft's internal filtration system. Everyone exposed to nuclear fallout or radiation underwent a thorough decontamination process before entering a 'clean'

An RAF Brüggen Canberra squadron deployed to its war dispersal site in 1957. *RAF Brüggen*

Before HAS were built, operational aircraft were given some protection in concrete or earthen blast revetments, as shown here at RAF Brüggen. *RAF Brüggen*

Pilots on DHS (QRA) at Marxwalde were accommodated in crude, but adequate and well-concealed hardened shelters. *Author*

This MiG-21M is using a standard fit of two SPRD rocket 'bottles' to reduce the take-off roll. *Jürgen Gruhl*

Lorry-mounted searchlights were used to illuminate the thresholds of permanent and reserve airstrips during night exercises. *Author/Cottbus Museum*

Redundant MiG-21 decoys at Preschen in 1990. *Klaus Schmiedel*

All LSK/LV Wings housed their air traffic controllers in low profile, well protected bunkers, with limited all-round visibility, but this 'aerial farm' gave away its position. *Norbert Hess*

In peacetime, local and approach air traffic was controlled on RAF airfields from very obvious control towers, with good, all-round visibility – but alternative facilities were ready for use in exercise and war. *Author*

The standard HAS in the LSK/LV (left) could accommodate a single MiG-21, whereas that in RAFG could shelter two Jaguars, two Buccaneers (wings folded) or two Tornados. *RAF Brüggen*

The reserve airstrip at Warbelow, a few miles from its parent base at Laage, was much used in exercises, but not easy to recognise from the air at high speeds and low level. *Hannes Mallwitz*

A Jaguar fighter-bomber from RAF Brüggen operating from a new stretch of autobahn near Hamburg, optimised for the purpose but as yet unopened in 1978. *RAF Brüggen* environment. To judge a wing's competence in planning, briefing, flying and debriefing a typical mission for the wing, aircrew members of Taceval team (drawn from other NATO air force units in the same role), could select any operational pilot with whom they wished to fly on an equivalent war mission, in the wing's two-seat aircraft.

A Taceval could continue for three or four days, 24 hours a day, usually terminating for a strike/attack unit with a mass launch of all the wing's aircraft, followed by an assessment of how well NATO standards had been met, including a 'qualification phase' on a weapons range, monitored by a member of the team. At the end of the evaluation, the base and its units would be awarded marks from one to five (one being 'excellent' and five being 'failure') for every aspect of performance within each of the four categories: Readiness and Reaction, Operations, Support Functions and Ability to Survive. The marking tended to be ruthless, one unit perfect in every other respect but making a small mistake when launching its nuclear force, had its final mark downgraded from 'One' to 'Five' – and failure. These evaluations identified shortcomings which could be remedied, and when a unit was judged to be weak in one or more areas, it could expect an early return of a Taceval team. The Jaguar Strike/Attack Wing at RAF Brüggen, on which the author served in 1977–79, was believed to have been the first strike/attack wing in AAFCE to achieve the ultimate accolade of 'Four Ones'.

The Warsaw Pact appeared to have no single, formal evaluation organisation to match that in the West, operational effectiveness of each NVA wing being rated by headquarters staff, against the universal criteria, during the monthly operational exercises 'Gefechtstags', and in random exercises involving two or more of the Warsaw Pact air forces. These staff officers kept themselves current in the aircraft and up-to-date with the latest concepts and procedures, often taking part in the periodic 'Kommandeursflugtags' (Commanders' Days), when flying was reserved for the division and wing executives and supervisors. On these special days, the wings might operate from dispersed sites, in simulated war conditions and often under air attack, practising operational turn-rounds (OTRs) in full NBC kit.

There is no doubt that RAFG and the NVA took NBC play very seriously.

Chapter Four

East German Fighter Wings

If a man hasn't discovered something that he would die for, he isn't fit to live

Martin Luther King, 1963

Jagdfliegergeschwader 1 (JG-1): Cottbus & Holzgau

The origins of JG-1 can be traced back to Flugplatz Cottbus, on the western outskirts of the town; it was there that the embryo air force of the NVA, the 'Luftstreitkräfte der NVA' began to take shape in 1952. Overseen by Oberkommissar Wolfgang Reinhold, what would become JG-1 developed somewhat covertly in 1953 as '1.Aeroklub Cottbus' (No.1 Aero Club Cottbus), flying training beginning there on the Yak-18 and Yak-11, with guidance and technical support from the Soviet Air Force already in residence on the airfield. Progression from the piston-engine Yaks to two-seat MiG-15s began in the first half of 1953, but was halted shortly thereafter, and the MiGs returned to Russia, because of the worsening economic situation and civil unrest in East Germany. The pilots in the pipeline continued their training on the Yaks, simulating as far as was possible the fighter tactics they would use when jet flying began again. In this way the club continued to evolve, becoming Fliegerge-

schwader 1 (FG-1) on 1 July 1956, following the formation of the NVA. Commanded by Hptm Klaus Baarß (Chapter Two), JG-1 became part of 1.LVD, with jet training resuming shortly thereafter on single and two-seat MiG-15s. MiG-17Fs and MiG-17PFs were added to the inventory during the following year, these early single-seat fighters being supported throughout their service with JG-1 by the two-seat MiG-15UTIs. In 1961, FG-1 was re-named Jagdgeschwader (JG-1). With very few experienced German pilots available (even fewer with jet fighter experience on the WW2 Me-262s) to act as instructors and mentors (pending more politically acceptable replacements), it was inevitable that there would be some growing pains. However, with the help of Russian instructors, strict discipline and tight supervision, the accident rate for MiG-15s and MiG-17s was low. In their first four years at Cottbus, there were two fatal accidents, one of these resulting from an ejection at 300 ft, and only five minor incidents, while in the final five years of their service with JG-1, there were thirteen accidents, four being lost (three with fatal consequences), two suffering major damage and seven minor damage.

In 1965, JG-1 entered a new era of truly supersonic flying with several variants of the MiG-21, the transition to the first of these new aircraft, the two-seat MiG-21U and single-seat MiG-21PFMs, being complete by the end of 1966. A succession of MiG-21SPS, MiG-21SPS/K and MiG-21MF fighters followed, supported by two-seat MiG-21US and MiG-21UM operational trainers – the latter continuing to serve until the dissolution of the NVA in 1990. On 7 October 1967, JG-1 was granted the honorary title of *Fritz Schmenkel*. For much of this long period, the accident rate was about average for the LSK/LV wings, but it was to the great credit of the wing that none were recorded during the last four years of its operation. Other flying units also operated from Cottbus, one of the first being a target towing facility for ground-based and seaborne AAA and for gun-armed fighter aircraft (Chapter Three).

In October 1977, Oltn Jürgen Gruhl was posted to JG-1 from JG-8 at Marxwalde, where he had flown 166 hours on the MiG-21MF, to convert on to the MiG-21SPS and spend the next three years flying a total of 209 hours in 392 sorties on this aircraft, for an average of 32 min/sortie. Despite the low average of 9 hours/month, he became qualified to carry out interceptions against manoeuvring targets and to engage in two v two combat at all heights, by day and night, in all weathers, and was cleared for instrument penetrations down to the minimums permitted. He found the MiG-21 to be very reliable, technically uncomplicated and easy to maintain, and never experienced any serious technical failure in the air. The aircraft's engine started without external aids and OTRs could be achieved in 10–15 minutes; there were no problems operating from grass runways (with take-offs often assisted by two pods of SPRD rockets), while touch-down speeds of 270 km/hr (145 knots) presented few difficulties. Jürgen believed that in some respects the aircraft compared favourably in flight with an American rival at the time, the F-104 Starfighter; both aircraft could accelerate very rapidly in reheat to M2.0+, albeit with a high fuel consumption, and perform very well in the supersonic zone, particularly in the vertical plane, but with their high wing loading, neither turned well at subsonic speeds. Armament fits depended on the variant, but in all cases the pilot was provided with an efficient gunsight and radar scope to make the best of a radar which had critical limitations. Jürgen recalls that the squadrons at Cottbus were each expected to have 12 aircraft on the line every morning, but that it was not unusual for his squadron to have 16–20 available, including the two-seat MiG-21UMs, ready to replace any aircraft found to be unserviceable on start-up, he and other MiG-21 pilots confirming that, as a result, they rarely had to abort a flight. Many NATO squadrons could not boast of such a luxury; some had one or two aircraft on strength above their establishment, as 'in use reserves', but a number of sorties planned for a day would expect to be lost due to technical problems. Much, of course, depended on the sophistication of an aircraft's systems, which in turn determined its war fighting capabilities, prompting the perennial arguments over the respective virtues of sophistication and simplicity. The official line, often supported by aircraft industries, called for expensive sophistication, on the grounds that fewer aircraft, containing 'state of the art' equipment, would be needed to achieve the same results as larger numbers of those which were less complicated. There were some, however, who favoured the latter option, preferring larger numbers of relatively simple, more robust aircraft, less prone to technical defect or susceptible to battle damage, easier for the pilot/crews to manage during intensive operations and requiring a minimum of ground support. Protagonists of the MiG-21 might claim that their aircraft fell within this latter category, and, with the lead-in training they had been given (Chapter Two), none of the ex-EGAF fast-jet pilots interviewed found any difficulty in converting to the MiG-21, quickly absorbing any differences in the aircraft's systems, performance and flying characteristics from the earlier MiGs.

Promoted to Hptm, Jürgen Gruhl left Cottbus in September 1980 to undergo a year's political training at the Berlin-Grünau Military Academy, before being appointed the political officer on 3.JS/JG-7 at Drewitz, where he flew 20 hours in the MiG-21M and 'MF', before being given command of 2.JS/JG-1. In 1982, JG-1 moved from Cottbus, in the wake of several accidents in the local area, to Flugplatz Holzdorf, a recently completed airfield east of Jessen (Elster). Holzdorf offered three separate dispersals, with a total of 46 HAS and eight open pans; it had a single concrete/asphalt runway, 2419 m (2650 yd) long, with a parallel taxiway of similar length and a hardened grass strip of 1800 m (1960 yd). The wing remained at Holzdorf, with the MiG-21, for the remainder of its life in the NVA.

The author and his chief adviser, Gert Overhoff, a highly respected fast-jet pilot from the GAF, were much impressed by Jürgen Gruhl's professional expertise, epitomised by his career achievements and supervisory appointments in the LSK/LV. He offered clear, honest and balanced views on air combat training with the MiG-21 on JG-1, which sought to develop the basic manoeuvring skills taught on FAG-15 at Rothenburg (Chapter Two), in a step-by-step approach, while illustrating, *inter alia,* the thought, meticulous planning and close supervision which went into the preparation for each flying sortie. Every attempt was made to capitalise on the fighter's strengths and take account of its shortcomings, within the limited flight time available. A flight leader would put together a sequence of 'canned' manoeuvres, each of which should have already been flown separately, to show what could be included in combat to achieve a desired result, be it offensive or defensive, tailored to the circumstances and proficiency levels of the pilots involved. NATO fighter pilots might observe that the LSK/LV had simply given names to the manoeuvring of fighters into various modes of attack or defence, in which opponents must, in live combat, adjust their power settings and speeds, rates of turn, climb and descent, and 'G' loading, according to their opponents movements. With infinite variables, the need for flexibility remained paramount, and Gruhl did not disagree with this. He stressed that the LSK/LV pilots fully accepted the need to adapt their tactics to whatever threat they faced, and this type of handling exercise was only expected to develop a pilot's skills, show what could be achieved and to generate confidence in the capability of his aircraft.

In one of the first of these 'canned' manoeuvres, 'Gabel' (Fig.1, page 89) postulates an attack by a pair of aircraft on a target approaching from below in the forward hemisphere. When the leader called: 'Gabel left/right' (depending on the direction from which the attack was to be mounted), both fighters carried out a turn-about at 4'G', the lead descending to maintain a speed of 700 km/hr (380 knots), the wingman remaining level with reheat engaged to create an attacking position from 1,000–2,000 m (3,300–6,600 ft) above. It was, of course, unlikely that a wary and experienced adversary would have allowed this situation to develop to his disadvantage. 'Haken' (Fig.2) was an academic reaction to a head-on attack from above, on either the leader or the wingman flying in a standard tactical formation. On the command 'Reheat and Haken left/right', both aircraft accelerated to 850–950 km/hr (460–520 knots) and on a further call of 'Manoeuvre' they executed a 4'G', 45–60 deg climbing turn into the attacker(s), until achieving a height separation of 2,000–2,500 m (6,600–8,200 ft) and an airspeed of 650 km/hr (350 knots), when a level turn would be made on to the target. In the later stages of the turn the position of lead and wingman, and their responsibilities, could be reversed, with the wingman carrying out the attack. Jürgen went on to describe several other illustrations of these basic manoeuvres, including 'Winkel', 'Knoten', 'Lasso' and 'Dach' – about which the same comments may be made.

Mix 2, illustrates a combination of these separate manoeuvres, integrated into an academic combat scenario. While many of the basic parameters, such as height separations, 'G' loading and manoeuvring speeds, were standardised to simplify training, they would of course, be infinitely variable in actual combat. Other than when specified, wingmen were required, at all times, to maintain visual contact with their leaders.

In the 2/2005 edition of the Luftwaffe's magazine, Jäger Blatt, former LSK/LV pilot Michael Wegerich, who served on JG-1 at Cottbus and Holzdorf, from 1977 to 1987, described a 'Mach und Höhenflüge' (M & H) supersonic and height flight he needed to complete to qualify for the next level in his flying career: LK.I (Chapter Three). The author is grateful to him for allowing an abridged and edited version to be included here. While the sortie did not go quite to plan, he achieved what was required of him, in a commendable illustration of his ingenuity and determination. This was a challenging sortie, flown in MiG-21SPS of JG-1 at Cottbus in the summer of 1980, to test Michael on the accelerations, decelerations and aircraft handling required in the transonic/supersonic zone, the optimum climb profile, fuel management, and judicious use of reheat. Moreover, he was very conscious that, with the fuel he had been allocated, there would be no chance of a second pass, and while this would not be his first M & H flight, previous sorties of this type having been flown in the MiG-21F-13 and the MiG-21MF, which had different characteristics. For the qualification he now sought, he would need to bring back cockpit film of a successful interception and simulated 'kill', showing timely acquisition and identification of the target with IFF, correct procedures to achieve a speedy lock-on and missile launch, terminating with a satisfactory break-off from the engagement.

On previous occasions, with an element of surprise and fuel economy very much in mind, and given the necessary support from the radar controller, Michael had favoured pulling up into a climb from 13,000 m (43,000 ft), at M1.8, to position 10 km (6 nm) behind the target, enabling him to achieve a 'kill' by launching his missile at about 5–6 km (3 nm) at 15–16,000 m (50,000 ft). He would then cancel reheat and descend in a glide, with a commensurate saving in fuel – but on this occasion it would not be that simple.

On that bright summer's day, Michael and OSL Rissel, the pilot assigned to fly another MiG-21SPS as target, reviewed and updated the plan they had made for the sortie on the previous day, noting the weather, air traffic procedures, frequencies and callsigns, etc, before dressing in their cumbersome pressure suits and walking to their aircraft. External, cockpit and safety equipment checks were all satisfactory and the pilots 'fired-up' their aircraft to be at the runway threshold for the 'Technischer Kontrollpunkt' (last chance) checks, before getting airborne at their allotted times. The target launched first, climbing to 12–13,000 m (40,000 ft), on a heading of 240 deg and accelerating to M1.2, before reversing course over Leipzig on to a north-easterly heading and continuing to accelerate to M1.5, at 18,000 m (59,000 ft), approximately over Torgau/Wittenberg.

Meanwhile, Michael had taken off from Cottbus and been handed over to an experienced fighter controller at the wing's nearby GCI site, which monitored his acceleration, initially to M1.2, as he climbed on a south-westerly heading. The timings, accelerations, turning points, angles of bank and procedures, on the part of both controller and pilot, were now crucial to positioning the fighter, ideally 20 km (11 nm) behind and below the target. As he rolled out on a north-easterly heading and accelerated to M1.8 in the climb to 18,000 m (60,000 ft), Michael believed that he should have been about 10–12 km (6 nm) behind the target – and that it should have been visible on his radar scope. It was not, despite the controller calling it ahead at 7 km (3.5 nm) and then 5 km (2.7 nm). This was not how it should have been, and never had been in Michael's experience, but a glance at his altimeter gave the clue why; he had climbed through the target's flight path at too steep an angle to 19,000 m (62,000 ft), 1,000 m (3,300 ft) above the target's height and outside the narrow beam of the MiG-21's radar. He immediately lowered the nose of his aircraft hoping that the radar would then pick up the target, but in fact he saw it first visually and promptly manoeuvred to cover it with the cross-hairs of his optical sight, changing the radar mode from 'search' to 'interrogation' to confirm the required IFF return. As soon as his radar acquired the target, and achieved a lock-on, he simulated a missile firing, holding his aim, albeit with great difficulty for the 12.5 seconds necessary to allow for the time of flight of the missile, and for his camera to record a 'hit'. The rapidity of these actions enabled him to break away from the target just before the missile would have hit, at which point he announced calmly to the GCI controller that he had achieved his objective. He then cancelled reheat and turned on to the heading he was given to recover to base. Only then did he realise that his engine had flamed out, with the rpm having stabilised at 78%, the exhaust gas temperature (EGT) registering zero and the throttle having no effect, a result, he assumed, of flying through his target's turbulent wake, which made it difficult for him to hold his aim. The correct procedure was now to report the flame-out, but Michael did not. With great presence of mind he realised that this would have negated a successful sortie, that because his aircraft had not yet been fitted with the new 'System Automatischeskoi Registrazij Parametrow Poletow' (SARPP) cockpit recorder, which would have recorded the flame out automatically, and that no one on the ground could help him in the next few minutes, there was no sense in reporting the flame-out. Such were the thoughts of a pilot who had 750 flying hours in the MiG-21, who had plenty of height in which to

attempt a re-light, the procedures for which he had practised only a week before in the simulator – so he kept quiet. As he descended, at 600 km/hr (325 knots), through 9,600 m (32,000 ft), he pressed the air-start button (having ripped off the safety cord which prevented its accidental operation). Within a few seconds, the crucial green ignition light illuminated to show that the system was working, and Michael was able to advance the throttle from 'stop' to 'idle', the success of his copy-book air-start signalled by a rise in the EGT. A standard recovery took him back to Cottbus, where he complained about the broken cord. With film from the sortie confirming a successful interception, and post-flight analysis of the data recorder revealing no in-flight anomalies, Michael earned an 'above excellent' assessment, and NATO fighter pilots would appreciate the way in which he had rescued success from potential failure.

Michael Wegerich went on to qualify as a flight commander and offered the author several more accounts, already published elsewhere, two of which served to remind fighter pilots to always expect the unexpected, and to be aware of the difficulties they might face in a jamming environment. Normally, another of the unit's MiG-21s, a Soviet MiG-23, Su-24 or similar jet aircraft acted as targets for practice interceptions, but the two stories which follow relate to something quite different. The first of these began in daylight with four MiG-21s of 2.JS/JG-1 on 'Alert Status One' (cockpit readiness) within their HAS, crew chiefs in attendance, expected to get airborne within four minutes of the order to scramble. After being held for 60 minutes, four fresh pilots took over, with Michael as their new leader and they too settled in for what might be a long and uncomfortable wait. They were aware that the weather was not ideal, with low cloud, light rain and a light westerly wind, but they were well briefed on the taxiing sequence, silent procedures, *et al*, and were happy to scramble 30 minutes later, under orders to expedite their taxiing and to use the easterly runway despite a tailwind component. At the runway threshold they received a succession of green lights (to minimize radio communication), lined up on the runway, engaged reheat and were airborne in pairs within the time expected, checking in with their assigned GCI frequency when safely airborne and expediting their climb to 10,000 m (33,000 ft). It was now clear that there was more than a degree of urgency attached to this task. On reaching a speed of 600 km/hr (325 knots), Michael cancelled reheat and watched his flight join up in clear air, before re-engaging 50% reheat, accelerating to 900 km/hr (490 knots) and climbing at an angle of 20 deg through another cloud layer in close formation. This was the first time that any of them had flown through dense clouds with four aircraft in close formation using reheat, so tensions were high, but after 90 seconds they broke out into the clear blue sky above. Almost immediately, Michael spotted two giant aircraft, flying about 1.5 km apart, some 2,000 m (6,500 ft) above and only a few kilometers ahead, heading east – and had his first sight of a Soviet Tu-16, strategic bomber. The fighters were now in tactical formation and closing in on their target at 1,000 km/hr (540 knots), at the same height, their radars showing that they would soon be through the firing bracket, but all Michael's requests for permission to complete the interceptions were denied. With every chance that his flight would soon overtake the bombers, Michael ordered power to be reduced to idle and the speed brakes to be extended, but his orders were no longer being acknowledged – or carried out – and very shortly thereafter the MiGs were flying line abreast, with a pair either side of the Tu-16, as if escorting them. Targets and fighters were now 150 km (80 nm) east of Holzdorf , in Polish airspace, the latter without any communication with their parent GCI or between aircraft. Assuming that their task was now over, Michael led his aircraft away from the bombers and turned through 180 deg to take up a westerly heading for base, shortly thereafter beginning to receive weak signals from the GCI controller and from his wingmen. It was now clear that the Tu-16s had been very effective in jamming the fighter pilots' communications, and it only remained for them to make a routine recovery to Holzdorf, where they landed 30 minutes later. None of the MiG pilots should have been surprised by this experience; they were all trained to expect their on-board radar to lock on to the strongest signal, in this case one emitted by a jammer, that a time delay in a radar return could result in incorrect range indications, while a phase shift could cause inaccurate angular information – and that they could lose their radio communications. However, there was no substitute for practical lessons in the air, and they had just had one.

In the second lesson, it was rumoured that Tu-16s would again be acting as targets, but this in itself presented no particular problem because the bombers would provide bigger than usual radar returns, leading to higher detection ranges and more stable signals for the MiG's radar; moreover, they would probably not execute the evasive manoeuvres which could make interceptions more difficult – but there would be other surprises in store. This time Michael was on his own when he launched into the night from cockpit readiness, with minimal airfield lighting. Take-off, climb and approach to his target were routine, and he broke into the clear between layered cloud which shielded him from the stars above and lights on the ground below. Under close GCI control, he now finalized his preparations for a simulated launch of his beam-riding RS-2US, AA-1 'Alkali' missile. Confirming his target with IFF, he switched to attack mode to reveal a strong blip on his radar and began to close to his firing range, but then the target on his screen made a positive movement to the right. This presented him with a major dilemma: should he follow this signal, which might have been generated by ECM, in which case the attack mode would be broken and he would lose his target, or trust the original plot when the bomber was indeed turning right – with possibly the same result? He chose the latter, and with his controller then reporting: 'Target straight ahead, range 5 km', he knew that he had got it right; the Tu-16 had used angular off-set jamming – but he had not fallen for it. To complete the interception, Michael increased speed, hoping to use a position light on his quarry to lock on and fire. Although he must have been closing fast on his target, the MiG's radar showed hardly any closing speed and a range well in excess of that reported by the controller, which convinced him that his range information too was being jammed. From then on he relied wholly on the controller, needing only to see something of the target, even a silhouette against a slightly brighter background, to simulate his missile launch – but that night he got more. Just when he thought that he was nearing his minimum firing range, 'a strong, glaring white light exploded in front of his MiG', blinding him and causing him to pull up and away to the left, back into the darkness, until he was again able to focus on his cockpit instruments. The interception was over; perhaps against the odds, Michael had overcome the jamming and again learned about ECM the hard way; his respect for the Soviet bomber's jamming capabilities had increased and he no longer saw them as easy targets – particularly at night and in cloud.

JG-1's main reserve or auxiliary airstrip was at Alteno, 80 km south of Berlin, while a second strip, known to be earmarked but its location not confirmed, was believed to have been a highway strip near Ruhland. One JG-1 squadron would invariably deploy to Alteno during an exercise, with between four and twelve aircraft, and be expected to operate there, in simulated wartime conditions, for several days or even weeks. In 1985–87 this task fell to 2.JS/JG-1, commanded by Michael Wegerich, all of his pilots required to be proficient at landing and taking off from such an airstrip in the MiG-21, to gain their LK.I qualification. When the author flew over the derelict airfield at Alteno in 2008, and visited it by road in 2010, he found evidence of the main airstrip, running east-west, probably of 2,000 m (2,200 yd) and flanked by grass strips of similar lengths either side, the approaches still clear of all obstacles but with few give-away features in the immediate area. Tracks led from the outlines of a perimeter track to some 12 aircraft hides in the woods to the north, which also helped to conceal basic accommodation for the support personnel. There may also have been a small, hardened aircraft dispersal area to the south east of the runway. Wegerich had got to know Alteno well while on a previous tour with JG-1 as a junior pilot, carrying out his first circuit there in a MiG-21UM, at 500 m (1,600 ft) and in excellent weather, after which he flew a solo sortie there in a MiG-21SPS. He remembers the shortage of landmarks to aid navigation and the need to pass north of Lübbenau (8 km east of Alteno) to cross the nearby autobahn at a particular point on a runway heading of 260 deg, but with no further help on a 'long finals' over a forest – to make a difficult touchdown. Some months later, now a more experienced pilot on 1.JS/JG-1, he returned to Alteno with the whole squadron, on a silent (no communications) combat training sortie at low level. They arrived in the area at a height of only 50 m (160 ft) to find that the visibility was down to 2–3 km (0.5–1.5 nm), well below

the published minimum for the exercise of 4 km (2.2 nm). At this point, Michael had difficulty establishing his position, but he could just see the MiG ahead, and followed it into the circuit, lowering his undercarriage and flaps on its cues, and seeing the runway in time to make a safe landing.

On a later exercise, as a young Hptm, Michael Wegerich was given the task of flying the Flugleiter, OSL Seeger, in a MiG-21UM to Alteno, where he would then act as Seeger's deputy – and this time the weather was excellent. They landed without incident, but not before the rest of the wing's aircraft checked in, 10–15 minutes earlier than briefed, and were calling for clearance to land, the Flugleiter and his assistant rising to the occasion, in exemplary fashion, to give the necessary clearance from the cockpit of their MiG-21UM.

Equally successful was another exercise during a Gefechtsflugtag at Holzdorf, when Michael led his squadron to Alteno early one morning, the chief engineer and his party having gone ahead by road to provide the necessary support. However, for reasons not explained, the road party was not there to meet the aircraft, after the pilots had completed their practice interceptions, they and the resident party being left to 'turn round' the aircraft themselves (refuelling, replenishing compressed air, oil and oxygen, and carrying out tyre checks etc) – some learning what not to do when fuel spurted out in all directions! However, hard work by all had every exercise aircraft ready for tasking by the time the support party arrived.

Some of these exercises worked like clockwork, as was the case with 2.JS/JG-1 during Michael's tenure in command, when the squadron's 12 aircraft were released from 'Bereitschaftsstufe 1' (Readiness State 1) and ordered to remove their operational missiles, suggesting that the flying phase was about to begin – and so it was. At 2300 hrs, the wing commander ordered the whole squadron to deploy forthwith to Alteno and report, within three hours, when all 12 aircraft were again at Readiness State 1. With no forewarning or lead time for the road party to travel the 80 km (43 nm), this was a challenge, but the deployment pack-ups of essential equipment were checked regularly, always ready to go, and the advance party was on its way within 30 min, followed by the aircraft at 0030 hours, each pilot with an assigned task to complete en route, and an hour later they all arrived at Alteno. Good weather, tell-tale lights on the ground and searchlights illuminating the runway threshold simplified the approach and landing, after which feverish activity by half the usual servicing party and the pilots, with 'all hands to the pump', had all the MiGs ready for re-tasking within three hours. It had been a hard day's night.

As commander of 2.JS/JG-1, Maj Michael Wegerich led a detachment of 12 MiG-21SPS and one MiG-21UM to Astrachan in the summer of 1986, for live missile firings against the Soviet high speed La-17 drone. This may have been the first time the Germans had taken their own aircraft to Astrachan, hitherto they had flown Russian MiGs on weapons training there. The pilots had been chosen carefully and given special training, while the aircraft and their radars were the best available. Ahead, was a momentous 3,300 km (1,800 nm) round trip for the short range MiGs, via the Ukraine and four refuelling stops. They set off, almost totally reliant on the obsolescent radio compass for navigation, each cockpit crammed full of unfamiliar maps, a complete file of 'questionable' letdown procedures and some 120 travel visas. Despite difficulties with flight clearances in Russia, the usual meticulous planning and preparation by the pilots paid off and all ended well. The ground party travelled in the relative luxury of a Tu-134 to Astrachan, where the temperature in the desert was +30 deg C, but even the normally very vigilant customs officials failed to question the need for so much 'aircraft de-icing fluid' – which came in very handy for the inevitable social programme with the Soviet hosts who, since 1985, had lived under a new rule of 'no alcohol'.

Following a lengthy introduction to local procedures, which emphasized complete, central control of all flying activities – with little left to the individual, Michael Wegerich flew the first sortie, simulating a missile delivery against a Soviet MiG-23, at speeds and an altitude in excess of those for which the Germans had trained, his MiG-21 suffering compressibility effects in the transonic zone. He again led from the front on the first live firing, with two R-3S missiles, starting from 12,000 m (39, 000 ft) at M1.4, and expecting straight vectors to the La-17 target, but instead he was given a succession of erratic turns, ranging from 'hard right' to 'hard left', which at that speed used a lot of airspace and fuel, as he closed rapidly on his target, with nothing yet showing on his radar scope. He finally acquired the La-17 visually and was able to release his missiles successfully to achieve a 'kill'. It transpired that the Russians had lost control of the La-17 at a crucial time, and then suffered a complete radio failure; this was no copybook exercise, but with commendable determination, Michael had again rescued success from failure. The 'de-icing fluid' was also a great success, and the Germans returned to Holzdorf safely, well pleased with their efforts.

With their long-standing, world-wide commitments, the RAF were highly experienced in long distance deployments, made easier with the introduction of AAR from the 1960s. Cold War exercises took RAF squadrons from Germany and the UK to America and Canada, while squadrons, flights and individuals flew regularly to the extremes of NATO in Europe (Italy and Norway), during routine training, without any undue formalities. However, neither AAR nor long range sorties were envisaged for the RAF units in Germany, should war break out.

In September 1984, Jürgen Gruhl, now a major, left JG-1 to attend the Military Academy in Dresden, during which time he flew 20 hours in the MiG-21 before graduating in July 1987 with a diploma in military science. He then returned to Holzdorf to command 2.JS/JG-1, qualifying as an instructor pilot, and was promoted to OSL in October 1988, to complete his final three years of service in the NVA as the wing's deputy commander flying training, for a total of 224 hours on the MiG-21. Jürgen could look back with pride on a highly successful 16 year career in the LSK/LV; he had followed the standard pattern of training for his time, earned a succession of rapid promotions and achieved much on the flight line, backed by the necessary academic training, all of which promised very well for his future in the NVA, only to have this cut short by reunification. From October 1990, Jürgen became responsible for the disbandment of JG-1 and transfer of its aircraft to Drewitz, for subsequent disposal. Selected to serve in the unified Luftwaffe, he accepted a reduction in rank, and completed his service as a major, flying his last flight in the MiG-21 on 27 March 1991.

Major Hannes Mallwitz had built up valuable experience during time on JG-1; he had flown 1,000 hours and gained his LK.I qualification on the MiG-21SPS, performed the duties of instructor pilot, flight supervisor and flight safety officer on the wing staff and become a well qualified weapons practitioner. He recalls that his weapons training on FAG-15, JG-3 and JG-1 had depended largely on synthetic scoring devices within the cockpit, with live air-to-air gunnery and missile firings over the Baltic in LSZ II, where he once scored a hit against a M6/M6T 'Airborne Small-Size Target'. He also fired a RS-2US, beam-riding missile successfully against an La-17 target on detachment to Astrachan, practised with air-to-surface weapons on ground ranges in the GDR and the semi-submerged ship wrecks in the Baltic, before leaving JG-1 in 1984, very well qualified to fly the Su-22 (Chapter Six).

At Cottbus and Holzdorf, JG-1 had forged

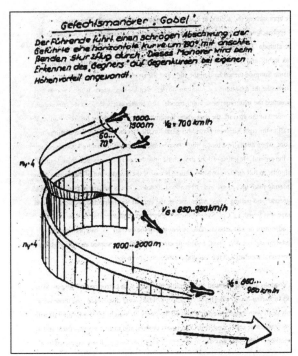

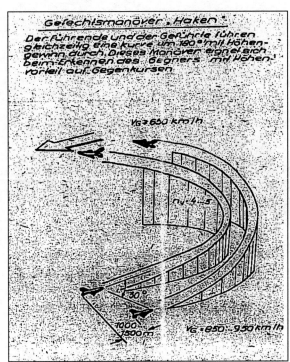

Fig. 1 'Gabel', one of the basic air combat 'canned' manoeuvres for early combat training on JG-1 in the MiG-21. *Jürgen Gruhl*

Fig. 2 'Haken' postulates a head-on attack from above. *Jürgen Gruhl*

Mix 2. Advanced air combat training involved complicated combinations of the basic manoeuvres. *Jürgen Gruhl*

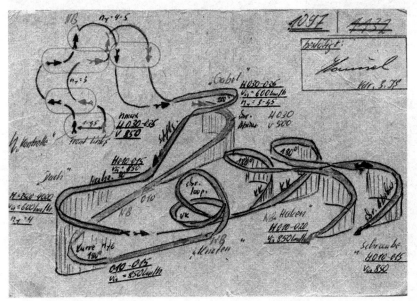

FG-1 celebrated its first birthday at Cottbus in 1957, this momento signed by the Klaus-Jürgen Baarß: squadron commander. *Jürgen Gruhl*

OSL Schulz, JG-1, debriefing Hartwig Richter after a MiG-21 sortie at Holzdorf. *Hartwig Richter*

MiG-21 pilots of JG-1 at Holzdorf. *Hartwig Richter*

Fighter Pilot. Jürgen Gruhl, JG-1, at Flugplatz Holzdorf. *Jürgen Gruhl*

MiG-17 No.009, now in retirement at Peenemünde Museum. *Author*

Combat Pair: A pair of JG-1 MiG-21s based at Holzdorf in 1990. *Jürgen Gruhl*

Proud to the end: JG-1, MiG-21SPS 'Weisse Hai' (White Shark) *Jürgen Gruhl*

Michael Wegerich, JG-1, flying a training interception one night from Holzdorf, found a Soviet Tu-16 bomber. *Author's Collection*

a proud history and did not go out with a whimper. On display as part of the farewell ceremony on 26 September 1990, was one of their MiG-21SPS (No.441), resplendent in a livery of white gloss and decorated with coloured insignia, to earn the endearing name 'Weisse Hai' (White Shark). It was not alone in the sky over Holzdorf and Cottbus that day, JG-1 launching all of its available MiG-21s for a total day's flying of 38 hours. The last recorded MiG-21 sortie from Holzdorf was on 19 April 1991.

Jagdgeschwader 2 (JG-2): Trollenhagen

Located on the northern fringe of the garrison town of Neubrandenburg, known for its tank barracks and military industries, Trollenhagen spawned an airfield in 1934. In WW2, it was developed by the Luftwaffe for flight training and as an aircraft assembly facility for the Focke-Wulf and Dornier aircraft companies, as such attracting considerable attention from Allied bombers – particularly from August to October 1944. The archives reveal no significant activity at Trollenhagen during Russian occupation of the airfield from 1945 to 1956, after which a 2,293 m (2,500 yd) runway and support facilities were constructed for jet fighters, and the airfield came to life again in 1961, as the home of JG-2. The genesis of JG-2 was very similar to that of other wings in the LSK/LV; originated at Bautzen in 1952, flying Yak-18 and Yak-11 trainers, the wing underwent several structural, location and name changes before entering the jet age at Rothenburg as FG-2, with the MiG-15UTI and MiG-15bis, before moving to Trollenhagen with MiG-17Fs in 1961, where it became JG-2 – part of 3.LVD. Leutnant Rudolf Müller was posted to FG-2 at Trollenhagen after completing OHS at Bautzen in 1960, converting there to the MiG-17F during 1961, but his stay was short-lived; in October 1961 he was transferred to JG-3 at Preschen.

The MiG fighters were not the only military aircraft to operate from Trollenhagen; Zieldarstellungsstaffel 33 (ZDS-33), the squadron of Il-28 'Beagle' target-towing aircraft, arriving there in 1971, the year JG-2 was granted the name 'Juri A Gagarin', in memory of the Soviet cosmonaut. In addition, Verbindungs-flugkette 33 (VFK-33), a small liaison flight, was based there to support the headquarters staff of the collocated 3.LVD. This consisted initially of two Yak-18A trainers, replaced in 1974 by two Z-43 light communications aircraft, together with three or four of the larger, single-piston engine An-2s.

Re-equipment with the MiG-21PF began in 1966, followed by the 'PFM', 'SPS', 'SPS/K', 'M' and 'MF', supported by a succession of two-seat operational trainers – all of which Andreas Schrodel flew on JG-2. Andreas spoke for many of his comrades in regretting the absence of an internal gun in the earlier variants, thus having to depend on IR and/or radar-guided missiles, so he welcomed the 'SPS/K', while commenting on the detrimental effects of 'podded' cannons on an aircraft's manoeuvrability. It had long been the RAF's policy to have guns built into all its fighters, whether they be for self-defence or offensive combat, thus providing the additional firepower and avoiding unnecessary drag, and the lessons of SEA were quick to endorse this policy. While podded cannon provided the only immediate option for some aircraft already in, or coming into service, many future designs would have guns built in. Such was the case with the NVA's MiG-21M and 'MF'.

'Benny' Luther joined JG-2 on 1 September 1985, and remained on the wing until it disbanded in 1990, flying the MiG-21PFM, 'SPS', 'M' and 'MF'. Like many others, he took five years to reach the front line from the start of his GST at Neustadt-Glewe and Schoenhagen on the Z-42, before attending OHS, during which he flew 200 hours on the L-39 and 220 hours on the MiG-21SPS. Interestingly, if GST is not included, this total of 420 hours in three years of training in the EGAF, is almost identical to that of 423 hours accumulated by the author in the RAF, in three-and-a-half years – 30 years before. In JG-2's final years, Andreas and Benny were deprived of 'live' air-to-air gunnery training, but they did deliver R-60M IRH AAMs against M-6 or RM-3V targets in LSZ II and trained, live, with the 23 mm cannon and unguided rockets against maritime targets in the Baltic and on the overland range at Peenemünde (Chapter Three).

Towards the end of the Cold War, concern grew over the risks involved in ejecting from MiG-21s equipped with the SK-1 ejection seat, those serving on JG-2 reminded of the hazards all too dramatically on 6 May 1988, at Trollenhagen, when Maj Liebert had no sensible alternative but to eject from his MiG-21PFM on take-off, outside the seat's limits, following a bird strike which caused his engine to fail. His death may have been the final straw, and it is said that the pilots on JG-2 were then given the option of not flying on the wing until all its MiG-21PFM/SPS fighters, or their seats, had been replaced – but apparently no one took up the offer. Fortuitously, enough MiG-21Ms and 'MFs', fitted with the KM-1 ejection seat, had become available as replacements.

Major Liebert's accident was far from being the only sad loss during JG-2's 38 year lifetime. The records show that, between 1961 and 1968, six MiG-17F/PFs were written off and five pilots killed; two more suffered major damage and a further seven were involved in lesser incidents – mainly when landing. From 1968 to 1988, five pilots were lost, nine 'PFM/SPS' and SPS/K MiG-21s were written off, one colliding with a Soviet Su-7 in the air near Penzlin, and eleven more suffered various degrees of damage. From 1972 to 1989, there appeared to have been no fatal accidents in the MiG-21SPS, but one pilot ejected safely from a 'SPS/K', near Neubrandenburg in April 1982 and another collided with an 'SPS' on the auxiliary airstrip at Warbelow in September 1980. In the 38 years, a total of four pilots were killed in accidents to JG-2's two-seat trainers (MiG-15UTI, MiG-21U, MiG-21UM and MiG-21US), but there were eight successful ejections, while three other 'two-seaters' were damaged .

Contrary to some reports, JG-2 did not spend all the Cold War years in its home at Trollenhagen; the records show that the wing, or parts of it, made several visits to the nearby Soviet bases of Tutow, Damgarten

Peter Martin, an instructor pilot on JG-2, in the rear seat of a
MiG-21UM at Trollenhagen.   *Source Unknown*

This MiG-21UM served with JG-2 at Trollenhagen and JG-1
at Holzdorf until the end.   *Jürgen Gruhl*

This MiG-17F, once on JG-2, is now in retirement at
Trollenhagen.   *Author*

Frank Hoffmann, a squadron commander, and believed to
be deputy wing commander of JG-2, in a MiG-21M.
                                        Source Unknown

This MiG-21SPS/K, showing the twin 23 mm cannon below the
fusalage, served with JG-2 until the end.   *Museum*

MiG-21PFM, No.821, flew with JG-2 in the 1970s and
went into retirement at Cottbus.

                                        Author's Collection

2JS/JG-2, detached to Peenemünde in 1986.

Benny Luther

Happy Flier. Captain Andreas Schrodel, a pilot on JG-2, at Trollenhagen in 1989.

Andreas Schrodel

Benny Luther aboard a MiG-21M of JG-2 at Trollenhagen in 1990.

Benny Luther

Final Fling. A MiG-21M taxies out of its HAS at Trollenhagen in the final days for JG-2.

Author's Collection

and Wittstock throughout the 1960s, flew from Köthen during Exercise 'October Storm' in October 1965 and was detached to Stendal from May to September 1969. The wing appears to have been largely static throughout the 1970s, but it was on the move again in the 1980s, 1.JS/JG-2 carrying out a 'successful' exchange visit to the Polish Air Force squadron at Zegrze Pomorskie in September 1980, one of the Polish squadrons being hosted back at Trollenhagen in 1987, and the wing spent a year (autumn 1983/84) at Garz, while work was carried out at its home base. Missile training took part of the wing to Astrachan in Russia in 1987 and 1988 and there were further visits to Wittstock.

With reunification fast approaching, JG-2 flew its last sorties on 27 September 1990, and when it disbanded on 10 February 1990, its inventory included 31 MiG-21M, 12 MiG-21SPS and 8 MiG-21UMs. However, the base lived on, administered by Bundeswehr units accommodated primarily on the southern side of the airfield. Trollenhagen then acted as a diversion for the Luftwaffe MiG-29s based at nearby Laage – and later for its Eurofighter Typhoons. Also, NATO air forces used the base for air exercises and when the author visited in 2007 and 2008, huge IL-76 transport aircraft were using the airfield to move military equipment to and from NATO operations in Afghanistan.

Jagdgeschwader 3 (JG-3): Preschen

The Soviet 2nd Army took over the old WW2 Luftwaffe airfield at Preschen, 25 miles south-east of Cottbus, on 24 April, 1945, and

in 1951 the Bau-Union-SEd Construction Companie of Dresden began reconstruction there, for it to become one of the eight airfields in the GDR for the Soviet 'frontal bombers'. The first Il-28 'Beagle' tactical bombers took up residence in 1954, before work on the big base was complete; ultimately it would have a 2,500 m x 90 m (2,750 x 100 yd) concrete runway, dispersals for 40 aircraft and a three kilometer taxi track connecting the airfield to a war reserve airstrip of 2,400 m (2,600 yd) on the autobahn at Forst. The airfield was taken over by the NVA in August 1956, FG-3 moving there from Cottbus in the following December, with the MiG-15UTI and MiG-15bis. They were joined in October 1957 by the first of 53, ex-Soviet MiG-17Fs, built to various standards, with different cockpit instrumentation, which made life difficult for the groundcrew and pilots.

On 1 January 1961, FG-3 was renamed JG-3, with Maj Wolfgang Gleis in command, and became part of 1.LVD by the end of that year, a year which also saw the withdrawal of the single-seat MiG-15s and MiG-17Fs from 1.JS/JG-3 and 2.JS/JG-3 and their replacement by MiG-19s, for which the pilots and technicians had undergone training in the USSR. 3.JS/JG-3 continued to fly the MiG-17Fs in a largely training role. JG-3 would be the only wing in the LSK/LV to be equipped with these high performance fighters, 12 MiG-19S 'Farmer C', day fighters going to 1.JS and 12 MiG-19PM 'Farmer D' to 2.JS. The work-up of both squadrons was rapid, 1.JS becoming operational and mounting DHS with the 'S' by day in 1961, while 2.JS committed the 'PM' to

DHS in the limited night/all weather role in the following year. Meanwhile, 3.JS had continued to fly the MiG-17F and joined the alert force in 1963.

In 1967, the first aircraft to use the war reserve airstrip on the autobahn at Forst, work on which had yet to be completed, was believed to be a MiG-19, flown by a Russian pilot, destined for the main runway at Preschen, but he saw the straight strip of roadway first and landed, thereafter having to weave his way between equally surprised vehicle drivers going about their lawful business. Fortunately, the traffic was light and the MiG was brought to a halt without incident; the words of the Russian pilot, on discovering his mistake, are unrepeatable here. When subsequently cleared for specific flying operations, all entry points to the strip were sealed off and civilian vehicles diverted on to local roads.

Despite its impressive performance, the MiG-19 was not generally popular in the LSK/LV; it was unreliable and difficult to maintain, and during its time at Preschen six were destroyed in major accidents, with six more damaged beyond repair. Attrition and general unserviceabilities led to the disbandment of one of the MiG-19 squadrons in 1963, the second soldiering on with a mix of 'S' and 'PM' until 1968.

After spending a year flying the MiG-17F at Trollenhagen, Rudolf Müller was posted to JG-3 in October 1961, to continue flying the aircraft with 3.JS until 1962, when he was included in a party of 25 carefully selected pilots from JG-3, all with 110 hours or more on the MiG-17F, and sent to Krasnodar, in Soviet Russia, to convert to

the MiG-21F-13. As there was no two-seat version of the MiG-21 available at that time, the Russian instructors used the MiG-15UTI to teach the Germans such techniques as were applicable to this new delta-wing aircraft, particularly in landing. All 25 pilots passed the three month course on the MiG-21F-13 and returned to Germany in July 1963, only to find that they had to maintain their currency on the MiG-21 with JG-8 at Marxwalde, pending the arrival of JG-3's own aircraft in October 1963. Rudolf spent the next nine years at Preschen flying the MiG-21F-13, mainly in the air defence role but with some training in the aircraft for offensive operations. For the latter, he recalls that the weapons delivery profiles included 45 deg dive-bombing from 2,200 m (7,000 ft), level/'laydown' deliveries and low approaches to pull-up for launching the unguided rockets .

Rudolf was among the many in East Germany who believed at that time that NATO was the potential aggressor, and was given to understand that, within the LSK/LV's concept of operations, JG-3 would be committed to the protection of the airspace around the frontier of the GDR with Czechoslovakia, in the area of the Erzgebirge mountain range, together with the protection of Dresden and the industrial centres of 'Schwarze Pumpe' Boxberg and Jaenschwalde. The MiG pilots were briefed that the greatest threat from NATO would come from the south-west, from what was known then as the 'American Zone' of the FRG, initially in the middle airspace but for most of the Cold War at low level. Against this latter, most difficult threat, Rudolf recalled setting up search patterns across likely NATO approach routes, at heights around 2,400 m (8,000 ft), hoping for target acquisition visually or with guidance from the local radars. Training against An-26 transport aircraft flying as targets at 8,000 m (27,000 ft), he also added some detail on how JG-3 might attempt to destroy NATO's AWACS E3A, with the MiGs expected to transit at low level through holes blasted in NATO's Hawk SAM belt on the IGB, before pulling up towards the E3As in full reheat for missile launch at 6,000 m (20,000 ft). They accepted that, using this tactic, they would suffer heavy losses from the Hawk and Nike SAM sites, any fighters protecting the AWACS and from a shortage of fuel – given the short range of the missile armed MiG-21s and the apparent lack of plans for them to operate from Soviet bases closer to the IGB.

Erwin Nützmann had joined JG-3 in 1967, direct from OHS (Chapter Two) and would remain with the wing throughout his career until 1988. Flying the MiG-21F-13, the 'SPS', 'M' and 'MF' fighters, and the two-seat trainers, he earned his LK.III status in 1967, LK.II in 1968 and LK.I in 1969, and rose rapidly through the ranks to qualify as an Oberflieger (pairs leader), flight instructor, Kettenkommandeur (four-ship leader), Leiter (flight supervisor), and Stellvertreter (deputy squadron commander), to become Kommandeur (squadron commander) of 3.JS/JG-3, in 1977. By any standard, he had a very good flying career in the LSK/LV. In 1971, the JG-3 was privileged to be granted the name: '*Vladimir Komarow*', in honour of the Soviet cosmonaut killed when the brake parachute system designed to soften the landing of his spacecraft malfunctioned.

In the first half of the 1970s JG-3 began re-equipping with the MiG-21MF, with the more powerful Tumansky R-13–300 engine giving it a significantly better performance than the 'M', it was a more popular aircraft. In 1973, when JG-8 was ordered to send 12 MiG-21Ms to Syria, to make good its losses in the Yom Kippur War against Israel, JG-3 was ordered to send 12 of its MiG-21MFs to Marxwalde to replace them, and to revert to flying the older, less capable MiG-21F-13 and MiG-21SPS. It was not until 1982 that all three air defence squadrons on JG-3 were operating the 'MF' again, some of which came from Peenemünde when JG-9 converted to the MiG-23MF/ML.

Meanwhile, in 1974, a new LVD-1 unit had begun to form at Preschen: Aufklärungs-fliegerstaffel-31 (AFS-31), an independent reconnaissance squadron, initially within JG-3, and made up of MiG-21F-13s, MiG-21Us, pilots and groundcrew from 3.JS/JG-3. AFS-31 built up slowly, increasing its strength progressively as more airframes became available from FAG-15, and by 1976 it was fully established with four flights, each of four MiG-21F-13s. From January to December 1977, all four Preschen squadrons were deployed north to the war reserve/satellite airfield at Garz, on the island of Usedom (now Heringsdorf civil airport), while their home base was refurbished. There, 1.JS and 2.JS occupied well prepared HAS sites, but 3.JS and AFS-31 had to operate in the open from revetted dispersals. In 1981, Rudolf Müller, who had been flying the 'MF' on JG-3 since 1972 and was now a very experienced fast-jet pilot, was transferred to AFS-31, to spend the next three years on tactical reconnaissance (tac recce) duties in the MiG-21F-13. In 1982, AFS-31 was re-designated AFS-47 and transferred to the Führungsorgan der Front-und Armeefliegerkräfte (FO FAFK), the new frontal aviation command (Chapter Six).

Hannes Mallwitz had proved his suitability for pilot training during GST, before spending three years at OHS, rather than the four years on the standard course because of a pilot shortage on the front line. This abbreviated course comprised two years of jet training on the L-29 Delfin followed by a third on the MiG-21F-13, in which he flew 78 hours before joining 3.JS/JG-3 at Preschen in 1976, where he converted on to the MiG-21SPS. Within the next year, he reached the grand total of 350 flying hours, was judged proficient in high level interceptions and basic weapons delivery and qualified for his LK.III classification. He was then selected to attend the challenging four year course at the Monino Soviet Air Force Academy in Moscow, where the German students spent the first year improving their Russian language skills, the second on mathematics and the sciences, the third on aircraft systems and operations at squadron and wing levels, and the fourth on all aspects of higher command and organization of air/land operations. Graduating in 1981, Hannes returned to JG-3, where he quickly built up his flying hours, now on the MiG-21M, and was given command of 3.JS/JG-3, in the rank of captain. Having achieved his LK.II qualification, he was appointed to JG-1's wing staff (See JG-1, above).

After graduating from OHS in 1981, Klaus Schmiedel was posted to 3.JS/JG-3, initially to fly the MiG-21SPS. He learned fast, to become a fully-fledged LK.1 operational pilot before moving to 2.JS in 1983 to fly the 'M' and 'MF', and play a full part in DHS as he progressed rapidly to become a four-ship leader, instructor pilot and ultimately deputy squadron commander – with promotion to captain in 1986. Klaus also liked the way the MiG-21 handled; he was very impressed with its combat speed, and its ability to manoeuvre at 7'G' with weapons attached. However, he too was frustrated by the aircraft's lack of range and the shortcomings of its RP-21 radar, which was even more marked when the emphasis changed from upper airspace to low level operations against manned aircraft and cruise missiles, which he admitted would have been a very difficult challenge for the MiG-21s in war. He found take-offs assisted by the two SPRD rockets exhilarating, and had good reason to be grateful for the training they received on short, grass airstrips, when one of his comrades misjudged his landing speed and blocked the main runway at night while he was airborne. Klaus, following behind, had to overshoot, with barely enough fuel to reach his alternate in rapidly deteriorating weather, but he was able to land safely on an unlit grass strip, with only the airfield's peripheral lights and his aircraft's landing lights for guidance. This was but one of many salutary reminders for the pilots of the problems caused by a lack of fuel aboard the MiG-21s. Given that no maps were available to them, Klaus thought that there were no plans for

JG-3 to move westward with any Warsaw Pact ground offensive.

Two squadrons from JG-3 were at Garz again in 1982, during which time the MiG pilots had an unplanned meeting with Swedish Draken fighters. It seems that the German pilots may not have been fully aware of new Swedish airspace restrictions, published in one of those vast volumes of regulations which fighter pilots of all nations find hard to digest, prohibiting practice interceptions in IMC, on what was known as the 'northern route' over the Baltic. Be that as it may, the pilots of JG-3 proceeded with a demanding but well thought out 'two-v-two' training exercise, involving only those pilots qualified to LK.1 standards, which followed the original route at 5,000 m (16,400 ft) in IMC . The first pair completed a successful interception, without seeing a Swedish Draken which the leader of the second pair had spotted in their area during a temporary break in the cloud. While there was no question of a 'near miss', this breach of regulations had been observed, and the following day 'officialdom' demanded details of the flight from the Germans, in which the flight leader admitted having flown the northern route but apparently failed to mention the Drakens. The matter was not allowed to rest there, the evidence accumulated from both Swedish and German sources concluding that an international violation had indeed taken place, and retribution would follow – in a story which became known as the 'Swedish Punch'. In the event, the flight leader survived with an entry on his records which remained there when he returned to

civilian life, but in December 2002, the Swedish honorary consul in Leipzig told him that the incident was no longer of interest to them. Many other military pilots have similar stories to tell – which they file under heading of 'occupational hazard'.

In 1983, elements of JG-3 took part, for the first time, in a joint exercise with the Polish fighter wing at Krakow. Hitherto, exercises of this nature had been rare, and even rarer when the Soviet Air Force was included, but those who took part were quick to proclaim its value to all. Other than in exercises such as the monthly 'Gefechtsflugtage' and the 'Kommandeursflugtage', the squadrons at Preschen ran their daily flying programmes from 'peacetime' flight lines, with frequent rehearsals to ensure that they could deploy to the war sites within minutes. Survival scrambles were also high on the training agenda, with 1.JS and 3.JS invariably launching from the main runway, heading west, while 2.JS took off between the two in the opposite direction and AFS-47/TAS-47 taxied the 3 km to operate from the autobahn strip.

Rudolf Müller left AFS-47 in 1985 to return to air defence duties on JG-3, flying the MiG-21MF. He was joined in that year by Frank Scholz, straight from a four year course at the OHS, where he had flown the L-39 at Bautzen and MiG-21 at Rothenburg. Frank was posted to 3.JS/JG-3, but within a year he was transferred to 2.JS/JG-3, flying the MiG-21M and the 'MF' on both squadrons. Asked about his weapons training, Frank confirmed that they trained on the GSch-23 cannon, the S-5 unguided rockets and bombs, by day only, but the RS-2US beam-riding, and R-3S IRH missiles by day and night; both in rear hemisphere attacks only. During the 25 years in which the MiG-21 served with JG-3, the wing was believed to have lost a total of 13 single-seat aircraft, with eight ejections and four pilots killed, and to have had a further 10 badly damaged on the ground, a relatively good accident rate in the circumstances at the time.

The spirit within JG-3 appeared to remain alive and well throughout its relatively short life, as exemplified by the 'Flugräte' club. Exclusive to JG-3, a pilot could become a 'Flugräte' on achieving 1,000 hours of flying on the MiG, then go on to become a 'Oberflugräte' with 1,500 hours, a 'Hauptflugräte' with 2,000 hours and 'Generalflugräte' with 2,500 hours. Rudolf Müller, a founder member of the society, one time chairman and a staunch supporter throughout its life, Siegmar Pastor and Erwin Nützmann were among the first to achieve 2,500 hours. The Flugräte, with their slogan: 'Sicher ist Sicher' (roughly: 'Safe and Sure') found many reasons and ways to celebrate their social rituals, initially in members' gardens, but as the society grew, in the wing's mess.

Throughout the Cold War, the combat elements of the Soviet Air Force in the GDR, and the EGAF, evolved largely from a succession of Mikoyan and latterly Sukhoi fast-jet aircraft; this evolution reached a defining point with the MiG-29. On 1 November 1986, Oberst Manfred Skeries was appointed Chief of Interceptor Forces, with direct responsibility for introducing the MiG-29 to JG-3 at Preschen. He would lead a group of specially selected pilots and senior officers from the division and wing, including the commander (designate) of the first MiG-29 squadron, and his three deputies, to Russia, to familiarize themselves with the aircraft. The chosen men left Schönefeld for Moscow on 10 May 1987, in an Il-62 of the Government Air Transport Wing at Marxwalde, to begin their conversion two days later, but progress was hampered by language difficulties with the Russian documentation, the lack of crucial training publications and copying facilities, a refusal to accept the NVA medical records and an insistence on local examinations. Gradually, however, these problems were largely resolved, and the NVA pilots passed the necessary academic examinations, to begin their final preparations for flight on 10 June 1987. The experienced Manfred Skeries, with his 2,000 hard-earned flying hours (in some 3,900 short but very busy fighter sorties) was the first to take to the air in a two-seat MiG-29UB, on 16 June, and on the following day, after two dual sorties and a check ride, he went solo in a MiG-29A, 37 days after arriving on the base. All the pilots in his party did likewise in the week that followed, with none encountering any significant problem. True to expectations, the Germans found the aircraft to be a pilot's dream, seated in the comfort of a more spacious cockpit than they had been used to with its MiG predecessors, with all controls ready to hand in excellent cockpit ergonomics. They revelled in the aircraft's powerful and responsive engines and splendid aerodynamic qualities, which combined to give an unprecedented performance. Consolidation, basic air combat manoeuvres and navigation exercises came next in the steep learning curve, and the whole syllabus of 15–18 flying hours, inter-dispersed with sporting events and appropriate celebrations, was completed on schedule, culminating in a 'very impressive' final parade in Lugovoj. The German pilots returned to Preschen on 30 July, this time aboard an NVA Tu-134, to face a nine-month wait for the first of 24 MiG-29s (20 single-seat and four dual aircraft), to arrive in the GDR, during which time the German pilots had to maintain flying currency on the MiG-21MF at Preschen.

A welcoming parade greeted the formal arrival of the MiG-29s at Preschen in April 1988. Hitherto, every attempt had been made to keep the whole MiG-29 project secret, so it came as some surprise that one cameraman was granted permission to record this memorable event – but it transpired later that his camera (by design or accident?) had contained no film. Secrecy remained the game even after the aircraft had arrived at Preschen, with other pilots on JG-3, some of whom were scheduled to join the programme later, denied access to the aircraft. As Klaus Schmiedel, who would become one of the chosen few, put it: 'It was as if a glass screen had been erected between the MiG-29 squadron and the remainder of the flightline'.

'Flugdiensttag', 3 May 88, was the first full flying day for the MiG-29s of 1.JS/JG-3, and nine days later the now chief of the NVA's air defence force, Manfred Skeries, was quite rightly chosen to display the new aircraft at Holzdorf, before a group of VIPs which included the Soviet Secretary of Defence. The local conversion programme got underway at once, with the four two-seat and ten single-seat MiG-29s now at Preschen, but without a flight simulator, the building in which it was to be housed having yet to be completed because of a lack of funds. However, with training and engineering support from the Russians, the first of these trainees completed the course in the first half of 1988, on time and without incident. 1.JS was then quick to work up its pilots to an operational standard, and with more aircraft arriving before the end of the year 2.JS followed suit in early 1989.

Klaus Schmiedel satisfied all the prerequisites for the MiG-29 programme; since 1983 he had flown 630 hours in the MiG-21, and had no difficulty converting to the MiG-29 within the prescribed syllabus, adjusted to each pilot's proficiency and progress, and consistent with the resources available. He recalled that the first solo in a MiG-29A could be expected after seven sorties/three hours in the MiG-29UB, and that a further four to six weeks of MiG-29 flying was usually needed (depending on the weather and resources) for a pilot to reach a classification of LK.I on the aircraft. Klaus, too, was greatly impressed by the aircraft's powerful, responsive engines and extremely good handling characteristics, and with an auto pilot which could recover the aircraft safely from any unusual flight attitude with the press of a button. He also spoke very highly of its radar/weapons system, which gave the all-important 'look-down/shoot-down' capability, and the IFF/computer interface which prevented the aircraft's advanced AAMs from launching against friendly aircraft.

Within a year, 1.JS/JG-3 was fit to assume DHS duties, day and night, VMC and IMC, and both squadrons quickly became proficient in most forms of air combat involving two and four aircraft, ground-attack and tac recce. In the last year of the aircraft's short life within the LSK/LV, roughly 30% of the training was devoted to practice interceptions at low level, 30% against targets up to 4,000 m (13,000 ft), and 28% up to 18,000 m (60,000 ft) – some against supersonic targets. The remaining 12% involved air combat training, all in a mix of day/night and VMC/IMC conditions. To exploit the aircraft's versatility, every MiG-29 pilot was required to complete seven weapons sorties satisfactorily, two of which had to be with live weapons, to operate effectively in an NBC and ECM environment, from alternative airstrips, in radio silence and minimum lighting at night, and to carry out visual reconnaissance. The pilots were expected to complete this very full and daunting programme, and to remain proficient, with annual averages of 80–90 hours, although instructor pilots, with their extra duties, were known to fly as many as 120 hours in the first year. More demanding exercises were planned – but they succumbed to reunification.

Major Gunter Fichte was also among the first to convert to the MiG-29 at Preschen, later to become one of the squadron commanders on JG-3. He recalls carrying out five landings with a Soviet instructor in the two-seat MiG-29UB, before his first solo in the MiG-29A, in a basic transition course

of 16 sorties, at a time when the new aircraft's serviceability left much to be desired, and its potential had yet to be realized. Crucially, a lack of technical documentation denied servicing teams the opportunity to achieve and maintain their new aircraft in peak condition, while the NVA hierarchy, determined to keep the accident rate low, tended to limit the flying programme to the lower risk training sorties. Progressively, however, the specialists on the ground found ways and means of developing the systems, and in the air it is believed that some of the more inquisitive pilots exceeded their mandate and explored ever more ambitious manoeuvres.

During the 25 years that the MiG-21 served with JG-3, the wing is believed to have lost a total of 13 single-seat fighters, with 8 ejections and 4 pilots killed, and to have had a further 10 badly damaged on the ground, a relatively good accident rate in the circumstances. No MiG-29s were lost.

When it disbanded, on 30 September 1990, JG-3 had on strength 20 MiG-29A, 4 MiG-29UB, 12 MiG-21MF and 3 MiG-21UM, supported by 216 officers, 299 NCOs and airmen/airwomen, and 28 civilians. Thereafter, the unified German Air Force, recognizing that they had acquired a very potent air weapons system, retained the two MiG-29 squadrons at Preschen until December 1994, before moving them to the new base at Laage, south of Rostock, where a flight simulator had been installed, and they continued to exploit the full, spectacular capability of the MiG-29 until 2004, when the majority were sold to Poland – for a token sum of one Euro each.

Interviews with pilots from JG-3 provided constant reminders of the dedication to the work ethic in the EGAF, and a willingness to tolerate the continuous high states of readiness for the defence of their homeland – against the perceived threat of a surprise attack by NATO forces. This was reflected in the overall lifestyle of the NVA pilots, with these demanding operational commitments clearly affecting family life and leisure pursuits. Attitudes, working and living conditions varied from wing to wing, but Klaus Schmiedel confirmed that there was no RAF-type crewroom/coffee bar culture on the flight line at Preschen, in which the pilots could meet and relax between and after flights or commitments on the ground (even if their intensive programmes had allowed). In this, NATO pilots did indeed have the advantage, their squadron crew-rooms being the central hubs of activity, whether flying was taking place or not, and it was not uncommon for them to be venues for 'beer-calls' after a day's work. EGAF bases did have communal 'Personaldienstgebäude' (personal service buildings) for their flying equipment and other purposes, and a wing 'Kulturhaus' (Culture House), with restaurants for officers and NCOs, cinemas and libraries, but these were quite unlike the messes the RAF provided for their off-duty officers,

NCOs and airmen. The RAF Officers' Messes in Germany, based loosely on traditional rituals and rules, were very popular and lively places throughout the evenings and weekends, and in many cases separate bars were available for pilots coming off flying duty, or others who were 'improperly dressed' for the main rooms in a Mess. In the EGAF, single officers and the many others who were waiting to be allocated married quarters, shared twin-bed rooms in barrack blocks, Klaus Schmiedel living in one for two years before his wife joined him, and until which time he was able to visit his family on one weekend only in every month. In the RAF, bachelor officers and those waiting for family quarters lived in well appointed single rooms, with staff on hand to attend to all their domestic needs. Consistent with sufficient manning being available to meet the published alert states, married officers and other ranks occupied married quarters on, or close to the base, in military hirings or private accommodation. Leave rosters were also determined against alert requirements, but it would seem that the NATO entitlements were more generous than those in the NVA. What effects these different lifestyles might have had on operational effectiveness in war, will never be known.

MiG-17Fs also served with JG-3 in the latter half of the 1950s.
Rudolf Müller Collection

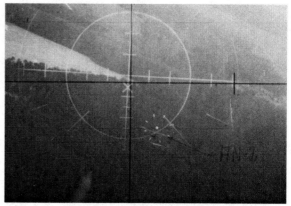

Flying a MiG-21MF of JG-3, Hannes Mallwitz had an NVA
An-2 transport in his gunsight.   *Hannes Mallwitz*

The MiG-19 served on JG-3 from 1961 to 1968.
Rudolf Müller

MiG-21 pilots from 2.JS/JG-3 at Garz in November 1977.
Rudolf Müller Collection

Congratulations. Hptm Klaus Schmiedel achieves 1000 flying
hours.   *Klaus Schmiedel*

Maj Erwin Nützmann achieves 1,500 flying hours on
3.JS/JG-3 at Preschen, in 1980.   *Erwin Nützmann*

Rudolf Müller, JG-3: Professional Fighter pilot.   *Rudolf Müller*

Klaus Schmiedel indulging in some age-old ground training
for air combat.   *Klaus Schmiedel*

JG-3 briefing 'al fresco'.   *Klaus Schmiedel*

Klaus Schmiedel with pilots of 2.JS/JG-3 at Preschen.
                                          Klaus Schmiedel

MiG-21Ms of ARS-47 prepare for a night reconnaissance sortie at Preschen. *Rudolf Müller Collection*

Flugplatz Preschen. *Rudolf Just*

Bereiche für Flugzeuge und Personal am Flugplatz Preschen von 1960-1994

The DHS (QRA) facility at Preschen, changed with the Cold War years. *Rudolf Just*

Major Erwin Nützmann rewarded for good work on JG-3, at a ceremony in 1980. *Erwin Nützmann*

In 1982, JG-3 visited the Polish Air Force at Posen. *Hannes Mallwitz*

Exclusive Club. The 'Flugrat' club was the exclusive preserve of the pilots of JG-3, catagorised 'Flugrat'(1,000 hours); 'Oberflieger' (1,500 hours); 'Hauptflugrat' (2,000 hours); 'Generalflugrat' (2,500 hours) & 'Luftmarshal' (3,000 hours).   *Rudolf Müller* Collection

On detachment at Garz in 1982, 3.JS/JG-3 had a chance meeting with the Swedish Air Force over the Baltic in the 'Schwerpunch'.   *Erwin Nützmann*

Executives of 3.JS/JG-3 in 1986 (L – R): Maj Schulz (Political Officer), Maj Schröder (Chief Flying Instructor); OSL Erwin Nützmann (CO); Maj Wilhelm (Engineer Officer); Hptm Grimmer (Admin. Officer).   *Erwin Nützmann*

A Memorable Day. Klaus Schmiedel flew his last sortie on JG-3, on 27 September 1990.   *Klaus Schmiedel*

Mig-29s arrive at Preschen in April 1988.

Rudolf Müller Collection

Michael Wegerich, who joined the MiG-29 force in its final year, flew his last sortie in the NVA aircraft, in its commemorative colours, on 27 September 1990. *Michael Wegerich*

End Game. Long time MiG fighter pilots OSLs Müller, Kilian, Pastor and Nützmann celebrate their last flights in the MiG-21 at Preschen. *Rudolf Müller*

Gunter Fichte commanded the MiG-29 Test Squadron at Preschen in 1989. *Gunter Fichte*

OSL Rudolf Müller, congratulated after his first flight in a GAF MiG-29 at Laage. *Rudolf Müller*

End of an Era. Formal and informal celebrations (or wakes?) on 2 October 1990 at Preschen, to mark the end of a proud era for JG-3, MiG-29 pilots with one of their aircraft, suitably adorned for its final flight before the disbandment of the NVA.

Rudolf Müller Collection

Jagdgeschwader 7 (JG-7)

Flugplatz Drewitz, cut from a forest between Cottbus and Guben, some 10 km (6 miles) west of the border with Poland, was established in the 1930s. In WW2 the airfield was used by the Luftwaffe, and thereafter by the Soviet Second Air Army, joined periodically by elements of the GDR's emerging aviation industry, before its refurbishment to become home for JG-7. A paved runway, 2,500 m (2,750 yd) long, was built in 1953, and flying began there with Yak-18 and Yak-11 training aircraft of No.2 Aeroclub in December 1954. FG-7, commanded by Maj Reinhold, took up residence in 1956, within the framework of 3.LVD, its first MiG-15UTI and MiG-15bis jets arriving in June 1956, followed soon after by MiG-17Fs; Maj Johannes Richter took command in 1959 and the IL-28s of ZDS-21, the target towing squadron, joined the wing in 1961, when FG-7 was re-named JG-7 and transferred to 1.LVD. Throughout the rest of the decade, the number of aircraft on the wing fluctuated, MiG-17PFs having been added to the inventory (with a commensurate reduction in MiG-17Fs) in 1965, followed by MiG-21SPS, MiG-21M and MiG-21US in 1969, resulting in an unusual mix of 26 MiG-17F, 16 MiG-21SPS, 27 MiG-21M, 6 MiG-21US, 10 MiG-15UTI, 5 IL-28 and 1 IL-28U (Trainer) – a total of 91 aircraft. This was big business. In 1971, ZDS-21 was re-named ZDS-33 and moved to Peenemünde, to join JG-9 within 3.LVD.

The primary role for JG-7's MiGs was of course, air defence, with the wing's secondary and very limited ground-attack capability rarely rehearsed by its fighters, but in 1971 Drewitz began playing host to the first of the EGAF's fighter-bomber wings, with the formation of 'Jagdbombengeschwader-31' (JBG-31) (Chapter Six). Initially, the new wing would make do with the MiG-17Fs rendered redundant when JG-7 was re-equipped with the MiG-21SPS and MiG-21M. In 1972, JG-7 was given the title of '*Wilhelm Pieck*', after a German WW1 and WW2 ace.

Gunter Fichte flew the 'M' on JG-7, after completing OHS and his jet training on the MiG-21F-13s and MiG-21Us with FAG-15 in 1973. From 1978, he also spent much of his time as an instructor in the two-seat trainers, all of this setting him up well to be among the first to fly the MiG-29 (JG-3, above). From the early 1970s, JG-7 and JBG-31 (later re-named JBG-37) shared the airfield at Drewitz, suggesting that joint exercises might have been laid on to mutual benefit, but those questioned could remember only two or three occasions on which this was organised in the years the two wings were together, and only one when the fighters escorted the fighter-bombers on simulated attack missions.

In 1985, Jörg Behnke joined 3.JS/JG-7 at Drewitz, to fly the MiG-21M, the wing's aircraft having now donned a more warlike camouflage in place of their original silver finish. Two years later he became an instructor pilot on the aircraft, holding that appointment until the wing disbanded in 1989. Commenting on typical external configurations (weapons and fuel tanks) for the MiGs on JG-7, Jörg recalls that for some specific, single-seat training exercises in the local area their aircraft were loaded with sufficient fuel for the assigned task plus a small reserve only, resulting in sortie times of only 12–20 minutes, with a minimum 'return home' fuel of 500 litres allowing one missed approach only on return to base. A lower limit of 300 litres was sometimes authorized for sorties in the MiG-21 trainers – but only when occupied by two pilots. This, coupled with the limitations of its RP-21 radar, meant that good GCI control and precise flying were essential if the pilot was to acquire his target on the first run, and complete his interception with a successful firing solution in a single pass.

Air-to-air gunnery with the MiG-21M on JG-7 in Jörg's time was targeted against the KT-04, while live AAM training was carried out against M6/M6T 'Small Size Targets' and high speed RM-3V target missiles for the IRH AAMs, both exercises making good use of LSZ-II, over the Baltic (see Chapter Three). For the latter, four aircraft would take off singly at two minute intervals, the first dropping an M6/M6T for its slow descent from heights up to 17,000 m (55,000 ft), the three 'shooters' following at heights above 10,000 m (33,000 ft) and at a speed of M1.2, which gave them very little time to gain a radar lock for their inert RS-2US missiles. Alternatively, single aircraft could launch their own RM-3V target, and attempt to engage it with inert R-3S or R-13M IRH missiles – again in the very short time available, so in both these demanding exercises a fast reaction was crucial to success – as it could be in an operational scenario. Jörg also recalls launching an RS-2US missile from his MiG-21M in the radar 'boresight' mode, without a target, simply

to practise the procedure of manoeuvring the aircraft to follow the missile's path as it headed for the Baltic Sea. For some, there were also detachments from JG-7 to Astrachan, for the pilots to develop their skills against the very demanding La-17 radio controlled, jet-powered target drone (Chapter Three). JG-7 pilots had little direct contact with their Soviet neighbours in the GDR, but Jörg was part of a small group of pilots and support personnel, including air traffic control officers and engineers from the wing, which took their aircraft to the local Soviet MiG-21 wing at Jüterbog, where their hosts provided some ground equipment and services. The programme began with official welcoming speeches but there was little opportunity to exchange professional experiences or make personal contact with their Russian hosts at their level.

Jörg described a successful MiG-21M supersonic interception training sortie, in which he closed on a target flying at M0.9 and 14,000 m (46,000 ft) at M1.6. As was always the case in the LSK/LV, the sortie was planned with great precision on a standard route, to be checked and cleared by a supervising officer on the day before the flight, with Jörg again very aware of the limitations of the aircraft's RP-21 radar and that his closing speed would be as high as 900 km/hr (485 knots). Given that his radar might pick up the target as late as 11 km (6 nm), and that it must lock-on by 5 km (3 nm), he would have very little time in which to complete the firing sequence – this whole phase being recorded in the aircraft's cockpit. Moreover, he would have enough fuel aboard for one pass only, with no re-attack possible. This was a challenging exercise for both controller and pilot.

On the day in question, the MiG-21US weather check, with two wing executives on board, launched on time and Jörg began the standard three hour pre-flight schedule (Chapter Three), during which it was confirmed that the weather was suitable for his exercise. Finally, having donned his pressure suit and helmet, which he said was 'a very uncomfortable procedure', he made his way to the flight line, acknowledged his groundcrew with the usual hand-shakes, and carried out the external checks on his aircraft. Having strapped into his ejection seat, he completed his cockpit checks, obtained ATC clearance and started the engine on time to meet his assigned take-off slot, giving the target, another MiG-21M, a five minute head start. With the MiG-21's simple and reliable systems, everything worked as it should, and the two aircraft launched from Runway '25' on schedule.

Take-off was also normal, Jörg cancelling reheat at 600 km/hr (325 knots) to conserve fuel, and switching to his assigned GCI frequency – quickly recognising the familiar voice of a controller he knew well. For the next 20 minutes he would be wholly dependent on this remote voice to guide him to an initial position 50 km (27 nm) directly astern of his target, necessary if his radar was to acquire the target without delay. The exercise route took him south-west from Drewitz, before the controller ordered him to accelerate and make a wide turn on to the target's heading of north-east. Jörg now used his experience and

judgment to optimize his fuel consumption and fly accurately at the prescribed altitude and speed, using the recommended angles of climb and bank. On reaching a speed of M1.6, a dot on the aircraft's radar screen confirmed that all the required parameters had been satisfied; the target was dead ahead at 14,300 m (47,000 ft), and a successful lock-on followed. Closing to a range of 4 km (4,400 yd), Jörg received the necessary growl from the R-13M training missile he had selected and pressed the firing button to simulate a launch. This had been a copybook interception.

Recovery to Drewitz, under GCI control, with the fair weather predicted and ample fuel remaining (he had 50 litres above 'Bingo' (the minimum fuel required at that point in the sortie), should have been routine, but in the flying business little can be assumed, and there was always the possibility of conflicting traffic on Airway A4, which lay across the route back to base. In the event, there were no problems, so Jörg throttled back to idle (85% at that height), and began to descend, and with a check of his engine instruments as he passed through 7,000 m, (23,000 ft), showing that all was well, he changed frequency to Drewitz control for positioning on a long final approach at 25 km (14 nm) from the runway threshold. It was then simply a matter of flying the airfield's standard, radar monitored recovery, making the final checks before touchdown and deploying the brake parachute on the ground. If the approach had to be aborted, Jörg knew that he had enough fuel to make one more attempt, and if the runway was blocked, he had the option of landing on the parallel grass strip.

As with all LSK/LV wings, JG-7 adhered strictly to the manning and aircraft requirements for the alert state in force, and regularly exercised their transition to war (TTW) procedures, including dispersal plans. To this end, the usual practice was for JG-7 to take 12 aircraft to its primary war reserve airfield at Klein Koris (Chapter Three), the ground support vehicles, including a mobile air traffic control, attempting to arrive at the airstrip before the fighters – but they did not always succeed. On one exercise the aircraft arrived first; the pilots were warned of an imminent air attack on the airstrip as the last of them was shutting down, and then ordered to get airborne again immediately, presumably in the knowledge that the aircraft would have enough fuel remaining to reach another suitable airfield. Get airborne they did, with pilots having done all that was necessary themselves, and with such commendable dispatch that the predicted airfield attack caught only two aircraft on the ground. On another occasion at Klein Koris, an over-zealous staff officer decided to test the squadron's reaction at 0300 hours on a summer's morning, and took it upon himself to initiate the alert system in the mobile control van. However, he triggered the 'scramble' button by mistake and could not prevent the first pilots leaping into their cockpits, starting their engines, taxiing to the runway and beginning the mass take-off, fortunately in the growing light of dawn. By the time competent controllers arrived at the van it

was too late to stop the take-offs; the aircraft were airborne and it was then a matter of deciding where they should land. First to be alerted to receive 12 thirsty fighters was the huge civilian airport at Schönefeld; then Drewitz was ordered to be ready for them, and finally they were recovered back to Klein Koris, where they all landed safely – and the story peters out. It could have been worse. In another surprise attack on Klein Koris, an An-2 sprayed the area with a red fluid, simulating a gas or chemical attack, but again the birds had flown and well practised NBC protective measures on the ground largely mitigated the detrimental effects of the attack.

In 1986, 3.JS/JG-7 was detached for a year to Garz/Heringsdorf, while work was carried out on the runway at Drewitz. There, in addition to routine air defence training in the neighbouring air-to-air range (LSZ-II), they had an ideal opportunity to rehearse their ground-attack/maritime attack role against surface targets on a range very close to the airfield and the semi-submerged, heavily damaged ships on the sea range off the Baltic coast, some 45 km (24 nm) to the west at Peenemünde airfield. In both cases Jörg recalls carrying out dive attacks from 900 m (3,000 ft), with unguided S-5 rockets, and strafing with the MiG-21M's cannon, taking care to recover from the dive above the ricochet envelope. On the air-to-ground range the pilots were required to adhere strictly to the published procedures, attacking the targets from one direction only and always with the first run 'dry'. With no accurate scoring system there, the results were assessed from the aircraft's camera recorder. Jörg claimed that MiG-21M's weapons sighting and cockpit switch procedures were simple, and cannot recall any of the 'switchery pigs' which were known to cause some NATO pilots embarrassment, if not trouble, particularly on those squadrons which contained a mix of aircraft with non-standard cockpit layouts, thereby inviting the inadvertent release of external stores (fuel tanks, bombs or rockets). Neither side was exempt from other 'incidents' on the weapons ranges, attributed to technical defect, target misidentification, pilot error or 'occupational hazard' (eg. bird strike), the author recalling the delivery of a small practice bomb from a Jaguar at night, with laudable accuracy but unfortunately against a new and unreported light array on a factory bordering Nordhorn Range, fortunately without damage or injury. On other occasions, range officers would report 'no bomb observed' after a 'live' bomb run, the final resting place of the errant weapon sometimes remaining a mystery to this day.

This was not the case on one Saturday afternoon in June 1986, when two UB-16 rocket launchers, each carrying three 57 mm rockets (3 with live warheads) departed inadvertently from a MiG-21M of JG-7 operating out of Garz, during a live weapons training exercise. Manfred Skeries, then Deputy Commander 1.LVD and Chief of Air Defence Training, was airborne with the Officer Commander (OC) JG-7, and heard the young pilot report that he had lost his rockets and both launchers, and Manfred was determined to find them, if only to avoid the tortuous weekend enquiry which would otherwise follow. OC JG-7 cancelled all further weapons training forthwith, and Manfred set up an inquiry which immediately concluded that all cockpit procedures had been correct, that there was no obvious technical defect and that the launchers had been lost *en route* to the range in use – rather than on the range itself. On that basis, search parties were set up to scour the area beneath the aircraft's flight path, drawing on all available help from the local air force, navy, police and Stasi units – but to no avail – and there were none of the expected calls from the public. It was then that Manfred came to the rescue, getting authority to offer a DM500 reward and to the use of the Mi-8 helicopter which had been acting as range monitor, to carry him, the JG-7 commander, the young pilot involved and his squadron commander, on a 'search and rescue' operation. This centred on an area in which the pilot had sensed that he heard a 'metallic thump' below his aircraft, but thought nothing of it at the time. Had he checked his weapons panel then he would have seen that the two lights which indicated that the pylons were occupied were no longer illuminated. Those aboard the helicopter quickly realized that their initial search from 80–100 m (260–330 ft) was too low, and raised the height to 200–250 m (660 – 800 ft), but still there were no sign of the launchers, no visible damage to property or any gathering of people to suggest that they had found their quarry. However, further calculations of the MiG's flight path eventually led to success, both launchers and their rockets being found in a cornfield just off the road to Anklam. There they met other military men searching the area, including a two-star NVA general who admitted that he had lost an entire tank company – and had no idea where to look for it. A deeper technical investigation subsequently revealed that the extreme humidity at that time had caused a short in the external stores jettison circuit. All's well that ends well; no incident statistic was logged, the helicopter crew was rewarded with the DM500, the hierarchy was happy and everyone involved took the rest of the weekend off.

In the 18 years between 1971 and the wing's disbandment in 1989, the author was able to trace the loss of eight MiG-21Ms and significant damage to 12 others. Jörg Behnke remembers one particularly tragic accident, on 16 March 1985, when the pilot of a MiG-21M was unable to maintain height following a hydraulic failure immediately after a rocket-assisted take-off from Drewitz, which disabled the afterburner's 'eyelids'. For reasons unknown, he failed to jettison the two (spent) SPRD rocket containers in the area provided for the purpose, and ejected successfully before his aircraft plunged into Juri-Gagarin-Strasse in Cottbus. Fortunately, the school at the point of impact was unoccupied at the time, but the jet caused serious damage, killing one civilian and seriously injuring a second. Thereafter, in the four relatively very good final years for flight safety on JG-7, there is only one other incident recorded, a typical landing accident to a MiG-21M in January 1988.

When the author suggested that the NVA officers had a relatively privileged lifestyle in the GDR, Jörg admitted that they enjoyed certain advantages over their civilian contemporaries, but pointed out that the airmen were committed to very long hours of duty maintaining very demanding alert postures. He, among others, was also at pains to claim that, while formal social functions in the EGAF may have been less frequent than in NATO, there were plenty of unofficial social activities at lower levels. Perhaps JG-7 was more fortunate than some other wings, with single and married quarters being hidden in the woods very close to their airfield, much now refurbished and occupied, and it was there that most of this socialising took place. Also, on the frequent occasions when the officers were confined to the base, or deployed to Klein Koris on exercise, their wives could depend on the friendship and support of their military and civilian neighbours in the local community. As for the Stasi, everyone was of course well aware of those of its officers who went about their normal duties in uniform, and many seemed unconcerned by the presence of others imbedded among them who remained unknown. In defence of the latter, Jörg made the point that they were often coerced or blackmailed into the Stasi ranks by nefarious means, remembering that one officer who had struck up a relationship with a Scandinavian girl was allowed to continue serving as a pilot only if he severed all contact with the girl – and became a Stasi informer. In another case, a pilot who was found to have too strong a liking for alcohol was grounded for a year, but was then allowed to return to flying only if he abstained and became a clandestine member of the Stasi. It was

A MiG-21SPS of JG-7, on a rocket assisted take-off, from Drewitz. *Rufolf Müller Collection*

This MiG-21SPS/K, carrying two UB-16 rocket pods, served with JG-7 and is now in retirement at Cottbus.
Author/Cottbus Museum

EGAF pilots were required to carry out regular cockpit drills in the aircraft they were flying, or on a simple ground training aid such as this – which shows the relative simplicity of the MiG-21's basic instrument display. *Author*

At one point, the spacious airfield at Drewitz was known to have had as many as 80 aircraft operating from it, and was a collecting point for many of the EGAF aircraft rendered redundant at the end of the Cold War. *Author's Collection*

JG-7 would deploy to this bare, grass airstrip at Klein Koris in war and exercise. *Author*

Hauptmann Gunter Fichte, flight commander on JG-7, in the cockpit of a MiG-21. *Gunter Fichte*

Jörg Behnke had his first flight in a MiG-21M on JG-7 in 1985. *Jörg Behnke*

Officers, NCOs and airmen of JG-7 in a proud farewell parade at Drewitz in 1989. *Jörg Behnke*

On 22 April 1970, the transfer of target facilities squadron ZDS-21, from 1.LDV to 3.LDV, was celebrated at Drewitz by all three organisations. *Peter Peil*

In October 1970, Drewitz hosted airmen from other Warsaw Pact nations at Exercise 'Waffenbruederschaft 70' (Brothers in Arms). *Peter Peil*

readily admitted that due care was taken in personal behaviour, to avoid attracting any unwelcome attention from the Stasi.

On 1 September 1989, JG-7 disbanded, its MiG-21Ms and UMs and some of its pilots distributed between JG-2 at Trollenhagen (31 'M' & 3 'UM'), TAFS-47 at Preschen (13 'M' & 3 'UM') and the newly formed TAFS-87 at Drewitz (12 'M' & 2 'UM'), leaving two squadrons of MiG-23BNs of JBG-37 and TAFS-87 (Chapter Six), as the only flying units remaining at Drewitz, their final aircraft count being: 18 MiG-23BNs and 3 MiG-23UMs on JBG-37; 12 MiG-21Ms and 2 MiG-21UMs on TAFS-87. Thereafter the base was used as a collecting and holding unit for all the NVAs fast-jets, pending their ultimate disposal.

As for Jörg Behnke, he was posted to FAG-15 as a flying instructor until reunification, after which he suffered a lengthy period of uncertainty, spending this time wisely learning English, until he was offered a place in the unified Luftwaffe. He began his re-orientation training on the Alpha Jet at Jabo 49, Fürstenfeldbruck, in 1992, went on to fly the F-4F with 72 FWG at Hopsten, so proving his worth with the wing on Red Flag and Maple Flag Exercises that he was posted to a prestigious exchange appointment at the USAF Flight Safety Centre at Kirkland AFB, New Mexico. At the time of writing, he is serving in the Flight Safety Directorate in the German MOD, in the rank of Lt Col.

Jagdfliegergeschwader 8 (JG-8)

Flugplatz Neuhardenberg (re-named Marxwalde during the Cold War) began life as a small grass airfield north-west of the village of Neuhardenberg in 1934, in the then Seelow district of Frankfurt (now Brandenburg). Pre-WW2, it was used by a variety of aircraft, such as the Heinkel He-72 training biplane, the He-112 fighter, the He-176 rocket-powered experimental aircraft, and the legendary He-111 bomber, large numbers of which would be seen over London in 1940. Presaging the future, another very important visitor was the He-178, the first aircraft to be powered by a turbojet, which went to Neuhardenburg from Rostock in August 1939 for its flight trials. Dornier Do-17 and Junkers Ju-86 bombers, the venerable Ju-52/3M transport, and the Messerschmit 163 fighter came and went throughout WW2, much of the airfield returning thereafter to agricultural use.

In 1955, the site was selected as the location for a NVA transport and liaison wing to support the East German MOD and NVA HQ at nearby Strausberg, their needs having hitherto been met by Soviet aircraft and their crews. This practice continued while the new wing worked up, with the help of Soviet airmen dressed in NVA uniforms, to become the 'Regierungs-und Verbindungsflieger Geschwader der DDR' (Government Communications Wing), operating initially from the well established airfield of Schönefeld, on the southern outskirts of Berlin. In 1957, two Il-14P 'Crate' transports were transferred to the wing from 'Deutsche Lufthansa der DDR', the East German carrier (later to be re-named 'Interflug'), one for immediate VIP use and the second to serve as a trainer and for general transport. Four more Il-14Ps joined them there in 1958, one of which, an Il-14P/S, had been built under licence in the GDR. In 1959, the unit, re-named 'Regierungsfliegerstaffel' (Government Air Squadron) moved to Marxwalde, although a special VIP reception centre at Schönefeld continued in use throughout the Cold War. Up-dating its expanding fleet of transports, including helicopters, throughout the Cold War, the wing became Transport Wing 44 'Transportfliegergeschwader-44' (TG-44), its tactical and strategic elements both available for use by the combat units of the LSK.

Meanwhile, work was being carried out at Marxwalde on a 2,100 m (2,300 yd) concrete runway, later extended to 2,400 m (2,600 yd), to accommodate a wing of MiG fighters, FG-8 moving there in January 1960, with MiG-15bis, MiG-15UTI and MiG-17Fs, under the command of Hptm Ralf Brandt. The wing was re-designated JG-8 in 1961, Maj Wolfgang Büttner in command from 1961 to 1968 – a long command by RAF and NATO standards, and in mid-1962, JG-8 had the distinction of being the first LSK/LV wing to operate the MiG-21F-13.

The MiG-21F-13 'Fishbed C' was, compared with its predecessors in the LSK/LV, a very high performance aircraft (Chapter Three: LSK/LV Fighters) and by all accounts it provided a good 'stepping-stone' to later variants of the aircraft, but it soon fell short as an operational fighter compared with its contemporaries in both the Warsaw Pact and NATO. In November 1964, JG-8 received its first 13 MiG-21PFM 'Fishbed F'; they were followed by 40 more 'PFM's in 1965, then by a succession of upgraded MiG-21s: the 'SPS', 'SPS/K', 'M', 'MF', and 'bis' (LAZUR & SAU), all supported by a number of MiG-21UM/US, operational trainers. The AS-7 'Kerry', beam-riding ASM fitted to the later 'M', 'MF' and 'bis' variants, increased their ground-attack capabilities, and all the MiG-21s at Marxwalde were known to carry 400 or 800 litre external fuel tanks on the centreline pylon.

When it was decided, in 1965, that the newly established parliament of the FRG should sit in the divided city of Berlin, the MiG pilots of JG-8 were treated to an exciting departure from their normal routine and the otherwise very strict regulations governing jet flying over and around Berlin. As part of the East German protest, selected pilots from the wing were authorized to join those from the Soviet Air Force in Germany taking part in 'large scale manoeuvres', effectively a show of strength, flying low and fast in reheat over the city. In April 1965, an NVA MiG was said to have flown directly over the parliament building at 100 m (300 ft), while Soviet Su-16 fighters 'buzzed' the Allied airfields at Tegel, Gatow and Tempelhof. All this heightened tension in the area again, bringing military forces of both sides to higher states of readiness until, gradually, everything returned to normal.

On 1 March 1972, the wing was awarded the name *Hermann Matern* (after the prominent SED politician), during its re-equipment with the MiG-21M and the MiG-21MF, but in 1973 JG-8 pilots were ordered to send 12 of their 'M's to Syria, to make good Syrian losses in the Yom Kippur War, these being replaced by JG-3 (above).

Already bearing Syrian numbers, markings and roundels, the MiGs were dismantled and transported, together with 12 pilots and 40 groundcrew, in giant Soviet An-12 'Cub' transports, via Budapest to Aleppo in Syria, where they landed in the wake of an Israeli air attack which left the airfield littered with burning aircraft. There they were re-assembled and test flown by the Germans, before being handed over to the Syrians. The support party then returned to the GDR.

The last aircraft to join JG-8's inventory were the formidable MiG-21bisLAZUR, 'Fishbed L' and MiG-21bisSAU, 'Fishbed N', the most capable fighters in the family. These fourth generation MiG-21s could be identified by their wider and deeper spine and additional RSBN (ILS) aerials on the fin and under the engine air intake, they were a little heavier than their predecessors and had slightly lower service ceilings but were otherwise similar in performance.

Harald Lares, hosting the author's team at Marxwalde in 2007, arranged a tour of the airfield, a visit to the wing's museum in a HAS and a meeting with his fellow MiG pilots. Harald had also followed the standard pattern of OHS training for his time, flying the L-29 at Bautzen for the first two years and the MiG-21U and MiG-21F-13 at Rothenburg in the final two years, with additional ground training at Kamenz. After graduating, he was posted to JG-8, where he flew the MiG-21U, 'UM', 'SPS', 'M', 'MF' – and his favourite, the MiG-21bis. He too confirmed that, compared with NATO pilots, they flew very few hours, blaming the locally poor weather, saturated airspace and

shortage of fuel, with the newly arrived pilots having the lion's share at the expense of the more experienced. Each of the three squadrons on JG-8 should have had 21 pilots on strength, but the records show that this was rarely achieved during Harald's time, when the average was 16–17. Harald cited one year in which he flew only 36 hours in the fighter, a figure which in NATO would have been thought dangerously low but, as elsewhere, the author found evidence that every minute of flying on JG-8 was very well spent.

The progressive flying training carried out at Marxwalde was little different from that on other LSK/LV wings, but with a notable emphasis on low level air defence over the Baltic. Harald explained that for this purpose they evolved a tactic in which one fighter in a screen of four flew at a height of 200 m (650 ft), to remain visible to the radar at Putgarten (on the northern tip of Rügen Island), and act as a two-way radio relay between the radar site and the three remaining aircraft searching the horizon from a height of 30 m (100 ft) asl. Such radio traffic as this would have been acceptable in war, in that it triggered immediate action and gave an enemy insufficient time to react effectively. However, in peacetime, with efficient NATO listening posts in Berlin, everyone at Marxwalde was fully conscious of the need for communications security in their training, and the procedures for 'silent' operations, on the ground and in the air, were adhered to rigidly, with much use made of coded lights and hand signals. For its secondary role, JG-8 made good use of the air-to-ground ranges at Peenemünde and Jerischke, Harald recalling that the MiG-21 could lose 50 km/hr (27 knots) when firing the fighter's twin 23 mm cannon. The JG-8 pilots interviewed were a little reticent on the subject of a nuclear capability, but it again seemed that a small group of selected pilots on the wing was given the relevant delivery training.

While the usual practice within the LSK/LV was for the operational pilots of 1.JS and 2.JS to bear the brunt of the stringent readiness requirements and other key duties, allowing 3.JS to concentrate on training, this policy was far from sacrosanct. Suitably qualified pilots on 3.JS helped meet primary requirements, and during the Cuban crisis of 1962 the alert posture was increased to a level which required all the pilots to be confined to base for a lengthy period. It seems that every individual involved at Marxwalde believed that this extra burden, and the high readiness states generally, were necessary to defend their homeland, and no one living within the regulation distance from their place of work could fail to hear the call to arms which initiated the many, irregular alert exercises. A cacophony of sound from very loud klaxons, loudspeakers and other means, all tested at 0600 hours daily, was used on the base and within the nearby married quarters, sometimes using coded messages with unexpected results. So it was that on one occasion an alert message disguised as: 'Mr Kabrinsy to the phone please', resulted in several 'Mr Kabrinskys' rushing to the phone. The wing was justly proud of its ability to launch 36 aircraft in the requisite timeframe, and many of these exercises

were held in radio silence. If needed, JG-8 also had the usual alternative grass strips on base, but also a straight but very narrow stretch of road (Route 167), now tree-lined, which could have been used in an emergency. The author, driving down this 'airstrip', would have viewed its use with considerable apprehension, especially at night – but as a last resort ...?

Michael Wegerich joined 3.JS/JG-8 in 1975, direct from OHS, and adapted quickly from the MiG-21F-13 he had been flying at Rothenburg to the heavier, more powerful and mission capable MiG-21M, and it was in this aircraft that he took part in a particularly successful mass launch of the wing's aircraft one sunny morning in 1977. Everyone knew that a practice scramble was planned, and each pilot had been briefed on the aircraft he was to fly, in which HAS it was accommodated, and in what order he was to start his engine and taxi. They were at cockpit readiness, with their groundcrew standing-by, when the order came to 'scramble', and within seconds the peaceful calm of Marxwalde was shattered by the growing roar of 36 aircraft starting up and beginning to taxi. The procedures had been well rehearsed, with 1.JS and 2.JS taking off on the main concrete Runway '27' and parallel grass strips, followed by 3.JS from the opposite end on Runway '09'. In the early days all the aircraft involved had to be in their respective positions before any clearance was given to take off, but good co-ordination between the pilots and their crew chiefs, and efficient handling by the airfield controllers, paid off, and after several practices the scramble was ordered direct from the HAS areas; with the aircraft taxiing in the right sequence and at minimum spacing – if perhaps at twice the normal speed of 30 km/hr. Practice had made perfect, and on this occasion the whole wing became airborne in less than 10 minutes from cockpit readiness, and in radio silence, to be rewarded with a new target of eight minutes, which was also achieved after a little more practice. It was ever thus!

In war, once the aircraft were safely airborne, whether for operational commitment or survival, JG-8 might recover one squadron at Marxwalde, send another to the nearby airfield at Müncheberg/Eggersdorf and the third to an unspecified airstrip. Being only 12 km (7 nm) miles south of Marxwalde, and thus reached quickly by a ground support party, Müncheberg was one of the EGAF's better reserve airstrips. The original site had been extended in 1965/66, when facilities were established specifically for the fighters of JG-8 and the transport aircraft of TG-44. Take-offs and landings were restricted to one direction only (240 deg) on three parallel grass airstrips, two of 2,100 m (2,300 yd), and the third of 2,350 m (2,600 yd) with 400 m of concrete at the threshold, this sometimes being the only one available for safe use in winter. Although radio beacons and flood lights assisted recovery of aircraft, Harald Lares believed that in peacetime exercises use of the airstrip required a cloud base of 300 m (1,000 ft). A concrete parallel taxiway, north of the runways, allowed access to a large apron for the transports and three dispersals, each for four fighters, were located under the natural camouflage of the forest on the northern perimeter of the airfield.

Having completed his conversion to the MiG-21M on JG-8, Michael Wegerich had no problem landing on the grass at Müncheberg, either in the 'US' or 'UM' with an instructor, or on his solo flights, using the normal approach procedures and landing speeds. True, the airstrip and touchdown point, although marked, could be difficult to distinguish from the immediate surroundings, and the height above touchdown hard to judge. Also, the nose wheel braking had to be disengaged to prevent the nose digging into any soft ground when the brakes were applied, and the harness straps tightened in anticipation of a rough ride on the uneven grass surface, but the aircraft's rugged design and low pressure tyres were up to the challenge. The flaps were raised as soon as the aircraft was safely on the ground, to reduce lift and a tendency for the aircraft to take to the air again, and to minimise damage to them from FOD, but with the parachute deployed very little braking was required, especially on soft ground, to reduce speed to the minimum of 60 km/hr (33 knots) recommended to keep the MiG from becoming stuck in the mud. Likewise, there should have been no difficulty taking off again on the grass strips, albeit with a slightly slower acceleration before leaping into the air, although the strips suffered badly from the use of reheat in a dry season. However, in another lesson learned by so many fast-jet pilots, Michael Wegerich was reminded, on one exercise at Müncheberg, that a sortie is never over until the aircraft has shut down in its dispersal – the right dispersal.

On that day Michael had made two earlier, uneventful flights at the reserve strip, and was perhaps relaxing a little as he taxied back to the dispersal he had used twice before that day – only to find that it was already occupied. He then remembered that, this time, he was flying a different aircraft from the two previous occasions, and from a different dispersal, so now he had to back-track against all the taxiing traffic, passing some puzzled supervisors in the command post. With his professional pride very much at stake he looked for an alternative route and decided to gamble on a one metre paved strip, with a mere 10 cm clearance either side of the wings between a 'Yield' sign and the tree line. Confident in his MiG's 'cross-country' capability, and his own skill, he guided the aircraft skillfully through the gap, running one main wheel on the paved track and the other on the grass, back to the correct dispersal and his waiting crew chief (who had probably seen it all before). Whether his gamble had been seen by anyone in authority, Michael will never know – but once again a pilot had proved that old maxim 'he who dares wins'!

Michael Wegerich had been quick to become combat ready, cleared to carry out interceptions by day and night, in VMC and IMC, and he recalled another story which will again strike a chord with many of his fellow fighter pilots – one of 'misidentification'. He was flying a MiG-21M at some 2,000 m (6,500 ft) above a cloud layer, looking for a target reported to be ahead, which was said to be closing fast with rapid changes in heading, and

which he quickly spotted as a 'dark shadow' against the cloud tops some 1,500 m (5,000 ft) below, head-on but offset to the left. Being in good visual contact, he was given permission to continue the engagement and made the necessary switch selections to bring up the appropriate sight picture on his gunsight for a gun attack (he had no missiles aboard), his target seemingly unaware or quite unconcerned by his presence as he descended for a 'slicing' attack. It just so happened that he had been preparing hard for his LK.II exam, and considered aircraft recognition to be one of his strong points – so he was convinced that this was an American F-111 'Aardvark', which had strayed into GDR airspace – a real coup! It was only when the 'Aardvark' pilot selected reheat that he noticed that this aircraft had only one engine – and was certainly no F-111! Gunsight film subsequently revealed this to have been a friendly MiG-23MF/ML 'Flogger', an aircraft not hitherto encountered by the pilots of JG-8 in their airspace; indeed, some did not seem to have been aware that JG-9, their neighbouring wing at Peenemünde, had been re-equipped with this jet many months before. Perhaps this incident underlined a problem inherent in the strict policy of security and 'need to know' which may have prevailed in the Warsaw Pact, with many officers and men at the lower levels knowing only that which was necessary for them to carry out their specific duties. Was it true that only those at the higher levels of command and control, selected officers in headquarters, military academies and libraries, were privy to the 'bigger picture'? This was not the case with NATO officers, who, depending of course on their security clearances, had easy access to – and indeed were encouraged to take an active interest in their nation's military intelligence and much of that available to their allies; invariably, they also maintained close relationships with their NATO neighbours, professionally and socially – to mutual benefit.

It was clear that JG-8 was an efficient fighter wing, capable of doing all that was asked of it by the LSK/LV, and that Marxwalde had been a very good operational airfield, perhaps in part because it was the home of the government transport and communications squadron. The author's team noted its long runway with clear approaches at both ends, and perhaps the most sophisticated airfield lighting system in the EGAF, that the HAS were well dispersed, with many partially concealed by natural camouflage, and while smaller (accommodating only one MiG-21), and probably less well constructed than those in NATO, that they were quite adequate. Vents allowed the aircraft to power up to 70% before exiting, and as a contingency against a technical failure or power cut, the 40 ton steel doors were mounted on a gentle slope, which enabled the author to open them single-handed; they were closed again under power, or with the help of a suitable vehicle. Conditions within the adjacent DHS (QRA) bunker were adequate, if very basic. Incidentally, none of the pilots interviewed knew of any instances in which their pilots were scrambled in earnest against a known or unknown intruder.

During its early years, FG-8/JG-8 lost only two MiG-17Fs, but, not surprisingly being the first wing in the LSK/LV to receive the new MiG-21s, the wing had seven accidents with the 'F-13s' in 1963 and 1964, the first being a serious incident on the ground which killed four people. Thereafter, the accident rate tailed off and JG-8 had, arguably, one of the better flight safety records with the MiG-21. One pilot was killed and two others ejected safely in four accidents to 'PFMs' between 1965 and 1967; four 'SPS' and 'SPS/K' were lost between 1967 and 1970, while between 1970–1973, two 'Ms' and an 'SPS/K' were written off and one pilot was killed during an ejection. There were no major accidents in 1974 and 1975, while in 1976 and 1977 the pilots survived ejections from two 'MFs' that crashed. In the eleven years that the MiG-21bis served with JG-8, nine of the aircraft were lost with one pilot killed and two surviving ejections. Harald Lares was one of the lucky two; his aircraft suffered an uncontrollable fire at Marxwalde on 9 March 1983, and he had to eject on the final approach at 200 m (600 ft), in such poor weather that friends who were watching did not see his parachute deploy. Fortunately, he walked away with only slight injuries – but they were enough for him to lose his flying category and be transferred to the air traffic branch.

These were not the only dramas at Marxwalde in the 1980s. Despite the LSK/LV's comprehensive radar system, and all the improvements to the MiG-21's radar, a 'bis' got lost in the skies above on one dark evening in November 1986, when the pilot had complete electrical failure (no navigation aids, R/T or external local lights), in adverse weather conditions on a local

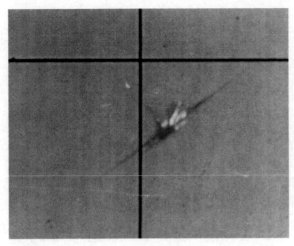

A MiG-21's sight picture of a simulated attack on a Russian bomber.   *Harald Lares*

Final Fling. JG-8's flight authorisation sheet for their final flying day: 27 September 1990.   *Author/Marxwalde Museum*

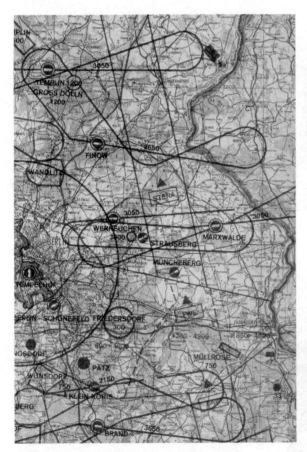

The airspace around Flugplatz Marxwalde was busy.
Author's Collection.

In WW2, Neuhardenburg airfield attracted the attention of Allied bombers, this hangar remaining heavily damaged in 1953 – to be re-built only after with the birth of the NVA.
Marxwalde History

MiG-17Fs served on JG-8 from the late 1950s.
Author's Collection

1.JS/JG-3, c.1977.   *Marxwalde History*

In 1979, JG-8 paid tribute to Colonel Sigmund Jähn, the first East German Cosmonaut, when he returned to his old fighter wing at Marxwalde.   *Author/Marxwalde Museum*

The last flying day for JG-8 at Marxwalde: 27 September 1990.   *Marxwalde History*

The airfield at Marxwalde during the Cold War – looking east.   *Marxwalde History*

flight. Although flying at an optimum height of 2,000–4,500 m (7,000–15,000ft) for the GCI, in a relatively small search area for the three other JG-8 MiGs looking for him, he could not be found, and eventually he ejected safely, landing a few miles from his base.

The last flying day for the MiG-21s at Marxwalde, 27 September 1990, began with the standard weather check, flown by the commander of JG-8, OSL Siegfried Lahmer, in MiG-21UM, No.243, after which all available aircraft and pilots were given, what would be for most, their last chance to fly the much loved MiG-21. The wing disbanded on 30 September 1990, the 'last call' conducted with proper ritual and ceremony; it was a sad day for a proud wing

Jagdgeschwader 9 (JG-9)

JG-9 began life in 1954 as part of No.2 Aeroclub at Drewitz, flying the Yak-18 and Yak-11, and was incorporated into the NVA as FG-9 on 26 December 1956, as it converted to the MiG-15UTI and MiG-15bis and thereafter the MiG-17F and MiG-17PFs, with which the wing moved to Flugplatz Peenemünde on 16 May 1961, to become JG-9 (within 3.IVD), under the command of Maj Klaus-Jürgen Baarß (Chapter Two). In 1964 twenty-seven MiG-21F-13s were delivered to JG-9, and in 1966 these were joined by MiG-21PFMs, the year in which the wing was granted the honorary name of *Heinrich Rau*. These were replaced in the latter half of the 1960s by the MiG-21SPS and 'SPS/K' , before the arrival of the MiG-21M in 1970 and the MiG-21MF in 1973, and

finally the MiG-21bisSAU/LAZUR – all supported by the progressively improved two-seat MiG-21 trainers. The first MiG-23MF 'Flogger B', all-weather air defence fighters, supported by MiG-23UB 'Flogger C', two-seat operational trainers, began to arrive at Peenemünde in 1978, to re-equip 2.JS/JG-9 , while the more advanced and operationally capable MiG-23ML 'Flogger G' joined 1.JS and 3.JS in 1982, all three variants remaining on strength until the demise of the LSK/LV in 1990. The characteristics of the MiG-23 air defence fighters are outlined in Chapter Three.

Having had his flying training in Russia (Chapter Two) and converted to the Soviet MiG-23MS there, Norbert Hess joined 3.JS/JG-9 at Peenemünde in 1983, to fly the MiG-23ML in the air defence role. Thereafter, most of his operational training was carried out over the Baltic, across likely penetration routes for NATO tactical bombers attacking targets in north-east Germany and Poland. From June 1978 until reunification, JG-9 had a total of 54 MiG-23MF and MiG-23ML single-seat fighters and MiG-23UB two-seat trainers, maintaining an average of 40 on the flight line. 1.JS and 2.JS were fully operational squadrons, each with 20 pilots, while 3.JS, predominantly a training squadron, had 24.

Norbert had found no difficulty converting to the MiG-23 in Russia, either in its general handling or operational role. He found the aircraft stable on the approach to land, albeit with a tendency to 'float' in the flare, when any backward movement on the control column was likely to cause it to 'rear up' again. The aircraft's accident rate was relatively low, attributed in part to the aircraft's robust construction, redundancy in its systems and an exhaustive trials and development programme, but it was also a measure of the pilots' carefully planned, heavily supervised and monitored sorties, and their self-discipline in keeping the aircraft within its limits. Spinning was forbidden, and while recovery actions were briefed, an inadvertent spin or any other departure from the prescribed limits could result in disciplinary action. NATO pilots might see such punitive action as deterring some pilots from taking their aircraft to the limits which could be required in combat, but the author heard several tales from EGAF pilots, 'off the record', which refuted such inhibitions. The initial and repetitive weather checks within LSK/LV's relatively small operating area meant that its pilots were rarely put to the test in conditions below their authorised limits, a safety factor which cannot be claimed by all air forces within the NATO's much larger 'playground'. The MiG-23 also had the advantage over other EGAF fast-jets, in having the SAU approach system (JG-8, above), which could take an aircraft down the glide path, on autopilot, to published weather minima. The aircraft's serviceability compared well with that of its predecessors, and the overall standard of maintenance was excellent, Norbert Hess recalling only one engine failure in the force throughout his time on the aircraft.

Operational training on JG-9 with the MiG-23s ranged from the simulated interceptions of the AWACS, through the full gamut of supersonic and subsonic targets in the middle airspace, down to the more likely threat of fast-jet intruders and cruise missiles entering GDR airspace at ultra low level, for which the aircraft's look-down/shoot-down capabilities were put to good use. Much of this training was carried out over the sea or on six pre-planned routes overland, known as the '600 Series', against other MiGs or the small and fast L-39 trainers flying at 50 m (180 ft) above the waves, with the fighters either at the same height or using their shoot-down capability from a height of 1,500 m (5,000 ft). No one interviewed could confirm the effectiveness of these procedures, and Norbert himself was quite realistic on their prospects of success against these difficult targets. He praised the MiG-23ML's RP-23D Saphir 'High Lark' radar, with its greater range (theoretically 45 km, against a 'fighter-size' target) and area of scan in azimuth and elevation than its predecessors, but Norbert believed that against such a target flying at 100 m (330 ft), its acquisition range might have been as little as 12 km (6.5 nm). Also, despite the superior speed of the 'ML', compared with that of the 600 knots (1,100 km/hr) flown by most of NATO tactical bombers of the day, the MiG would need to have been in an optimum position when sighting the target for a successful engagement. In the good radar environment over the Baltic, fighter control by ship or coastal radars should have been more effective than they were over land, but ECM and ECCM would have to be taken into account. None of the EGAF pilots questioned had been controlled by Warsaw Pact ships in the Baltic, by Soviet airborne early warning and control A-50 'Mainstay' aircraft, mobile NVA units or Soviet radar sites. Moreover, even if Soviet fighter controllers had been available, the majority of the LSK/LV pilots, having only a basic knowledge of the Russian language, would probably have had difficulty understanding anything but routine orders. Norbert recalls that, on JG-9, all his interception training had been carried out under the LSK/LV control from either the GCI radar close to Peenemünde at Pudagla, or Puttgarten, well forward on the northern coast of Rügen island (Chapter Five). Operations in conjunction with NVA and Soviet ships, shore-based SAM and AAA, were co-ordinated and de-conflicted by the GCI station assigned. Other than in the final days of the Cold War, when some LSK/LV pilots claim that they would have been given more discretion to fire on targets they had positively identified as hostile, without further authority, all interceptions were rigidly controlled, with fire orders issued from the ground. Most JG-9 pilots interviewed took the view that intruders flying very low and fast over the Baltic into the GDR from the north would have been dealt with by the Soviet Navy and Air Force, or the many and diverse AAA units ranged along the coast. The USAF, having flown at low level in the 1960s against MiGs, SAM and AAA in SEA, might suggest that the guns would have posed the greatest threat in that operating regime.

The more experienced pilots on the wing were also trained to intercept multiple targets expected in the NATO mixed force packages, which were known to be training in Europe and North America in 1980s.

NATO air forces were indeed rehearsing the co-ordination and execution of sometimes very large numbers of aircraft supporting high value offensive missions (Chapter Three), but the author believes that their employment within the scenarios expected was likely to have been very limited.

During the last decade of the Cold War, the wing maintained four MiG-23s on DHS at 10 min standby, typically armed with two R-23(T) and two R-23(R) missiles, and they were often put to the test in surprise scrambles. Despite being on the 'training' squadron, all LK.I and LK.II qualified pilots on 3.JS/JG-9 were eligible for DHS duty, and Norbert remembers being launched into the night from DHS against a Soviet Tu-16, identifying the supersonic bomber visually only as he broke off the interception at 2 km (1.1 nm). JG-9 was not going to be caught short.

Live firings of the MiG-23's short range R-60/R-60M IRH missiles took place against M-6 targets over LSZ-II. While Norbert agreed that the R-60M had a theoretical capability for head-on interceptions, given a sufficient heat source, such an attack was not viewed with any great confidence, and rear hemisphere attacks with the missile were more the norm. Some JG-9 pilots also had the opportunity to fire the R-23R SARH missile against La-17 targets at Astrachan, while air-to-air gunnery was practised against KT-04 targets, towed by L-39s over LSZ-II, but in the main, gunnery and missile deliveries were again simulated and recorded for analysis on the aircraft's integral cockpit recorders. The JG-9 training syllabus also included step-by step training in air combat, at a pace determined largely by a pilot's performance but, as with the other wings, it was hard to achieve the much vaunted goal of 'free-play', enjoyed by NATO pilots at earlier stages in their training on the front line. For example, Norbert, although he was acknowledged to be a very capable pilot, never reached that ultimate goal. As for JG-9's secondary role of ground-attack, much of the wing's 'live' bombing, rocket and gunnery training in the MiG-23 was carried out on the overland range just west of Peenemünde, or against the ship wrecks off the coast to the north of the airfield. Routinely, a helicopter would stand off as a range guard, when this was taking place, but there was no accurate scoring system.

In the latter decades of the Cold War, JG-9 forged good relations with their comrades in the Soviet, Polish and Czech air forces, with useful squadron exchanges and mutually beneficial exercises – including air combat training. Elements of the wing were known to have visited the Polish 34th Air Defence Fighter Regiment (MiG-21), at Barbie Doly, in 1975 and 1981, the 28th Regiment (MiG-23), at Slupsk, in 1982, and the Czech No.1 Fighter Regiment (MiG-23), in 1987.

JG-9 had its share of incidents and accidents. A total of 17 MiG-17F/PF were lost between 1959 and 1965, together with the lives of five pilots. The MiG-21F-13s had four accidents in 1964/65, with two fatalities, but only two MiG-21PFMs were written off in 1966–67, with no loss of life. Four MiG-21Ms were destroyed and two pilots killed

between 1970 and 1973, and the MiG-21MFs incurred the same number of losses between 1975–80. From 1978 to 1983 the wing also lost three MiG-23s, but no pilots, and from 1987 until the wing's demise, four MiG-23MLs were written off, with two fatalities. In the penultimate accident, on 4 November 1988, the pilot survived when the engine compressor in his 'ML' disintegrated during the take-off run, but he was able to abort the take-off and was rescued from the cockpit. The aircraft was repaired but never flew again, and can be seen at Peenemünde in the Technical and Historical Museum. The wing's final accident, at Peenemünde on 13 September 1990, was also the last to be recorded in the LSK/LV; it occurred at the end of a demonstration before the Defence Committee of the Bundestag, the pilot taking the 'ML' to its limits with much use of the reheat. The weather for the rehearsal on the previous day had been excellent but on the unlucky 13th the pilot, Maj Syrbe, entered cloud steeply, at about 200 m (650 ft) from the ground, and re-emerged in an 80 deg dive – from which there could be no recovery. A very sad finale indeed.

JG-9 ended its days on 30 September 1990, with a strength of 552 men and women, 10 MiG-23MF, 29 MiG23MLs and 5 MiG-23UBs – bringing to an end another proud episode in the LSK/LV's history. Five of its MiG-23s were transferred to the USAF, the remainder scrapped or sent to aviation museums.

As with so many of his comrades, Norbert Hess had been convinced that his home country was seriously threatened by NATO,

JG-9 flew ten versions of the MiG-21 between 1964 -1978.   *Jürgen Gruhl*

Maj Klaus-Jürgen Baarß commanded JG-9 when it moved to Peenemünde in 1961. He is shown here as a colonel in 1976, about to board a MiG-21PFM.

Klaus Baarß

Oltn Klaus Heinig with a MiG-17PF at Peenemünde in 1963.
Klaus Heinig

This MiG-23ML, in retirement at Laage, carries an IR-guided, AA-7 'Apex' AAM. *Mark Rourke*

Early MiG-23MFs had a marked tail-down attitude when on the ground, but modifications to the complicated undercarriage of later variants resolved this problem. This aircraft is now in retirement at the Cottbus Museum. *Author*

MiG-23MLs could be identified from the 'MFs' by the absence of a 'filet' between the leading edge of the fin and the fuselage.
Norbert Hess & Author's Collection

and he too devoted all his energies to its defence. As a result of this dedication, his good training and his diverse abilities, he had quickly mastered the MiG-23, to become a four-ship leader, flight supervisor, deputy squadron commander and ultimately commander of 3.JS/JG-9, while continuing to hone his skills in the air and on the ground for the wing's war role. Attendance at the staff college in Moscow, 1987–'89, helped ensure a bright future in the NVA, and at the age of 30, while still a captain, he was one of the youngest squadron commanders of a front line squadron in the EGAF; he became a major shortly thereafter and had been selected for further promotion when the Cold War came to an end. Overall, he and his fellow MiG-23 pilots were intensely proud of the aircraft and their abilities to accomplish the tasks they were set. Having excelled thus in the LSK/LV, Norbert was readily accepted into the unified German Air Force after reunification, and by 2009, when interviewed by the author, he had been promoted twice to become a lieutenant colonel in the Luftwaffe, serving in a prestigious appointment in the German Ministry of Defence.

Chapter Five

Command, Control, Communications and Intelligence (C3I)

'It is better to act quickly and err than to hesitate until the time for action is past'.

General Karl von Clausewitz

Many treatise on air power tend to dwell almost exclusively on the aircraft and their crews, while paying too little attention to the vital contribution of command, control, communications and intelligence (C3I), and other support functions which constitute the total team effort essential to effective air operations. Accordingly, this chapter pays tribute to all those involved in Cold War C3I, and what follows is an outline of the C3I functions from divisional level in the LSK, and from 2ATAF in NATO, down to operations on the front line. It also takes a cursory look at the systems, facilities and procedures for allocating tasks, the control of the fighter force, local ATC on the airfields and the crucial inputs to battle management made by the intelligence services – touching only briefly on the very complex, comprehensive and all-important communications networks.

Command and Control Structures

LSK/LV

The Soviet and East German air forces shared the responsibility for the air defence of the GDR from the IGB to the border with Poland in the east, and from the Baltic to the border with Czechoslovakia in the south, the Second Soviet Air Army predominating in the west of this area, the LSK/LV in the east. It follows that the Soviets would have borne the brunt of any air offensive by NATO aircraft penetrating overland from the west, while they and the East Germans could have seen action against intruders from the Baltic. All Command Post Exercises (CPX) and Field Training Exercises (FTX) involving the combined fighter, AAA and SAM units, were directed by the Warsaw Pact Air Defence Centre well behind the front line at Kiev, in the Ukraine, with all timings based on Moscow time (German time plus two hours). EGAF air defence operations were orchestrated at the LSK/LV HQ, collocated with the GDR MOD at Strausberg, and effected through its operational bunker at Fürstenwalde, known as 'Fuchsbau', where an up-to-the-minute 'Recognised Air Picture' (RAP) was maintained to show every activity within GDR airspace – and beyond. Based on this information, the HQ would then delegate tasks, or perhaps authorise autonomous operations in clearly defined areas for specific time periods, to its two air divisions: 1.LVD in the centre-south, with its war HQ at Kolkwitz (Cottbus), and 3.LVD in the north, with its bunker at Colpine (Neubrandenburg). No attempt is made here to discuss the *modus operandi* of command and control at the highest levels of command, where it must be assumed that the main exchange of information between the Soviet and NVA forces took place and joint battle plans were developed.

RAFG C3I WITHIN 2ATAF

Responsibility in NATO for the control of military airspace in the FRG was divided between 4ATAF in the south and 2ATAF in the north, its organization undergoing several structural and name changes throughout the Cold War, but this section will confine itself to snapshots of the RAF's involvement in 2ATAF. In accordance with policy directives from Allied Forces Central Europe (AFCENT), at Brunssum (Holland), and Allied Air Forces Central Europe (AAFCE), at Ramstein (Germany), the air effort in the north was orchestrated from the 2ATAF bunker at Maastricht, in the old Jesuit caves on the Dutch/Belgian border,

where the battle plans were developed. Implementation of these plans was then a matter for the two Sector Operations Centres (SOCs) at Uedem and Brockzetel, and the GCI radars, for the fighters, and the two Allied Tactical Operations Centres (ATOCs), at Kalkar and Maastricht for the fighter-bombers. All flying operations, on both sides, started with Air Traffic Control (ATC) at the airfields.

Air Traffic Control

LSK/LV

The development of air traffic control on NVA airfields began in 1952, when Russian P-8 search radars were installed and developed at the then People's Air Police airfields at Kamenz, Bautzen and Cottbus. Once the LSK/LV was fully established, control was exercised from single-storey, semi-hardened bunkers on the fighter airfields, each containing an air filtered cell for use in NBC conditions. Not all of these low profile control cells, sometimes hard to see from low flying aircraft, had a clear, all-round view of the local airspace, and thus relied heavily on radar surveillance to control air traffic within 40–50 km (22–27 nm) radius of an airfield, with cover out to 80 km (43 nm) on the extended centre lines of the main runway in both directions. Within this area, all air traffic was the responsibility of the airfield's 'Gruppe zur Leitung der Flug' (flying supervisors), commanded by a 'Flugleiter', a pilot experienced on the aircraft with which the wing was equipped and with the seniority appropriate to the flying planned. He would be assisted by a 'Gehilfe des Flugleiters', also a pilot, who in poor weather might deploy to an alternative control cell on the threshold of the active runway (as with the RAF caravan controller or USAF 'mobile' controller). The team included the 'Steuermann vom Dienst', a senior air traffic controller directly responsible to the Flugleiter for monitoring a P-18 (meter waveband) radar, to ensure aircraft separation in the local area, and for hand-over/take-over of aircraft to/from the wing's remotely located operations centre, 'Gefechtsstand' (GFS or GS). Another controller, the 'Landeleiter', was responsible for operating the 'Radio System Posadki' (RSP), a facility similar to the Ground Controlled Approach (GCA) or Precision Approach Radar (PAR) systems used in NATO. At set points from the airfield the fighters would be handed over to, or taken back from the associated GFS. As with any air force, the type of recovery to an airfield in the GDR depended on the weather, although the author gained the impression that, in the LSK/LV, regardless of the conditions, the majority of recoveries were 'straight in' approaches under radar control. However, Jörg Behnke (3.JS/JG-7) said that, given suitable weather, they had the option of a fast and low tactical recovery at Drewitz, on the NATO pattern, into a circuit height of 600 m (2,000 ft). However it was admitted that, with the MiG-21 lacking the lift augmentation devices of other fighters, the circuits were necessarily wide, and thus more vulnerable to any predatory fighters.

RAF

Similar air traffic procedures were in force at all the RAF's airfields in Germany, but with control of local traffic, on the ground and in the air, together with that of aircraft recovering to an airfield, conducted from a 'Control Tower', usually with a minimum of two stories, to give the 'local' controllers a good all-round view of the whole airfield and local airspace, albeit with a vertical structure highly visible to any unwelcome intruders. Accordingly, alternative facilities were created at Brüggen (without official funding, through local initiatives and improvisation) for all basic control functions; these were manned throughout every exercise – as they would be in war – and proved to be adequate for their purpose. In VMC, most of the resident aircraft, formations and single aircraft, would carry out tactical recoveries at high speed and low level, breaking upwards into a tight circuit, usually 1,000 ft (300 m) above ground level (agl), for stream landings, thus minimising their vulnerability in the circuit and the time taken to recover large numbers of aircraft. In peacetime training, these aircraft might then remain in the circuit to carry out several 'touch-and-goes' or low overshoots before their 'full-stop' landings – all of which called for maximum vigilance by the 'local' controllers. In addition, all RAF pilots had to complete a specified number of actual or simulated instrument approaches under radar control (the latter monitored by a second 'safety pilot' in a dual or chase aircraft) in specific periods – so pilots and controllers were well trained.

Squadron Leader Jerry Wilmot, the Senior Air Traffic Control Officer (SATCO) at RAF Brüggen from 1978–1981, explained the *modus operandi*. On this very active base, with its four big, nuclear-capable Jaguar fighter-bomber squadrons operating around the clock, the arrival and departure of many transit aircraft and practice diversions, ATC handled an average of 250 air movements a day. Jerry, with a staff of 50 fully qualified ATC controllers and assistants, was responsible for the safe and effective movements within the local airspace and on the airfield, and for ensuring that all the necessary support equipment, facilities and services, including the airfield surfaces, were kept fully operational. Strange as it might seem in today's aviation hazard and risk aversion culture, the grass on the airfield, right up to edge of the paved runway, was kept short by the resident flock of unpenned sheep, controlled by one shepherd and his dog. In addition, Jerry was appointed the Air Traffic Services Examining Officer, charged with the training and 'licensing' of all the ATC officers within his employ, and he was frequently attached for up to a week to act as the air traffic specialist on the AAFCE Taceval team (Chapter Three).

Brüggen was equipped with an Instrument Landing System (ILS) on Runway '27', its use invariably monitored by the PAR. The SLA 3C PAR permitted simultaneous talk-downs of transmitting units (single aircraft or pairs) spaced at 3 nm (5.5 km) intervals in trail, out to a distance of 8 nm (15 km). With the intensity of air traffic, it was possible for a newly arrived controller to achieve the 50 satisfactory PAR talk-downs he or she needed, under supervision, in a single day, before being allowed to 'go solo'. Brüggen shared an approach radar service with nearby Wildenrath, where for much of the Cold War a Plessey AR-1 radar was installed, providing assistance to aircraft out to 40 nm (74 km) from the two airfields. The aerodrome was also equipped with Tactical Air Navigation (TACAN) and a Non-Directional Beacon (NDB), but these aids would be switched off (weather permitting) in war and Tacevals, to deny their use by aircraft tasked with attacking the airfield. Middle and upper airspace management for the two bases was provided, respectively, by Clutch Radar (below) and Lippe Radar at Maastricht. During normal working hours the Radar Approach Room in the Control Tower would be manned by a watch supervisor, an approach controller and two talk-down controllers, while a ground controller and an aerodrome controller would man the Visual Control Room above. These six officers were supported by eight ATC assistants, one of whom would deploy to the runway caravan at the threshold of the runway in use.

As with all other elements of an operational RAFG station, ATC was always vulnerable to a 'no-notice' Taceval, and careers could stand or fall on the results. In 1978, Brüggen was the first station of its type to receive the highest accolade to be awarded by AAFCE, that of 'Four Ones'. Perhaps it was in a valiant attempt to retain its reputation that, in another Taceval shortly thereafter, 54 of the wing's single-seat Jaguars were launched in marginal weather, severely testing ATC when the conditions deteriorated further – with one controller (on exchange from the Royal Navy) having 24 Jaguars on his frequency at one time, spread over Germany, Holland and Belgium. Suffice it to say, all 54 aircraft were recovered safely, either at Brüggen or at suitable diversions, ATC living up to the words on its car stickers: 'Get 'Em Down Safely with ATC Brüggen'.

Clutch Radar

The occupational hazard of unexpected weather and very heavy traffic in the small 'Clutch' airspace between the Rhine and the Maas rivers, from Wesel in the north to the Eifel mountains in the south, led to the formation of 'Clutch Radar', an intermediate monitoring and control agency between the airfield ATC units within that zone, the area radars and, for the air defence fighters, their GCI controllers. Within the Clutch airspace lay Düsseldorf Airport, several small airfields, the NATO E3A base at Geilenkirchen and the three very busy RAF fast-jet airfields of Laarbruch, Brüggen and Wildenrath, each of which controlled its own local, departure and approach traffic. Initially an RAF unit, Clutch Radar was handed over to the Luftwaffe in 1978, OSL Joe Faber becoming its first commander. He headed twenty-five military radar specialists, working alongside their civilian counterparts at Düsseldorf Airport, using common radar equipment to handle all air traffic, military and civilian, within and in some cases beyond the primary Clutch area, plus movements in and out of RAF Gütersloh

and the tactical manoeuvring area above. Joe was well equipped for this challenging appointment; he began his training in the air traffic control branch of the GAF in 1959, had 'hands-on' experience at the GAF Terminal Radar Control Centre at Fürstenfeldbruck ('Fürsty Control'), as a controller on Fighter-Bomber Wing 34 (FBW-34), Memmingham, and in command of the ATC squadron on FBW-41, at Husum, Schleswig Holstein. His air defence experience came at the Control and Reporting Centre (CRC), Lauda, and he had responsibility for airspace management as a staff officer at HQ 4ATAF.

Within very strict guidelines, Clutch Radar was also authorized to initiate and monitor practice interceptions by 2ATAF fighters against low flying military fast-jets recovering to their bases under its control, and this worked very well on countless occasions, until an AIM-9 'Sidewinder', fired from an RAF Phantom FGR.2 sent an RAF Jaguar crashing to the ground close to a huge fuel processing site near Wesel. The Jaguar pilot, Flt Lt Steve Griggs, ejected from his stricken aircraft and landed safely nearby. It is said that the pilot of a Luftwaffe F-104, on seeing the whole incident while waiting his turn for a target, commented on the radio: 'These Brits play it for real – I'm off', and promptly returned at high speed to his base at Nörvenich. Although this incident occurred during Joe's command, he was not involved directly and Clutch Radar was in no way held to blame. Inevitably, with such a continuously high volume of air traffic under control, there were other incidents, some attributed to

NATO AWACS E3As were based at Geilenkurchen, West Germany.

Luftwaffe

Zentraler Gefechtsstand 14 (ZGS-14) 'Fuchsbau', was in overall command of the LSK/LV's two air defence divisions, and exercised its responsibilities in war and exercise from the Führungs-und-Beobachtungszentrum (FBZ) bunker at Fürstenwalde. *Rudolf Just*

'Dog Watch'. 'All hands to the pump' when RAF Brüggen was busy! *Jerry Wilmot/Dick Doleman*

Oberstleutnant Joe Faber, CO Clutch Radar (right), with Maj Klaus Fischer (centre), hosting an RAF Air Cdre (Brig.Gen) at Clutch Radar. *Joe Faber*

At the top of RAF Brüggen's ATC tower, 'Local' controllers (here in full NBC clothing) had a good all-round view of the whole airfield and surrounding airspace. Approach Control was situated immediately below.

Jerry Wilmot/Dick Doleman

Major Kleine and Unteroffizier Silke Werner in 1985; Silke was the first female Unteroffiziere to serve on JG-8's Air Traffic Control at Marxwalde.

Marxwalde Archives

Oberstleutnant Peter Peil, assisted by Oltn Opel as 'Steuermann' controlling KHG-67 helicopter flying at Cottbus, during a 'Kommandeursflugtag' (commander's flying day) on 1 September 1983. Mi-8 helicopters can be seen below air traffic control.

Peter Peil

An original (mobile) command post, used by FW-3, in the early days at Preschen. *Rudolf Just*

The entrance to the 1.LVD Operations Centre at Kolkwitz – now a museum.

Author

language difficulties. In one, the leader of a section of RAF fighter-bombers leaving Brüggen asked Clutch for clearance to depart at low level to the south (a standard procedure), but this was denied on the grounds that low flying was not permitted on that day, a German holiday. Being inquisitive, the pilot asked the nature of the holiday, putting the German controller on the spot because he could not think of the right word in English for 'Fronleichnamfest' (Corpus Christi), but he chanced his arm with: 'Happy Cadaver Day', leaving everyone on that frequency none the wiser, and the very puzzled flight leader seemingly with very little option but to accept the alternative of a high level departure.

After eight demanding years in charge of Clutch Radar, Joe Faber was posted to command the Upper Area Centre 'Lippe Radar' at the Eurocontrol Centre, Maastricht, and spent the last three of his 34 years of military service back at Kaufbeuren, as a full colonel in command of the Air Traffic Services School.

Fighter Control

LSK/LV

'Gefechtsstand' (GFS or GS), was a term used generally for operational command and control centres throughout the LSK/LV. The centre for 1.LVD at Kolkwitz, GFS-31, was manned in exercises as it would be in war by 50 officers and NCOs and some 100 other ranks, and fed directly with information from three 'Jägerleitstelle' (JLS), small radar surveillance and control sites, at Altenburg, Sprötau and Dadeburg, each

supported by a radar company or a local SAM unit. Every fighter wing was served by a GFS, effectively its wing operations centre and, with its associated JLS, capable of controlling fighters on to their targets. 1.LVD was responsible for JG-1 (initially at Cottbus and latterly Holzdorf), with its GFS at Schönewalde and a JLS at Hinzdorf; JG-3 (Preschen), with a GFS at Döbern and a JLS at Meißen; JG-7 (Drewitz), with automated fighter control at GFS Taubendorf, but no JLS, and JG-8 (Marxwalde) with a GFS at Müncheberg and a JLS at Wusterwitz. In 2008, the author's team was given a guided tour of the bunker at Kolkwitz, where many of the operational and domestic facilities remained evident. Deep underground, this hardened and filtered control centre was spread over three floors, each of 700 square meters, the executives being kept up-to-date with the overall air picture displayed on a Perspex screen, maintained by fast and efficient 'mirror-writers'. The basic equipment seemed simple and there was ample redundancy, the domestic arrangements frugal but adequate. A dormitory containing multiple bunks, spaced only a few feet apart, with barely five feet clearance from floor to ceiling, accommodated staff on duty but off watch, sleep perhaps made difficult by the noise of the air conditioning system. Eating arrangements also appeared to be very basic, and the provision of a bar which sold alcohol, such as that which existed in a similar NORTHAG/2ATAF War HQ bunker at Maastricht, would surely have been unthinkable in the NVA, but both these facilities had reserves of food and water –

Kolkwitz with enough of both to sustain life for up to 30 days if a nuclear 'lock-down' was necessary. In the event of a main and back-up power failure, luminous strips provided adequate guidance between sections of the bunker. Should Kolkwitz have been rendered unusable, the JG-3 GFS at Döbern would have taken over its responsibilities.

A similar operational facility for HQ 3.LVD (GS-33) was located underground at Colpine, east of Neubrandenburg; it was served directly by a JLS at Rövershagen and another at Saal. This smaller division presided over JG-2 (Trollenhagen), with a GFS at Pragsdorf, and JG-9 (Peenemünde), with its GFS at Pudagla, both of which had automated fighter control. Pudagla also had an additional search radar well forward on the island of Oie Greifswalder, and a JLS situated at Putgarten, the most northern point on the island of Rügen.

In addition to being in overall charge of his wing's assets, and for the safe and effective conduct of its training in peacetime, a Jagdgeschwader commander, a pilot, was responsible for his wing's operational commitments in exercises and war, as directed by higher HQs. In that role, he would be assisted by other experienced pilots, a 'Diensthabender' (fighter control shift leader), 'Steuermann' (senior controller), and a team of 'Leitoffizier' (fighter controllers).

A typical sequence of events following the identification of a hostile or unidentified track would begin with the generation of a task at HQ LSK/LV, or at a divisional HQ if authority had been given for it to act autonomously within a given area and

timeframe. The division would then hand down the task to a specific GFS, where the wing commander would decide which of his aircraft and controllers (GFS or JLS) to commit, taking into account (by reference to his 'tote') whether suitable assets were already airborne with sufficient fuel to carry out the task, or being held at readiness on the ground for such a purpose. The action would then pass to the ATC bunker on the airfield, and the GFS/JLS selected for the task.

Fighter control in the GDR evolved rapidly from the first attempts in 1954, using Soviet procedures and control equipment, with the embryo fighter wings using piston-engine Yak-11 trainers to simulate fighters, their tracks fed from P-8 radars and drawn with grease pencils on locally built horizontal, Perspex covered light tables, from which controllers calculated the necessary parameters for an interception and passed instructions to the pilots by radio. Initially, they were working with very limited information, but this improved as the P-8 radars were replaced in quick succession from 1957 by the more advanced P-10, P-12, P-25, PRW-10, PR-30 and PR-15 equipments. This evolution continued with the introduction, in 1962, of the P-36 and PRW-11 search and height-finding radars, giving better range and definition in a fast developing ECM and ECCM environment, and a radical shake-up of the whole organisation for fighter control. Local radar companies were subordinated to the fighter wings they served, and in the 1970s these became the responsibility of radar technical battalions: 'Funktechnisches Bataillone' (FuTB). For additional security, the GFS were built some distance from their airfields (typically 5–10 km), and while these were hardened, filtered and well-concealed, the radar heads of its associated FuTBs gave away their approximate positions. Further out, any associated JLS, again hardened, which also served as back-ups or alternatives to the GFS, were established with fully qualified fighter control officers, 10–13 in a GFS and 2–4 in a JLS, to meet the 24 hour DHS commitment. All EGAF airborne operations were conducted in Russian but in an emergency, and for ground communications, the Germans reverted to their native language.

In 1975, the more advanced P-37 replaced the P-36 and the whole network was enhanced further by the arrival of the Kabina K-66, a decimeter wave search radar with double radar antenna, which incorporated two PRW-13 height-finders, giving greater range, better discrimination and target acquisition at lower levels, together with increased protection against jamming. It was suggested that a single Kabina K-66 was only fully effective when supplemented by additional search and height finding equipment, making it a cumbersome system overall. Ultimately, the ST-68U (the first radar in the NVA with a 3D capability), which entered service at Putgarten and Lehesten, 20 km south of Saalfeld, in 1983, helped locate more targets at low level, and with low reflectivity. In the event that any of these units suffered incapacitating battle damage, or became unserviceable, there was more than sufficient redundancy to cover any gaps. Each radar unit was manned by a radar technical company: 'Funktechnische Kompanie' (FuTK), the whole organisation again being the responsibility of the wing commander, through his 'Stabschef' (Chief of Staff).

The NVA's fighter control procedures during the Cold War fell into two categories: traditional (manual) control, and automatic control. For simple, manual control, the controller identified the targets allocated to him within a GFS or JLS on a two-dimensional VDU, fed by radar returns to the FuTB, and added the information from a height-finder, provided on a second screen or by voice through his headset. He then gave the necessary instructions to the fighter pilot, by radio, to effect the interception and subsequently to assist the pilot in his recovery to base. In general principles, this mirrored NATO procedures. In an automated procedure, the controller took processed information from the same sources and entered it into an analog computer, which calculated the interception parameters and turned these into requirements to be transmitted by data link directly to fighters equipped with the 'LAZUR' system (Chapter Three). The aircraft's instruments then 'led' the pilot to the correct heading, airspeed and height, and added corrections where necessary, to achieve the ideal interception profile, without the need for verbal contact between controller and pilot, while doing much to mitigate the effects of ECM.

The training of fighter controllers began at OHS, Kamenz, with much of the early syllabus being common to all potential LSK/LV officers (Chapter Two). The course then became more specialized, with the students introduced to typical air situations, and simulating MiG-21 interceptions in the T-30 facility at the Soviet 'Elektron' training establishment, Sperenberg. This produced realistic scenarios and enabled a student's performance to be viewed on the spot and analysed in detail later for a debriefing. A more advanced system, the Polish IKS-80, was introduced at Kamenz in 1987, adding greater realism, and it was about this time that female students were accepted for training in the role.

Those who passed the controller's course at Kamenz still had a long way to go in their follow-up training on the front line to reach the highest qualifications in their specialisation. In the first year at 'the sharp end' they would have to react rapidly to unpredictable situations, such as ECM jamming, limited communications, manoeuvring targets in combat scenarios and the rapid hand-over of control to another agency. Having demonstrated their ability to satisfy these requirements, the students would become qualified at Level III. The demands increased as they progressed towards Level II, with the newcomers facing the more complicated automated control, random equipment defects and having to handle two fighters, first against one target and then against two targets simultaneously. In this second year, they were also tested on the control of fighters against ground and sea targets. Year three was particularly challenging, with all the previous tasks repeated in ever more difficult circumstances, working with up to three pairs of fighters committed against three targets simultaneously, sorties

involving live weapons deliveries – and with more equipment defects thrown in. Following the successful completion of all this practical work, there was a final examination at the LSK/LV HQ, Strausberg, which had to be passed before the award of Level I certificate.

With the continuous evolution of threats, aircraft, tactics and control equipment, throughout the Cold War, fighter controllers in the LSK/LV could never rest on their laurels having achieved Level I. The monthly exercises were ideal vehicles for the development of new control procedures, for example those needed to intercept cruise missiles and NATO early warning aircraft, or to integrate army mobile radars, the controllers also taking part in the evaluation of new concepts under consideration at the NVA Air Academy in Dresden. From 1981, the controllers were flown in training aircraft, on sorties which simulated fighter operations, to give them a better 'feel' for the problems faced by the fighter pilots, and the success of this policy led to the use of the wing's two-seat MiG trainers, to demonstrate typical interception sorties more realistically. A fully equipped An-2 airborne classroom was also brought into use to give the fighter controllers an insight into basic air navigation.

After passing a rigorous selection process, Rudolf ('Rudi') Just was accepted for training as a fighter controller at the OHS, which by this time was enjoying the status of an academic university, and began his career there in September 1975. The course included detachments to the fighter control simulator complex at Sperenberg four times between February 1977 and April 1978, to control a virtual MIG-21, 'flown' by instructors against typical targets, with his every action supervised and recorded for 'post-flight' analysis. In 1976 and 1978, he was also given 'hands-on' training at the GFS for JG-8 at Müncheberg and JG-3 at Döbern, and graduated from OHS in August 1978, as a second lieutenant (Ltn) in the fighter control branch, with a degree in engineering. He reported to JG-3 in September 1978 and remained there until December 1979, accommodated with the other wing officers, including pilots, at Preschen, but working in the GFS at Döbern. There, each watch was manned by a crew of four, headed by a supervisor. Newcomers had to work hard to obtain the five licenses they needed to become fully-fledged controllers, and these Rudi achieved in his first year. He was then qualified in navigational support, subsonic and supersonic interceptions (manual and automatic), silent interceptions with LAZUR, interceptions in IMC conditions and control of air combat manoeuvres, after which he became an instructor and was licensed to control helicopters. In December 1979 he was transferred to the JLS at Meißen, where he remained until reunification.

All GFS and JLS within the LSK/LV were standardized in their basic functions, manning and procedures, albeit with some variations in radar equipment, and the GFS at Döbern, served by FuTB-31, was typical, with three teams rotating every 24 hours to maintain a continuous watch at all times, a duty which could be expected every three days. Rudi outlined a typical week for him at Döbern: the 24 hour shifts began at 0700 hours, the programme thereafter depending on whether it was a flying or non-flying day for the wing. The latter would start with a formal briefing and weather forecast, analysis of the previous day's flying and preparations for the next, with the controllers given their tasks to study in detail, complete their planning and seek the necessary clearances. They were then tested on what was required of them before being cleared to exercise these responsibilities on the following day. This whole process was usually completed by 1500 hours.

A flying day would also start with a formal briefing and weather forecast, followed by a review of the tasks ahead, the facilities required (weapons ranges *et al*) and special warnings (similar to NATO's NOTAMS). The utmost priority was always given to the wing's DHS, flight safety and the launch of the wing's weather check, 1 hr 30 min before the beginning of the full flying programme, which was normally planned in two, six-hour periods. A fighter controller's schedule for these standard two-day cycles would then be repeated, with some variations subject to the tasks assigned and inter-dispersed with free days for those coming off 24-hour shifts, the routine also succumbing to pre-planned or 'no-notice' exercises. In addition to his service at Döbern, Rudi spent much of his time as one of three controllers at the JG-3 JLS, Meißen (Scharfenberg-Naustadt), with FuTK-314. Here too, from 1979 to 1984, a 24 hour watch was maintained at all times, but thereafter they were held at 30 min readiness at night, this being relaxed to 45 min from 1987. Their duties reflected those described at their parent GFS at Döbern, albeit on the lesser scale. Standard procedures were said to have existed in the NVA for the de-confliction of fighter, AAA and SAM operations in peace and war, with all parties involved required to adhere strictly to their assigned responsibilities, but the author could find no evidence of a pre-planned system to minimise fratricide, such as existed in NATO.

Fighter controllers were inevitably involved in some of the incidents and accidents which occurred in the air, and such was the case in 1984, when Rudi Just was on one of his several detachments to the JLS at Steinheide (Thüringia). Steinheide was one of many Soviet and NVA helicopter sites forming a continuous chain along the IGB, each with an associated JLS to assist in border surveillance. On this occasion Rudi was controlling three helicopters simultaneously (one Soviet and two NVA), which were looking for a low level intruder believed to have crossed the border from the west – in poor visibility. Amid some confusion, the Soviet and one of the NVA helicopters met head-on, with a mere 50 metres (55 yd) separation, at about 100 m (330 ft agl), in a very near miss which could so easily have been a disastrous mid-air collision. The investigation cleared Rudi of any blame, and the mystery intruder escaped back across the border.

On another occasion, a Mi-24 helicopter from Cottbus, carrying a border surveillance team to replace Rudi and his comrades at the end of their tour of duty, was unable to land at Steinheide because cloud covered the landing site, 900 m (3,000 ft) asl, and the pilot was ordered to divert to Meiningen, where the weather was better. The crew spent the night there and made a second attempt to reach their destination early the following morning, but for some reason they took off 30 min later than the 0700 hours departure they had planned to avoid the fast deteriorating weather. This delay proved fatal; in his attempt to reach Steinheide, the pilot collided with the cables supporting a Soviet communications aerial, one man aboard jumping to safety before the helicopter crashed, killing the remaining occupants. Again, Rudi was exonerated from any blame.

Throughout his career Rudi had been involved primarily in the close control of fighters, becoming particularly familiar with the P-37 search radar and the PRW-11, PRW-13 or PRW-17 height-finders; he controlled every type of fighter and fighter-bomber in the EGAF, and had extensive experience controlling helicopter and transport aircraft. He was promoted to Oltn in 1980 and to Hptm in 1984, worked with JG-3 during an eight week detachment to Garz/Heringsdorf, carried out regular continuation training, with up-dates on procedures and proficiency checks at Sperenberg, took courses on NATO tactics and equipments and, in 1983, participated in a Warsaw Pact exercise at Wroclaw, Breslau. Rudi had had a busy, successful career, and in an appropriate finale, he was one of the first to be licensed to control the new MiG-29 at Preschen – his service in the NVA coming to an end there on 27 September 1990.

By courtesy of the commander, Col Dederich, Rudi arranged for the author's team to visit the old Cold War GFS bunker at Schönewalde, which became operational in 1982 when JG-1 moved from Cottbus to Flugplatz Holzdorf, there to be welcomed and hosted with great consideration by Maj Michael Hanowski and some of the officers and NCOs who had served there in the NVA. They explained the use of their now obsolete Cold War equipment, the P-18 and P-37 search radars, supported by PRW-11, PRW-13 and PRW-17 height-finders, which provided good radar cover in the middle and upper airspace, well beyond the NVA's specific area of responsibility – but not down to the heights at which NATO aircraft were training. Although close control had been the norm, some controllers claimed to have had some experience with a simple system of 'broadcast control', similar to that of the RAF's 'Rat and Terrier' procedures (Chapter Three), based on random transmissions of target position relative to a fighter. They agreed that their cover at ultra low level was very poor and that fighters would have had to be airborne (i.e. on CAP) in order to have any chance of engaging high speed, low flying intruders, also that terrain masking, continuous changes in heading (snaking) and the type of ECM transmitted by the USAF's EF-111A could have confused them. At the other end of the spectrum, they had little difficulty following the paths of the ultra-high flying USAF SR-71 and U-2 reconnaissance aircraft with their P-37 and P-14 radars, and the visitors were shown a photograph of a radar scope which traced the flight paths of a USAF SR-71 over the GDR and the track of a Soviet MiG-25 'Foxbat' from Werneuchen which failed to intercept it, together with those of a NATO AWACS and USAF tanker aircraft on station within NATO airspace. None of those questioned knew of any successful interceptions at these very high altitudes, either by the NVA or the higher performance fighters of the Soviet Air Force.

Having completed the fighter controller's course at OHS in 1979, Armin Schulz was posted to the JG-1 GFS at Striesow for his 'on the job' training, and it was not long before he was 'thrown in at the deep end'. In 1981, he was on duty at Schönewalde when a Polish airline pilot, flying an An-24 aircraft belonging to the national carrier, LoT, began his escape from Poland to West Berlin. As soon as his intentions became clear, Polish MiG fighters were scrambled to intercept the aircraft, but they were unable to make visual contact in bad weather before their quarry crossed into the GDR. Meanwhile, two MiGs of JG-1, on DHS at Cottbus, had been scrambled to take over from the Poles, but the take-off of one was delayed by a technical defect, leaving Armin to control the two aircraft separately, with all three aircraft now flying in the very poor weather. Photographic evidence from the radar scopes, taken at the time, showed that every sensible effort had been made to close in on the An-24, but the MiG pilots were unable to gain the visual contact with the airliner necessary to encourage the errant pilot to land at an NVA airfield in the east, and the uninvited guest eventually reached the American base of Tempelhof, Berlin, safely. There was general agreement that Armin Schulz, apparently left alone to make several vital decisions himself, in very trying circumstances, had acted in a highly professional manner. Fortunately, there was no suggestion that the MiGs should have fired warning shots (or worse) against the airliner, and a major international incident was averted.

Armin, who contributed much to this text, progressed quickly to senior controller, became a 24-hour shift leader in 1983 and subsequently a chief controller at Schönewalde. On promotion to major in 1989, he was posted to HQ1.LVD, as a senior specialist in fighter control, and shift leader in the bunker at Kolkwitz. His Log Book records that, during his time with JG-1, he logged 3656 'live' interceptions, including 525 using automated control, many of which involved manoeuvring targets and, as a mark of his expertise, he was selected to participate in live operational weapons deliveries in Astrachan, in 1984, 1986 and 1989.

Notwithstanding the high degree of standardisation throughout the LSK/LV, the strict discipline and a seemingly rigid adherence to flying training syllabi issued by higher authority, several of the senior pilots and fighter controllers in the EGAF assured the author's team that the LSK/LV continued to develop its tactics and procedures, with every new threat and improved equipment, throughout the Cold War. Staffs were in place for this purpose at the NVA HQ, Strausberg, to examine theoretical ideas

submitted by the NVA Air Academy in Dresden, which might then be evaluated by the fighter wings. Nor were 'bottom-up' initiatives ignored, those considered to have good potential being evaluated on the spot by wing staffs, and perhaps put to the test in the air on the monthly divisional or wing exercises (Chapter Three).

Armin Schulz confirmed that, if the situation required it, control could be delegated from the LSK/LV HQ, 'Fuchsbau', via an air division down to a GFS, for specific time periods within well-defined areas, and that the control agencies on the ground were responsible for the integration and de-confliction of fighter, SAM and AAA operations within specific areas of the GDR. He recalls playing a leading part in one such exercise in 1.LVD, to trial a new variation of the combat manoeuvre 'Skorpion' – which did not go quite to plan. The targets were provided by pairs of MiGs from JG-8 at Marxwalde, flying a pre-planned route at a height of 7,300 m (24,000 ft) and speed of 1,000 km/hr (540 knots); they were authorised to complete one evasive orbit when intercepted by the defenders within a specified exercise area. The 'defenders' comprised a succession of 'six-ships' from each of the participating wings, JG-1 electing to fly one pair as a decoy, leaving two pairs to engage the 'intruders'. The decoys hoped to catch the attention of the target with a head-on attack, zooming up from a height of 1,200 m (4,000 ft), before breaking off to be ready to assist in the interception if required. Meanwhile the two pairs flew below and 6 km (3.5 nm) behind the target, ready to administer the *coup de grace*. Initially, everything went as planned, but just as the main force engaged reheat and pulled up behind their targets, the leader spotted a huge, four-engine transport on the same heading, between them. Up to that point, the exercise had been carried out with a minimum of voice communication – but no longer; in the words of one of the pilots: 'the formation simply exploded, with MiGs flying in all directions and their pilots not knowing who was who!' Armin' s meticulous and explicit exercise profile, planned so assiduously, typified the effort which went into these sorties – but success could never be guaranteed. Considering the extensive coverage provided by overlapping Soviet and NVA radars in that area, the continuous monitoring of forewarned aircraft movements, the strict procedures and very detailed preparation of these exercises, this incident, which could have led to a major accident, might seem surprising, but as every airman knows: even the best laid plans … Of course a comprehensive 'wash-up' followed, revealing a number of causal and contributory factors. The uninvited guest at the MiG's party was a Soviet Air Force Il-20 reconnaissance aircraft from Sperenberg, about which the NVA knew nothing; although under radar control, it had vanished at a critical time, in what was called the equipment's 'cone of silence', after which it changed heading and became mixed up with the fighters – which were also lost temporarily from the ground radar's cover. With an accident happily avoided the event was conveniently forgotten, perhaps because of a strange lack

of convincing evidence and the political implications; there was no retribution and harmony prevailed.

Uwe Senf was also accepted by the EGAF for training as a fighter controller, and estimates that in his three year course at the OHS some 40% of the syllabus was of a political nature, the remaining 60% being devoted to all forms of military training: leadership, organization, personnel management *et al,* practical work in the fighter control simulator at Kamenz and four weeks 'live' training at the JG-1 GFS at Striesow. In 1982 he graduated, with a degree in engineering, and was posted to Schönewalde. Thereafter, he followed a similar pattern of 'on-the-job' training to that described for Rudi Just, playing a full part in JG-1's activities within the standard two-day cycle. Like Rudi and Armin, he quickly achieved the necessary qualifications for DHS duties, to control interceptions and combat manoeuvring at all heights and in all weather – after which he became an instructor, also working with Soviet and NVA helicopters on border surveillance. Uwe was promoted to Oltn in 1984 and to Hptm in 1987.

Questioned on the NVA's C3I mobility, Uwe cited one occasion on which the JG-1's GFS moved to a new site, with all its equipment, and became operational within the 24 hours demanded by an exercise scenario – but only just. Armin Schulz also recalled similarly successful detachments by road to Garz, and another to Bautzen, adding that a GFS was expected to operate effectively at reduced capacity while some of its components were broken down, moved and brought into operation at a new

This Kabina K-66 'Back Net' decimeter wavelength search radar at JLS, Wusterwitz and GFS Pudagla, had a theoretical range at low level of 50 km (27 nm) against targets at 200 m (650 ft).

Rudolf Just

Rudi Just controlling his last flight on JG-3 from Neustadt (JLS Meißen) before reunification. *Rudolf Just*

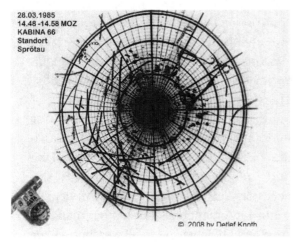

Another Kabina K-66 PPI display from Sprötau, indicating the tracks of a USAF SR-71, a supporting KC-135 tanker, an E3A, and a MiG-25 'Foxbat' which launched from Wenauchen, but failed to engage the high-performance recce aircraft.

Armin Schulz

A mobile P-18-2 'search radar, which operated on the meter waveband in conjunction with a mobile identification radar 'Parol-4'. *Rudolf Just*

Armin Schulz was given a jet familiarisation flight at Holzdorf, in a two-seat MiG-21, flown by the commander of JG-1. *Armin Schulz*

P-37 'Barlock' at Elmenshorst. *Rudolf Just*

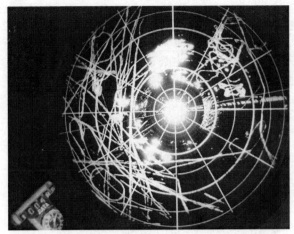

Another PPI display from the Kabina K-66 at Sprötau, showing two tracks (left, upper and lower) of a NATO E3A AWACS on patrol west of the IGB.
Armin Schulz

LSK/LV staff and trainee controllers practised realistic interceptions in the Soviet simulator complex at Sperenberg.
Armin Schulz

Armin Schulz had his controller skills tested to the full in his early days at Schönewalde, when a Polish airliner defected to the USAF base at Tempelhof, Berlin, on 22 August 1981, the tracks of the airliner, Polish and EGAF MiGs recorded here.
Armin Schulz

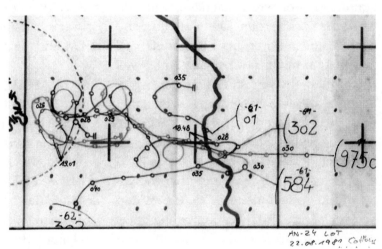

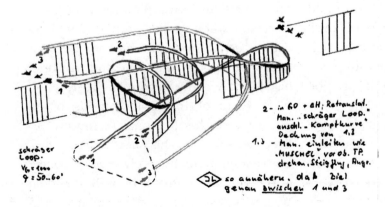

In another example of the meticulous planning and recording of flights in the LSK/LV, senior pilots on JG-1 evaluated suggested modifications to add effectiveness to a standard combat training manoeuvre 'Skorpion'. Their well laid plans were disrupted by an unplanned visit into their tactical training area by a recce version of a Soviet Il-20, resulting in an impressive, unrehearsed and very unorthodox manoeuvre. The 'wash-up' was inconclusive, and with no harm done, the matter was laid to rest.
Armin Schulz

location, before the remainder followed. In any event, the author was again assured that, should one of the control elements in the NVA's network be rendered unusable, others in the neighbourhood, all with full access to the air situation, were ready and able to take over its tasks seamlessly – and this again had been proved during periodic exercises.

With the JG-1 JLS located well west at Hinzdorf in the predominantly Soviet area of responsibility for air defence, the author's team raised again the possibility of confusion over which agency should do what, the possible duplication of effort and inadequate handovers, and that some vital information might not be sufficiently well circulated in the very short timeframes that might be available. While Uwe accepted that there was an overlap in radar cover, he stressed that flexible arrangements and well rehearsed procedures should have avoided any confusion. He confirmed that the all-important communications were provided by each wing's radio section, while good use was also made of the comprehensive network of land lines, incorporating strategically positioned outlets, linking all the prepared deployment sites. This should have allowed the full air picture, fed from all sources including, perhaps, information from the Soviet A-50 'Mainstay' Airborne Early Warning (AEW) aircraft, to be displayed throughout and beyond the NVA's area of responsibility, for all elements of the air defence force to see at a glance and react without delay, but uncertainty remained over the ability of the system to detect very low flying aircraft.

The author, having spoken to many LSK/LV officers, pilots and controllers, and visited their facilities, above and below ground in the GDR, could not fail to be impressed by the professional pride and enthusiasm of the officers within the LSK/LV C3I organisation. However, while simplicity, mobility and redundancy had their attractions, as did the repetitive training which brought pilots and controllers together in aircraft cockpits and in their domestic co-location, he was left with a feeling that the profusion of bi-lateral control agencies, and the rapidity of events inevitable in the 'fog of war', had the potential for confusion, delays and misunderstandings.

RAF in 2ATAF
From 1945 until the mid-1950s, the RAF manned, maintained and operated all the C3I facilities in north-west Germany, beginning the Cold War with Tp.14 and Tp.15 search radar (with IFF), and Tp.13 'nodding horror' height-finders, this proving to be a satisfactory combination at the time.

Flying Officer Ken Senar had flown Vampires in the ground-attack role, and was a fully operational F-86E 'Sabre' fighter pilot on No.93 Squadron at RAF Jever, in north Germany, when he was grounded in 1955 with a reduced medical category. He then became a fighter controller, and this brief glance at RAF fighter control in 2TAF, in the early years of the Cold War, is based primarily on his personal testimony. To prepare him for his new career Ken underwent an intensive eight week course at the Fighter Control School, RAF Middle Wallop, a WW2 Battle of Britain station in southern England, and on graduation in December 1955 he was posted to No.537 Signals Unit (SU), RAF Borgentreich.

RAF Borgentreich, an hour's tank drive from the IGB, had a domestic site near the village and the operational facilities some two miles away, across difficult tracks. The equipment consisted of a single Tp.15 and two Tp.14 radars, for high and low level work, and three Tp.13s – all fully mobile. No.537 SU was also responsible for two small radar out-stations, located closer to the IGB, one at Waggum (Brunswick) the other further north; their primary role was to monitor air movements within and close to the three air corridors from the West to Berlin. RAF Borgentreich had a nominal strength of 24 officers and 180 men, responsible, with their supporting technical teams, for fulfilling the two distinct functions of reporting unidentified aircraft movements and the control of fighters, as required, 24 hours a day, 365 day a year.

Ken Senar was soon put to work, albeit under close supervision. On 22 December, he carried out his first practice interception (PI), with two RAF Meteor NF.11 night fighters operating at 25,000 ft (7,600 m), each taking its turn to be target and fighter. The gun-armed NF.11, while inferior in performance to that of the fighters then coming on line, was equipped with an equally obsolescent but effective Airborne Interception (AI) radar, operated by a specialist navigator seated in tandem behind the pilot. Other NATO air forces in Europe were equipped with the single-seat F-86D or F-86K night fighters, with pilot operated AI radars. For aircraft with fully

serviceable AI equipment, the controller might merely bring the target into the fighter's radar scan, but for those not so equipped (Sabres, Hunters, Venoms and Vampires), control would continue until the pilot had visual contact. In six months, Ken had achieved the 100 successful interceptions necessary for him to become a fully-fledged controller, qualified to work, day and night, without supervision.

Most of the control work at 537 SU consisted of routine PIs with the local fighter wings, at heights of about 30,000 ft (9,100 m) for the older fighters and 40,000 ft (12,200 m) for the new Sabres and Hunters, using parallel/head-on and quarter attacks, but Ken recalls some interesting diversions. On 29 June 1956, he was involved with an RAF Comet returning the Secretary of State for Defence and a party of senior RAF officers from the Moscow Air Show to the UK. Two Russian MiG-15 fighters had escorted the aircraft to the IGB at 41,000 ft, where a pair of Hunters was to accompany it the rest of the way through German airspace. The Hunters had taken off late, but Ken derived great satisfaction from bringing them to the rendezvous and in visual contact with the Comet on time, using a parallel/head-on interception. In the following week he carried out four PIs, with two pairs of Meteors, and in conditions of moderate jamming he resorted to 'broadcast control' (Chapter Three). For this he used whatever sporadic traces he had, with the Craig Computer Plotter and 'dead reckoning', to give a running commentary on his best estimates of the target's position, track and altitude. As a result, two of the four Meteors were able to complete successful interceptions against four Lincoln bombers operating their ECM equipment. They were taking part in Exercise 'Guest', held monthly for ECM training in Germany to make controllers aware of the difficulties radar and radio jamming could give them, and to encourage them to practise any intercept procedures that might remain available (eg. broadcast control).

Ken had become fully qualified just when East and West seemed to be heading towards WW3, with an increase in military tension on both sides of the IGB and more activity in the air very evident on the radar scopes. Being only a 'stone's throw' from the GDR, Borgentreich also became a hive of activity on the ground, with Ken made responsible for the unit's ground defences, evacuation and demolition plans, in addition to his primary role of fighter controller and secondary duty as officer-in-charge of the Station Cinema. All this was a very tall order for a young flying officer not trained in such additional skills, but Ken gave his all, acquiring weapons, ammunition and explosives, and the necessary secure storage, while drawing up the vital contingency plans, and he was soon *en route* back to the UK for an Atomic, Biological and Chemical (ABC) Warfare Course at Winterborne Gunner. This fighter controller was a very busy man.

While Ken was away in the UK, the RAF ACB and German construction companies were putting the finishing touches to four big new radar stations in the British zone of West Germany, at Brockzetel (Aurich),

Udem (Goch), Borgentreich/Arnhausen (Warburg) and Breckendorf (Schleswig Holstein), manned initially by the RAF and available for use by all NATO air defence fighters. These four units became operational in 1957, equipped with the new Tp.80 search radars, and an array of four to six Tp.13 height-finders. The Tp.80 operated on the S-band, centimetric (3 Ghz), at 235 – 300 pps, with a peak power of 2.5 Mw, and had a published maximum range of 220 nm (400 km), so it could 'see' well into the GDR and out over the Baltic to the north, providing clear returns, in all directions, up to 50,000 ft (15,200 m), and it was able to discriminate between two targets flying one mile apart at 150 nm. Thus it was now easier for the controllers to identify individual aircraft within a tactical formation, and because the aerials were mounted as high as possible, and on pedestals, the hitherto permanent echoes and reflections from high ground were also much reduced, improving low level coverage. Indeed, in some conditions of anomalous propagation 'Anoprop', caused by a temperature inversion in the lower atmosphere which effectively split the radar beam, with one part 'hugging' the earth, extraordinary ranges could be achieved at low level. However, this phenomena, often prevalent in the early morning, was usually short lived (perhaps no more than an hour) and could not be relied on operationally. Otherwise, the new radar remained subject to the earth's curvature which, as with all radars at that time, limiting its low level range. Heavy cloud and precipitation were generally visible on the centimetric radars, but this could now be reduced with the latest ECCM equipment, perhaps enough for the controllers to see aircraft through the clutter, and more effective IFF equipment helped differentiate between friend and foe. While the new radar offered many improvements in performance over its predecessors, the huge Tp.80 array (75 ft (23 m) long and 25 ft (7 m) high, on a fixed installation, was a very prominent and lucrative 'soft' target for hostile fighter-bombers.

On his return from the ABC Course, Ken Senar found that No.537 SU no longer existed, having become No.210 SU, with a single Tp.80 and four Tp.13s occupying a new site at Auenhausen, a few miles northwest of Borgentreich. The site was already operational, with many improvements in the overall organisation, back-up power and communications network. Heavy steel doors helped protect the bunker, while airlocks and a sophisticated air conditioning/filtration plant re-circulated the air trapped therein, to enable operations to continue in NBC conditions. Four cabins doubled the control capacity which had been available to 537 SU, and space was provided for a realistic controller training simulator.

Ken carried out his first interception on the Tp. 80 on 17 January 1957, when he was allocated two pairs of Hunters looking for 'trade' – to wit any military aircraft within the controller's purview which might act as a target. This was a very popular alternative, for both controllers and aircrew, to splitting a pair of the same type of aircraft for 'canned' PIs, because it had an element of the unknown, the reactions of a target being difficult to anticipate – and always with the possibility of a little simulated combat. For this, the two ATAFs published general regulations, to which each nation added its own rules. Interception of civilian airliners was, of course, prohibited, as was unbriefed combat, but a sighting pass on military aircraft and a single evasive turn by the target became a generally accepted practice, and some squadrons tended to interpret the rules very liberally, in order to take advantage of this potentially very useful opportunity training. Indeed, it was not uncommon, in the 1950s, for one squadron to telephone another (or several others) to arrange a rendezvous at, say: '40,000 ft over Dummer See at 1100 hrs', and as a result the author often found himself on a very steep learning curve in highly disorganised, multiple aircraft, mixed-force combat. At such times, a controller's task was temporarily suspended when battle was joined, until the 'fight' was over and the combatants needed help to get 'home'. While there may have been some risk involved in this practice, with some pilots running short of fuel in their enthusiasm and having to divert to an airfield other than their own, the author does not recall any accidents attributed to this *ad hoc* combat during his time, and is sure that it did much to help pilots get to know their aircraft's strengths and limitations – and their own.

In February 1957, Ken completed 50 PIs with the Tp.80, and was soon able to control two pairs of fighters on separate PIs simultaneously, while in June, in Exercise 'Skittle', he had five aircraft under control at the same time and carried out a successful interception on a USAF RB-45 by a Swift FR5, forced up from its usual habitat at low level by weather (perhaps with the author aboard?). The tempo continued to be high throughout 1957, the NATO fighter pilots eager to have the assistance of the increasingly competent controllers at the four new radar sites.

From 16–23 September 1957, Ken was detached to No.348 SU at Udem, to observe and assist in the NATO Exercise 'Counterpunch'. In a truly international gathering, he was accommodated with French, British, Dutch and Belgium officers, 14 to a room in a barrack block, all of whom mixed well and spoke English – except the French, who preferred their own company and language. At work, they were joined by Women's Royal Air Force (WRAF) controllers, Ken acting as mentor to those under instruction. He recalls one who checked in with an RAF pilot using her callsign: 'Bedmate', which elicited an immediate response of: 'Loud and clear, strength five darling – I hope I don't suffer a bent weapon!'

Back at Auenhausen, the routine was sometimes broken by unusual incidents, such as that which Ken experienced on one morning in September 1957. It was while he was walking towards the Airmen's Mess to carry out his duties as Orderly Officer, that he heard the noise of jet engines approaching from the south, a most unexpected sound on a weekend when NATO aircraft would not normally be flying – but it was not a NATO aircraft. As it flew directly overhead, below a cloud base at about 1,000 ft (330 m), Ken could see clearly the red stars of a twin-engine, Russian Il-28 'Beagle'. He raced to the nearest telephone to call the radar site and raise the alarm, but by the time everyone had collected their wits, the Beagle was out of sight to the north. It was assumed later that the aircraft was a reconnaissance version of the Il-28, on a photo mission to cover the Rothwesten and Auenhausen GCI sites, the newly formed No.757 SU (Gee navigation) unit at Borgentreich and the listening post at RAF Sharfoldendorf – or that it was merely checking NATO's reaction. It is not known whether there were any repercussions from this blatant border violation.

Of greater concern was the sight of what appeared to be massive jamming in north-east Germany, seen by several GCI sites early one summer's morning in 1957, just as dawn was breaking. Interest within 2ATAF increased as the mass of returns intensified and drifted south over the GDR, until the controllers realised that they were watching nothing more than the sunrise! On another occasion, sharp eyes noted mysterious 'paints' heading over the Baltic into Denmark, at unknown heights and very high speeds (estimated at 'thousands of knots'), before vanishing. In this case it was concluded that the traces came from meteorites passing through the earth's atmosphere. There was more reason to be concerned, on one October night in 1957, when the radars at Auenhausen saw multiple clusters of aircraft launching from their respective bases in the GDR. Ken was the 'nightwatchman' that night, and was quickly in the forefront of the 2ATAF reaction; he immediately called everyone on his shift to his post and opened up further lines to HQ No.83 Group to warn them of an increasing number of plots, estimated at 100 plus – now being reported also by other GCI units. The tension increased when all the plots suddenly turned simultaneously on to a westerly heading, bringing a very senior officer on the line from higher headquarters. Notwithstanding the paucity of resources immediately to hand, Ken was ordered to man a single control cell with what he had and call up reinforcements from the domestic site at Borgentreich. This he did, and shortly thereafter he had two pairs of night fighters positioned on a north/south patrol line, safely west of the IGB. The USAF at Rothwesten were clearly unhappy with what they considered to be a rather tardy and low key reaction by the RAF, and set about adding to the defence of this particularly vulnerable region between the British and American zones of West Germany – but they would have been a little late. The 'raid' was rapidly approaching the IGB, dropping 'window' to add to the drama until, with 20 nm (37 km) to go to the border, all the aircraft turned through 180 degrees and returned to their bases. Nineteen fifty seven was indeed a year of high drama for politicians and the military.

In October 1957 Ken carried out his first interception with the RAF's new arrival in Germany, the two-seat, delta-wing Javelin N/AW fighter (Chapter Three), and on 12 December 1957, he completed the final PIs of his career, controlling two Canadian CF-100s in parallel/head-on interceptions.

Looking back, he is sure that at no time in his service with Nos.537 SU or 210 SU did either unit have any break in their surveillance duties, with alternative means or improvisation always serving to redress a problem. Ken had learned fast and done well, both as a fighter controller and as an all-round RAF officer, and on 18 December he was rewarded with promotion to flight lieutenant.

While Borgentreich/Auenhausen was in the south-east corner of 2ATAF's area of responsibility in Germany, No.101 SU at Brockzetel was in the north-west, close to the border with Holland and the North Sea, near the town of Aurich. Its development was very similar to the other three Tp.80/Tp.13 sites, built by the RAF's ACB in the same timeframe and coming on line in 1956/57. With the GAF growing rapidly thereafter, Luftwaffe GCI controllers were soon under training at Brockzetel, and the site was handed over to the Germans in December 1960. The British radars were eventually replaced by a succession of new equipments, and as the air defence environment within NATO's Central Region devolved into geographical sectors, Brockzetel became Sector Operations Centre 1 (SOC 1). For the remainder of the Cold War, SOC 1 was commanded by an RAF air commodore (Air Cdre) and manned by multinational teams, but with five RAF wing commanders continuing to exercise their tri-partite responsibilities for specific aspects of airspace control over the FRG (see below), one RAF controller being on duty at all times – and Wg Cdr Barrie Palmer was one.

Barrie was posted to SOC 1 as a sector

controller in 1978, and with his previous experience serving him well, he was soon 'operational'. His duties included the production of the RAP, authenticating messages which changed the alert states and initiating the necessary measures therein, while monitoring, making and reporting changes to force levels. He found the performance of the Tp.80 and FPS.6 height-finders to be 'very good', except in heavy cloud conditions, when an L-band Tp.84 radar, albeit less precise, was his preferred choice, while that of the Hughes Air Defence Radar (HADR), which replaced the Tp.80, was 'very good all-round'. On the low level threat, Barrie looked forward to developments in the look-down/shoot-down capabilities of the Allied fighter force, and their further integration with AWACS, and felt that point defence against low level intruders was best served by SAM/SHORAD forces.

Regarding the tripartite agreement, allocating responsibility for the integrity of West German airspace to the RAF, USAF and FAF, it was the duty RAF wing commander's responsibility at SOC 1 to scramble the QRA to intercept, interrogate and take any further action deemed appropriate, in any violation of FRG airspace. For these duties, it was essential that Barrie and his colleagues were familiar with the Rules of Engagement, and could lay their hands on the necessary Standing Operating Procedures (SOP), together with the numerous other publications well prepared for every likely contingency. Likewise, they had to remain aware of activities in neighbouring air defence sectors, have a working

knowledge of the Ballistic Missile Early Warning System (BMEWS), force survival and dispersal plans, local defence plans and NBC procedures, fighter CAP and AAR plans, utilisation of AEW and AWACS, and AAFCE-wide airspace control plans for de-conflicting aircraft, SAM, AAA and SHORAD operations. Barrie found this a very demanding but satisfying role.

Air Commodore (Brig Gen) John Nevill, a very experienced fighter/ground-attack pilot, became Sector Commander at Brockzetel in June 1985. He had Operational Control (OPCON) of some 27,000 personnel (German, Dutch, American and British), within JG-71 'Richthofen', (GAF F-4s), Wittmund, No. 32 Squadron (USAF F-15s), Soesterberg (NL), two RNLAF F-16 squadrons at Leeuwarden (NL), numerous Nike and Hawk SAM units, and many facilities, including the USAF 606th Tactical Air Control System (TACS) and the GAF Low Altitude Radar System (LARS). Additional USAF fighter squadrons were earmarked to reinforce the Central Region in war, and SOC 1 would have received some of these units.

The 606th TACS, introduced into north Germany in the 1970s, was based at Basdahl, some 30 km from Bremenhaven. In war, this fully mobile self-supporting GCI facility, with its TPS-34 radar, could have operated from a number of carefully selected, covert sites in north Germany (never activated in exercises). The multi-functional LARS was said to have been able to detect large scale troop movements on the ground, as well as aircraft (including helicopters), flying at very low level in the border region. As such, it could have provided the first indications of an attack, impending infringement of NATO territory or airspace. In addition to radar data supplied by its own CRC at Brockzetel, the TACS and LARS units, SOC 1 received radar inputs from the CRCs at Visselhövede and Nieuw Milligen, the NATO E3A AWACS, and German naval ships at sea, data linked or passed by voice. Nieuw Milligen remained ready to take over the duties of SOC 1, should that become necessary, with the 606th TACS providing a further alternative, and handover/takeover procedures were practised regularly between these units in the later years of the Cold War.

As with all units within NATO, SOC 1's operational effectiveness underwent regular evaluations, in simulated war conditions, by teams of highly critical specialist evaluators, and did particularly well during John Nevill's time in a most demanding System Evaluation ('Syseval') of the whole integrated air defence system within its area of responsibility. The results showed how personnel from four nations, operating as one team in combining the various elements of aircraft, missiles, radar and C&R facilities, could achieve highly commendable results.

Airspace Management

A problem which occupied many minds, not least those of the strike/attack pilots who would be transiting across the IGB between East and West Germany, was that of de-confliction between the several air defence systems (fighters, AAA and SAM), to minimise fratricide, or 'blue-on-blue' losses.

In the NVA, this was largely the responsibility of the command and control agencies on the ground, but the author could find no standing procedures for this purpose, whereas NATO went to great lengths to safeguard their aircraft transiting through the 'Hawk' and 'Nike' SAM belts, and the Gun Defended Areas (GDAs) which protected important targets such as airfields. The effectiveness of these procedures, which were up-dated regularly, depended on strict discipline among all those involved, in observing the prescribed heights, routes, speeds and IFF settings for specific time blocks. NATO's Integrated Air Defence System (IADS) in West Germany was tried, tested and developed, throughout the Cold War, with the need to de-conflict fighter, SAM and AAA defences and minimise fratricide given great emphasis. Any Warsaw Pact aircraft attempting to cross the IGB and enter the FRG overland from the east, would have to pass first through the Low Missile Engagement Zone (LOMEZ), comprising MIM-23 Hawks, then the High Level Missile Engagement Zone (HIMEZ) of nuclear-capable MIM-14 Nike-Hercules SAM, and the low level Fighter Engagement Zone (FEZ). In 2ATAF, these assets were drawn from the West German, Dutch, Belgian and British member nations, who also manned their own point defences, especially around airfields, comprising short range SAM (e.g. Rapier) and GDAs (e.g. Bofors LAA). Special arrangements were made for allied aircraft to pass through these zones, in relative safety, based on IFF settings (changed at set intervals), safe speeds, height bands and lanes – but it would be naïve to believe that safety was guaranteed.

Intelligence

At the core of all Cold War political and military considerations, from the highest to the lowest levels, was the intelligence picture, and both sides invested great and diverse efforts into this imperative. The intelligence came in several forms and from many sources, but an inability to access reliable information on the Warsaw Pact intelligence organisations, coupled with some enduring NATO and national security caveats, has precluded more than a few general comments here.

High on the list of sources were airborne and satellite surveillance systems, typically with flights over Russia by US high-flying U-2 aircraft, and intelligence gathering over international waters by long range Soviet aircraft, such as the Tu-95 'Bear' and thinly disguised shipping, often hitting the headlines. Less visible and highly covert initiatives included 'radint' (radar surveillance), 'sigint' (communications), 'elint' (electronic), and 'humint' (human). These made use of increasingly sophisticated 'listening and looking' devices, attempting to intercept and analyse all forms of ground-to-ground, air-to-air and air-to-ground dialogue.

Berlin, being in the centre of East Germany, was a mecca for intelligence gathering by all four nations in residence there (Russian, American, British and French). Being very visible in Berlin's Grünewald, there was no disguising the

purpose of the Allies' military agencies working on the high ground of the Teufelsberg, listening intently to any radio communications on Soviet and NVA activities in the surrounding areas. All the EGAF pilots interviewed were conscious of being overheard by UK, US and French signals interception units in West Berlin, including No.26 SU, a specialist RAF signals intelligence unit with its receivers on 'the hill', and 'silent' procedures were high on their list of NVA disciplines. It can also be assumed that air traffic control radars at the three Allied airfields of Tempelhof (US), Tegel (French) and Gatow (British) would, *inter alia*, be able to observe Soviet and NVA military air movements well outside the Berlin Zone.

There were, of course, many agents embedded on both sides of the Iron Curtain, as well as disillusioned defectors who added to humint, a young East German pilot, Thomas Krüger, being one. While undergoing his pre-NVA GST, Krüger flew his Zlin Z-42M light aircraft from Schönhagen, Trebbin, to RAF Gatow, on 15 July 1987, where he requested political asylum. He was handed over to the civilian authorities and eventually granted West German citizenship, but his aircraft was returned to the East Germans, bearing these messages from the RAF: 'Come back soon', and 'Wish you were here', while on the flying control there was the added warning: 'Remove before the next escape'.

In addition to those aircraft whose primary role was that of airborne early warning/command and control, the USAF AWACS, Russian IL-76/A-50 'Mainstay' and the NVA's Mi-8 battlefield command helicopters, additional aircraft of various types were used by both sides in C3I roles. EGAF An-26 transports, specially adapted for sigint, may not have had the sophistication and capacity of the Il-22 'Coot B' of the Soviet Air Force, a dedicated sigint platform, but by all accounts it served its purpose well in contributing to the 'big picture'. Also, Su-22 pilots from Laage told the author that they made regular sorties at high level down the IGB, recording the electronic signatures from a wide variety of emitting sources in West Germany.

A strong and recurring theme throughout the author's research, has been the impact that the Stasi, the East German State Security Service, had on all aspects of civilian and military life in the GDR. Their effects on the civilian community have little place in this text, but their intrusion into military activities, already covered, bears some reiteration here. Regardless of their roles, every NVA unit operated under the watchful eyes of the Stasi officers serving with them; some held military ranks (usually captains at squadron level, majors on the wings) and wore military uniforms, but they remained responsible to their parent 'Department 2000'. Up to the early 1980s, these were full time appointments within a separate career structure, and involved formal political training in Russia, Dresden or Berlin, but later in the Cold War some of these officers also became fully operational pilots, committed to regular flying duties. Opinions among the officers questioned on the influence the Stasi had had on their lives varied widely, with some

seemingly wholly unconcerned by their presence, visible or covert, while others took them very seriously, but in both cases it could be concluded that the apparently good discipline and social behaviour within the NVA community, at work and play, might at least in part have been attributed to a Stasi presence. Again, political indoctrination, and what might be deemed propaganda, were high on military agendas, with two days a month devoted largely to that end, run by a political officer.

Perhaps paradoxically, one of the best sources of real time intelligence on East and West Germany military, political, security, industrial and social activities was born of the 'London Agreement', signed in November 1944 by America, Russia and Britain, which established the post-WW2 'Control Machinery in Germany' (France joined in March 1945) – and this bears a closer look. Article 2 of the agreement stated that 'Each Commander-in-Chief in his Zone of Occupation will have attached to him army, navy and air force representatives of the other commander-in-chiefs 'for liaison duties'. This arrangement was formalised in detail for the British and Soviet Missions in the Robertson/Malinin Agreement of 1946, the British team becoming 'The British Commander-in-Chief's Mission to the Soviet Forces of Occupation in Germany' (BRIXMIS) and the Soviet Mission 'SOXMIS'. The French established their liaison mission under the Noiret/Malinin Agreement in 1947, to be closely followed by the US with the Huebner/Malinin Agreement.

It is important to note that when these

agreements were set up, and for much of the Cold War, the Allies did not recognise the East German State, the NVA, Stasi or East German police (VOPO), answering only to the Soviet authorities. With the country divided into four Allied Zones of Occupation, each under its own military government, the status of the military liaison missions was a matter only for the respective Commanders-in-Chief. In the British case, BRIXMIS was based in Potsdam, in the Soviet Occupied Zone, but had its HQ in the old Olympic Stadium in the British zone of Berlin, while SOXMIS, accredited to the British Commander-in-Chief in the British Occupied Zone of Germany, made its home in the town of Bünde. The strength and composition of BRIXMIS varied throughout its life, with a mix of mobile 'tour' officers and other ranks, ideally German or Russian linguists, backed by a support team of technicians and craftsmen back in Berlin. In general, the BRIXMIS strength was drawn from the Army and the RAF in an approximate 66%/33% proportion, although always under the command of a British Army brigadier. In 1946, BRIXMIS was issued with 31 'tour' passes which allowed restricted travel throughout East Germany. Invariably, these 'tours' were carried out in parties of three, comprising one officer (equipped with a large selection of cameras and lenses from 85–1,000 mm), a SNCO or WO specialising in the recognition of Soviet equipment, and a corporal driver, drawn from either the Army or RAF. The Americans and French had similar, but much smaller missions (18 and 14 Soviet passes respectively).

As the Cold War escalated, the stated purpose of 'liaison' gave way rapidly to that of intelligence collection, with the tacit acceptance of all the parties, who understood the inherent value to them of their missions. In the first place, the constant surveillance and liaison they provided should have given vital early warning of any sinister or bellicose developments within the 'enemy camp', and hopefully prevent hostilities breaking out by accident or misunderstanding. Also, while both sides had good reason to hide some of their assets and intentions, it might be argued that revealing selected military strengths and political determination could be vital in deterring aggression. In any event, the missions always had much to tell their masters on their potential enemy's strengths and perhaps weaknesses, with real time or near real time intelligence.

While the GDR was recognised formally in 1972, the Allies maintained the supremacy of the Robertson/Malinin, Noiret/Malinin and Huebner/Malinin Agreements, and this continued to dictate attitudes on the ground, with BRIXMIS still refusing to acknowledge the GDR or answer to the NVA, VOPO or Stasi. This caused immense bad feeling among the East Germans, who were legally obliged to report any sightings of mission activity, and there were frequent incidents when contact was made. In a generally more aggressive attitude, mission vehicles were subjected to persistent tracking and interference by the Stasi, often amounting to ramming by the police and NVA. There is evidence that the GDR made approaches to the Soviets, seeking changes to the bi-lateral agreements to force the missions to recognise the authority of the GDR, but the Soviets declined, implying that they were content with the agreements and probably realising that one change would lead to another. In 1973, the UK then added to the tensions by establishing diplomatic relations with the GDR as a state and opening an embassy in East Berlin. The Foreign Office was now in a quandary, since this was at odds with the Robinson/Malinin Agreement, and threatened the very profitable intelligence role of BRIXMIS. In the end, the agreement remained in force, with the mission left to act as though East Germany was still the Soviet Occupied Zone, but, contrary to normal embassy practice, no military attachés were appointed to the embassy in East Berlin – a solution which did nothing to improve the mission's relationships with the East German state organs. So it was business as usual for the missions, the original agreements remaining unchanged until the end of the Zones of Occupation with the reunification of Germany.

Probably the best known BRIXMIS coup was the securing of valuable information on the new 'Skip Skin' radar and jet engines from a high performance Soviet Yak-28 'Firebar' fighter which crashed in Berlin's Lake Havel, in April 1966, after suffering engine problems. The Russians had denied the crew's request to save themselves and their aircraft by landing at nearby RAF Gatow and, as a result, they died in the crash. Being in their zone of Berlin, the British were able to resist Soviet involvement, allowing BRIXMIS to organise the salvage and inspection of the aircraft before handing over the wreckage to the Russians.

In a seemingly endless list of other useful 'finds' throughout East Germany, BRIXMIS tended, as ordered or on their own initiatives, to concentrate more on the greater threat to NATO from Soviet rather than NVA military forces. This is not to say that they neglected the NVA, which indeed sometimes had priority, and good information could often be obtained on tours which took them to the east of the GDR, where most of the NVA airfields, GCI sites and tactical ranges were established. For example, they were required to take soil samples from the latest EGAF airfields at Holzdorf and Laage, for assessment of airstrip vulnerabilities, in addition to observing ground/air exercises and weapons delivery profiles, and photographing new missiles, aircraft, military vehicles and radars, while monitoring troop and equipment movements. The missions were able to provide valuable information on such details as the size and shape of engine intakes and efflux, and all types of external load carried below aircraft operating at airfields and weapons ranges. Mission activity was not confined to the collection of technical intelligence; a vital task was to observe and report on weapons' profiles and procedures used at air-to-ground ranges, together with comments on the aggressiveness, or otherwise, of the aircrew operating both fixed-wing and rotary-wing aircraft. There was evidence that the NVA aircrew practised their tactics with more determination than some of their Warsaw Pact partners, their helicopters being seen to fly very low and aggressively – sometimes targeting BRIXMIS tour parties.

For more than forty years, BRIXMIS was on the front line, the only British military unit operating legally in East Germany, often well beyond its official mandate and under the eagle eyes of the Soviet Secret Police (KGB) and Stasi. In addition to the mission's ground based teams, RAF pilots on the staff in Berlin who were given authority to remain in flying practice on two, two-seat Chipmunk training aircraft based at RAF Gatow, *inter alia* acted as 'spies in the sky', flying at 800 ft (240 m) over the many Soviet and NVA military units within the 20 nm radius of the Berlin Control Zone. These units included particularly interesting sites such as the Soviet 'Foxbat' base at Werneuchen, the Soviet Army EW base at Schönwalde and the army barracks and training areas around Potsdam. With four eyes and cameras ideal for the purpose, the fliers gained a great deal of useful information on new Russian equipment and other military intelligence in and around Berlin. One NVA tank unit was clearly visible on the western side of Gatow airfield, through a wire fence which had replaced a section of the Berlin Wall, the East Germans explaining, with some strange logic, that this was a 'courtesy to the West'. However, it seems more likely that this was to provide a simple and convenient entry point for the NVA tanks if or when the expected attack on the Berlin Garrison took place. Plans for such an invasion were found post-Cold War, in a nearby command post, revealing that the Granz Regiment 34 'Hanno Günther' of the Grenztruppen der GDR, had the task of occupying RAF Gatow, and it was clear that these plans were continually updated up to the time of reunification.

Whereas more remote intelligence agencies could be 'spoofed' by sigint, or indeed by silence (the Warsaw Pact was adept at moving huge forces silently), BRIXMIS could hear and see what was going on on the ground, in detail, and was thus able to provide the formal intelligence community with a running commentary on events as they unfolded. In his final years of service in 2ATAF, the author got to know some of the carefully selected men in BRIXMIS, and developed a very high regard for their skills, ingenuity, courage and potential value to battle management – of which he was a part. He sensed, however, that they might have been considered the poor relations within the UK intelligence 'establishment', and indeed one BRIXMIS officer told him that he felt that Washington was more interested in their contribution than London. The author's battle management team in 2ATAF would consider this to have been a calumny; it often had the greatest difficulty getting specific and vital intelligence on targets in the GDR, the acquisition of such information being grist to the mill for the BRIXMIS airmen. For instance, he recalls asking several times, but to no avail, for the location of hardened grass and autobahn airstrips, which he eventually found for himself after the Cold War, together with several autobahn strips (Chapter Three). Largely unprotected, and therefore very susceptible to cannon fire and other air weapons, these were very lucrative targets when compared with those on the 'hardened' MOBs, which had a redundancy of operating strips and were very well defended. Again, the author's team asked for – but did not get – the locations of pre-prepared dispersal sites for the Soviet and East German Mi-8 and Mi-24 attack helicopters, which would have been worthy of attention in war. It is now clear that all this information was recorded somewhere in the vast intelligence libraries, but perhaps subject to over-zealous security arrangements, pending the outbreak of hostilities – when it might have been too late. On the other hand, BRIXMIS officers were aware that the technical intelligence staff within MOD UK valued highly what BRIXMIS could provide for them, particularly the detailed photographs of new weapon systems.

The author was privileged to have RAF Group Captain Andrew Pennington and British Army General Peter Williams, both of whom served on BRIXMIS, add to these notes on its activities. Andrew had completed Russian language training in 1979, to equip him for his forthcoming duties with No.26 SU in Berlin, and later he instructed military attachés and personnel destined for BRIXMIS at the Joint Intelligence School at Ashford, Kent, before being posted to BRIXMIS himself in 1985 – as a tour officer – and with promotion a year later he was appointed Squadron Leader Operations.

Andrew described one incident, in May 1986, which typified the work carried out by the Mission. He was travelling with a ground (Army) tour, which comprised a BRIXMIS army officer acting as tour NCO and an army corporal driver. The first target was a large oil refinery at Schwedt, close to the Polish border, north-east of Berlin, which involved standing-off to take a series of colour images of the fumes emitted, to enable scientists to monitor the output and quality of the refinery's product. There was very little traffic around, other than a Stasi car containing three Stasi 'narks' which had been following the tour car for some time, but this was normal practice and caused little concern, even when it took the lead and raced to the entrance of the refinery – but it was no match for the BRIXMIS Mercedes Geländewagen. However, as the tour party moved on, having taken the required photographs and intending to turn off the road on to a small track some short distance ahead, an East German-registered Wartburg saloon came speeding down the road towards them from the main gate, driven by a uniformed VOPO officer, accompanied by two other men in civilian clothes. After an abortive, head-on attempt to stop the BRIXMIS car, the Wartburg turned round and drove alongside, again trying to force it to stop, but the Geländewagen weighed 3.5 tons and the VOPO car came off worst in a number of side-swipes, as the two vehicles accelerated, neck and neck down the road, until the German crew gave up and the tour party continued on its way. While the incident had to be reported, this was a relatively minor encounter and the tour continued as planned, heading first towards Angermünde, with the intention of buying food there for the evening 'cook-up'. There they were ambushed by 14 VOPO vehicles, varying from large trucks to cars, and completely blocked-in on a one-way system with no chance of escape. Standard practice in such circumstances was to ignore the VOPOs and let the situation calm down before doing anything, so it was out with the flasks of coffee and on with a cassette of soothing music on the Geländewagen's radio/cassette player. This having achieved the desired effect, Andrew dismounted and sought out the senior VOPO officer to demand that he clear the road and let them go, on the grounds that he had no right to detain them, and that a Soviet officer be called to the scene. He then re-joined his tour colleagues in the Geländewagen for a two hour wait, during which time all traffic was at a standstill until the Soviet Kommandant arrived from the nearest garrison HQ, somewhat surprised by the scale of the detention. However, after speaking to the VOPO, he confiscated the British servicemen's Soviet passes, thereby confirming their detention and, after a number of long phone calls, they were formally accused of a flagrant violation of the local Permanent Restricted Area (PRA), and escorted to the Soviet External Relations Branch (SERB) office in Potsdam by the Kommandant. There, Andrew was given a good dressing down for his 'unacceptable behaviour' which it was considered verged on 'hooliganism' (a favourite Russian accusation), after which the passes were returned and the 'miscreants' were allowed to drive back to West Berlin. In retrospect, it was concluded that the ambush in Angermünde was a deliberate retaliation by the VOPOs, for the damage caused to their comrade's private car outside Schwedt.

Peter Williams had a similar story to tell, which again underlined the risks taken by BRIXMIS. On 12 August 1982, the new Chief of BRIXMIS, Brigadier John Learmont, joined Peter (acting as 'Tour NCO' and mentor) and their driver, Corporal John 'Benny' Boland, on what they might have expected to be a 'routine' ground tour – but well aware that anything could happen. The tour was planned to introduce the new Chief to the type of targets BRIXMIS might be called on to cover, some four or five a day for three days, while making him aware of the restrictions and dangers inherent in their travels. In the hope that it would help to keep them out of trouble, they used the Brigadier's shiny black Opel Senator, bearing his star plate, rather than a standard, matt green Opel or Range Rover tour vehicle.

The first day began well; they passed several points of interest as planned, including rail sidings, Soviet and NVA barracks and local training areas in Halle, noting the number, nature and insignia of every military vehicle they encountered, all the while conscious that their movements, since leaving Berlin, were being monitored closely by VOPO and Stasi operatives. From Halle they headed north-west through what was considered the low risk town of Magdeburg, then west to the IGB, where they turned south towards their intended night stop in the Thueringen Forest, skirting round a PRA at Halberstadt. It was then that the trouble started. As they moved south from Badersleben over a wooded ridgeline, an early warning radar site appeared, seemingly very close to their route south of Athenstedt, where a 'Mission Restriction Sign' (MRS) warned them to proceed no further. It was not unusual for the tours to ignore an unforeseen MRS; this being an East German sign in four languages prohibiting access by 'foreign liaison missions'. As such they had no legal status as far as BRIXMIS was concerned, since East Germany had not been included in the Robertson/Malinin Agreement. So the party decided to continue, temporarily losing sight of the radars as they passed through Athenstedt until they climbed over the far ridge, to find themselves immediately confronted by the radar site perimeter running along their route – and another MRS. The tour crew's reaction was instinctive, all camera and tour equipment being hidden as the driver was ordered to accelerate, the intention being to pass the site entrance at speed, but the NVA and Stasi were ready for them. One man leapt out of a ditch behind them to throw a 'Schlagbaum' barrier across the road to cut off their retreat, and as the Senator passed the main gate at some 60 km/hr, a huge NVA Tatra-148 truck emerged to strike it amidships with tremendous force, forcing it sideways off the road, only a line of small trees preventing it rolling over. This deliberate act of violence caused considerable damage to the BRIXMIS car, with several windows smashed and all the doors jammed; in Peter's words 'it was truly a miracle that no one was killed'. In fact, none of the party was hurt, although the driver was severely dazed. The brigadier remained in the car while Peter Williams climbed through a window to remonstrate, in German, with the many 'jubilant' NVA soldiers and Stasi officers who had rushed to the scene, and to demand the presence of a Soviet officer, while ensuring that no German could break into the wrecked car. The team then resorted to the standard ritual for these circumstances, that of making cups of coffee, and settling down to wait for the Soviet Kommandant from Halberstadt, and a recovery vehicle from BRIXMIS in Potsdam. As things calmed down, the East Germans themselves offered the men they had so nearly killed a disgusting version of their tea – interpreted by the team as a psychological victory in their favour, and perhaps a mild act of contrition.

The aftermath followed a familiar pattern. When the Soviet party arrived, the team surrendered their Russian passes, and that of their damaged vehicle, to the Kommandant, who then began his investigation into the incident, starting with statements from the NVA and the Stasi officers involved, then the British – all in accordance with published procedures. The brigadier and Kommandant then chatted amiably about their respective service lives, establishing a useful rapport, while Peter tried to find a telephone to enquire about their recovery, a fruitless search because no military telephone seemed to be available and every public booth he found in Athenstedt had been vandalized. The team and their 'hosts' spent a total of six hours huddled together in the front of the offending Tatra truck outside the radar site's main gate before the recovery got underway, amazingly with the Senator able to be driven aboard the low loader under its own steam, after which the team travelled back to Potsdam in the relative comfort of another BRIXMIS car.

On the following day, the brigadier had an unprecedented summons to the office of the Chief of the SERB in Potsdam, to be told that the Russian Commander-in-Chief considered him 'a hooligan', and to receive a 'formal rebuke'. That was an end to the matter, but thereafter BRIXMIS took more care over route preparation, and the Chief would never again rely on his shiny black car, or his star plates, to enhance his protection – from then he would tour in the matt green vehicles, fitted out for the purpose, and exercise greater stealth. This incident was considered to have been the most violent, deliberate assault on a Chief of BRIXMIS over the 44 year life of the mission's life, but the French mission had worse, when Adjudant-Chef Mariotti was killed in another ramming. This had been a dangerous 'game'. Interestingly, when the author was flying with a Hunter FR.10, armed reconnaissance squadron, his pre-planned war task followed a route, expected to be used by Warsaw Pact reinforcements in an offensive against the West, which took him past the same radar site at Athenstedt, and he felt that the greatest risk to him then would be from the ZSU-23/4 AAA defences around the site.

Much less information has been found about the Soviet/NVA intelligence agencies in East Germany, but SOXMIS was very visible in West Germany, as their huge black 'Zlin' cars toured with much greater freedom than did the BRIXMIS vehicles in the East, clearly gaining a great deal of military information without fear of being forced off the road – or shot. They could often be seen, quite openly, from the air and on the ground, outside weapon ranges and off the ends of NATO runways, presumably taking numbers, noting tactics and estimating weapons scores. Occasionally, as a token gesture, they were moved on by the civilian or military police, but the author is not aware of any serious incident. Surely in further attempts to extract military intelligence, SOXMIS invited NATO officers to their annual cocktail parties in Bünde, the author and his wife attending one, escorted by an RAF intelligence officer and hosted by courteous and inquisitive Russian officers, purporting to be in the Soviet Air Force but wearing rather new, somewhat ill-fitting uniforms. Despite the flow of vodka and gin, both sides showed proper caution, with probably little gained or lost by either side. Evidence that the Warsaw Pact had many informants in West Germany, in various guises, often amused the British forces. It was well known that classified or 'need to know' information, such as the start time of 'surprise' exercises or impending troop movements, could be learned first from a man in the local garage, while accurate facts on local military incidents, including aircraft accidents, albeit subject to a news blackout, were often heard of first on German radios. Intelligence was big business in the Cold War.

In the first years of the Cold War, the RAF deployed Tp.14 and Tp.15 search radars throughout north-west Germany.

Author's Collection

The British Tp.80 long range search radar, supported by an array of Tp.13 height-finders at Brekendorf, Auenhausen, Brockzetel and Udem, served well in the first two decades of the Cold War.

Author's Collection

Squadron Leader Andrew Pennington, serving as Operations Officer on BRIXMIS, 'on tour' somewhere in the GDR. *Andrew Pennington*

In August 1982, the occupants of BRIXMIS tour car Opel 'Senator 1', Brigadier Learmont, Peter Taylor and their driver Corporal Boland, were lucky to escape unhurt when it was rammed by a Soviet lorry outside Athenstedt. *BRIXMIS Association*

Major Peter Williams and Squadron Leader Pennington at Potsdam in 1988.   *Andrew Pennington*

In the mid 1950s, the RAF Airfield Construction Branch (ACB) laid the foundations for the CRC at Brockzetel.   *ACB*

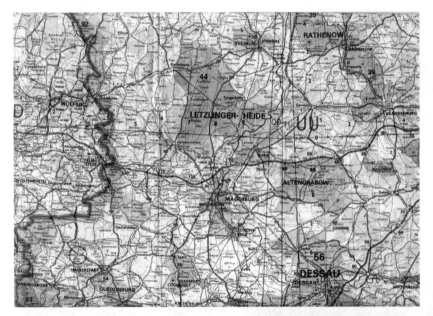

This cutting from the BRIXMIS map of the GDR, shows the Permanent Restricted Areas (PRAs) around the village of Athenstedt (lower left), where Brigadier Learmont & Peter Williams were rammed by a Soviet lorry.

BRIXMIS Association

A Meeting of Minds? Maj Peter Williams, Soviet Lt Col Savin & Sqn Ldr Steve Griffiths in Potsdam.
BRIXMIS Association

Chapter Six

Strike Force

Hit Hard, Hit First, Hit Often.

Admiral W F Halsey

EGAF Strike/Attack & Reconnaissance Force

Having been founded primarily to contribute to the Warsaw Pact air defences, the LSK/LV devoted little effort to its secondary role of ground-attack. In 1971, however, a large number of MiG-17Fs, rendered redundant when JG-7 was re-equipped with MiG-21s, were re-roled for offensive support, and retained at Drewitz, as 'Jagdbombengeschwader-31' (JBG-31), Fighter-Bomber Wing 31, signalling the beginning of an offensive addition to the EGAF. JBG-31 started life within the LSK/LV, but from December 1981 it came under the newly established FO FAFK, which became FO Führungsorgan Front-und Militärtransportfliegerkräfte (FMTFK) in 1984, to provide more direct air support for surface forces (land and sea). Commanded initially by Col Wolfgang Büttner, the FOFK set up its headquarters at Eggersdorf, until it was re-designated FMTFK, when it moved to Strausberg. This was effectively a third air division for the EGAF, comprising air force and marine (naval), fixed and rotary-wing

strike/attack, reconnaissance and transport support elements.

In the context of offensive support, 'strike' refers to nuclear operations, 'attack' to operations involving conventional weapons. Other than in the first years of the Cold War, when some bombers and fighter-bombers continued to make use of the middle and upper airspace, both NATO and the Warsaw Pact air forces accepted the need for their offensive forces to transit to and from their targets, in war and in training, at low level, thus reducing the chance of early detection by increasingly effective radar systems. With this switch in emphasis, together with the introduction of noisy, post-WW2 jet aircraft, air forces in both NATO and the Warsaw Pact countries found it increasingly difficult to secure agreement from civilian authorities for this training to take place in peacetime at low level. This was particularly true in the GDR, which had the additional problem of a relatively small training area for the very large number of tactical aircraft needing to use it, which is presumably why, to reduce the risk of mid-air collisions at low level, the Soviet and EGAF routinely flew on alternative days of the week, and were confined to a small number of low level routes – with which the pilots soon became all too familiar. Also, in an attempt to placate the anti-noise lobby, low flying was generally restricted (other than for specific exercises) to a minimum height of 100 m (330 ft). Meanwhile, NATO pilots had the advantage of being able to plan their own routes and fly down to 500 ft (150 m) over much of West Germany, and in some eight Low Flying Areas (LFAs), linked by specific routes, down to 250 ft (75 m).

Jagdbombengeschwader 31/37 (JBG-31/37)

As the first commander of JBG-31, from 1971 to 1973, Klaus-Jürgen Baarß was responsible for introducing seasoned fighter pilots from the LSK/LV, and newly qualified pilots coming direct from OHS, to the offensive support role at low level. The MiG-17F (basic details in Chapter Three) was a good aircraft for this purpose, but the work load was high. On the plus side, it was relatively simple and robust, could carry a useful weapons load of up to 2x 250 kg (550 lb) bombs or UB pods of unguided rockets, in addition to its powerful 37 mm and two 23 mm internal cannon, and had a performance quite adequate for ground-attack aircraft at that time – and it retained a self-defence capability with its guns. However, the aircraft's navigation suite was antiquated, with an unstable, none too accurate DGMK-3 slaved gyro compass, one ADF set which was difficult to set at night or in bad weather, no autopilot and a single four-channel (pre-set) VHF radio. The aircraft's range on internal fuel was poor, but it could be increased by fitting a variety of external tanks on two wing hardpoints, albeit at the expense of weapons and with significant limitations on performance and manoeuvrability. Moreover, the aircraft also had the unpopular SK-1 ejection seat, with one of three vertical positions having to be pre-set on the ground – with the seat removed. Despite these shortcomings, the fledgling fighter-bomber pilots had no difficulty converting to, or operating the MiG-17F in its new role; indeed, they liked the aircraft very much, finding it easy to fly, stable at low level, and, without external tanks, relatively agile in both vertical and lateral planes.

Leutnant Frank Born left OHS in 1979, having completed the course in three years rather than the normal four because of a temporary shortage of pilots on the front line. His course was the first to carry out all its flying training on the L-39 at Bautzen and MiG-21SPS at Rothenburg, the graduates expecting to be posted to MiG-21 air defence wings. However, volunteers were required to man JBG-31, due to be re-equipped with the exciting new MiG-23BN fighter-bomber, and Frank was among those who accepted the offer, thereby beginning his productive service on the MiG-17F. He quickly encountered a personal problem; being shorter than most of his comrades he had difficulty with the three-position seats, most of which were set in the mid-position and too low for him when it came to aerobatics, combat and weapons training. Indeed, it was said that 'Borni' was the only pilot in the NVA's fast-jet force who was allowed to fly the MiG standing up, and when a two-seat trainer taxied by, seemingly without anyone aboard, it was assumed to be crewed by 'Borni' and 'Franta', the latter a highly competent and experienced instructor – but also of less than average height. However, they both proved over the years that stature was no measure of a good flier. Perhaps it was partly because of their good consolidation training in the MiG-17F that none of Frank's training course lost an aircraft during his time in the EGAF.

Frank was also much impressed by the aircraft as an air-to-ground weapons platform. In addition to the facilities in Germany, JBG-31 had access to less familiar ranges and unlimited low flying in Poland, which provided invaluable tactical training when the German pilots visited Polish bases such as Pila, Miroslawic and Babimost, often for joint exercises. Whereas air defence pilots, exercising their secondary role of ground-attack, were invariably required to carry out 'dry runs' before 'live' passes, and from one direction only, Frank confirmed that selected fighter-bomber pilots were, in some cases, cleared for first run attacks (FRA), 'live', and to approach their targets from various directions, with guns, rockets and bombs by day – but only with bombs at night. Although no records could be found of the accuracies achieved, the JBG-31 pilots were very proud of their proficiency with the MiG-17F's hard-hitting 37 mm and 23 mm cannon, and the 57 mm unguided rockets, some launched horizontally from a height of 25 m (80 ft) at 700 km/hr (380 knots). 'Manöverkunstflug' (manoeuvring aerobatics), were authorized down to

1,000 m (3,300 ft) agl, before progressing to 'manöverreiche Luftkampf' (air combat tactics), but these involved extensive use of reheat which could reduce the duration of combat sorties to 20 min, landing with a minimum of 300 litres (530 lbs). Frank Born also recalls air combat against other German and Polish, but not Soviet MiG-17 units, although it remains unclear whether this was authorized or inofficial. As with the air defence wings, JBG-31 was subject to monthly 'Gefechtsflugtage', special exercises on the ground and in the air, planned and directed by the wing commander. Again, these would usually be staged under fully operational conditions, within an NBC scenario and often including off-base deployments to the wing's dedicated reserve airstrips, such as that at Alteno, where the divisional commander himself was known to appear unexpectedly, on the ground or in the air, to assess the wing's general preparedness and vulnerability to air attack. Initially, the MiG-17F pilots of JBG-31 were not committed to DHS, but during exercises the squadron was required to generate specified numbers of aircraft, within certain timeframes.

The records show that, from 1971 to 1979, only six MiG-17Fs were lost, in a mix of pilot errors, technical defects and operational hazards, an accident rate less than might have been expected with this aging aircraft – and as the fighter pilots adapted to the new role.

In 1979, JBG-31 took a further step into the offensive role, when it began to replace the MiG-17s on two of its three squadrons with one of a new breed of variable geometry fast-jets, the MiG-23BN 'Flogger F', supported by a small number of the two-seat MiG-23UB 'Flogger C'. The 'BN', with its wedge-shaped or 'duck-bill' nose sloping down from the cockpit giving the pilot a clearer view ahead at low level, differed in appearance from the 'MF' and 'ML' fighter variants, which had symmetrically pointed noses housing their radars. All the MiG-23s had a dorsal fin which was locked in the horizontal on the ground but extended to the vertical as the undercarriage retracted, to increase the aircraft's directional stability in the air. A mirror fitted above the canopy rail and two more within the cockpit improved rearward vision, while a pilot in the rear cockpit of the 'UB' had a periscope to give him a good view ahead, this being particularly useful on take-off, landing and taxiing. The controls in the 'BN' were optimised for low flying, giving the aircraft a very steady ride at the normal operating speed of 900 km/hr (500 knots) and making it an excellent ground-attack platform, whereas those in fighter and trainer variants were geared more to the interceptor role at higher levels. With the R-29B-300 engine, generating 10,200 kg (22,500 lb) thrust in reheat and 8,000 kg (17,600 lb) 'dry', a 'clean' aircraft could achieve M1.7 at height (wings at maximum sweep) and in excess of 1,000 km/hr (540 knots) at low level. The radius of action at low level, with a war load of four 250 kg (550lb) bombs, was 690 km (370 nm). An advanced Sokol-23M navigation and weapons system was effective at its best but not thought by some to have been wholly reliable. Four external pylons below the fuselage and one under each fixed section of the wing, could each carry 'dumb' bombs, of up to 500 kg (1,100 lb), 16 or 32 unguided S-5 rockets in UB containers, S-8s in UB-20 pods, or external fuel tanks. The inner wing pylons could each accommodate a single S-24 round or an AS-7 'Kerry', radio command guidance tactical air-to-surface guided missile, with a range of 10 km (5.5 nm), modelled on the very successful US 'Bullpup'. The 'BN' could also deliver the AS-11 'Kilter', Anti-Radar (AR) missile, with a published range of up to 160 km (86 nm), and the Soviet 'Razovare Bombovara Kassete 500' (RBK-500) Cluster Bomb Unit (CBU), a canister containing a number of anti-tank, anti-personnel or runway-cratering sub-munitions, dropped from 300 m (1,100 ft). It is believed that the wing also had access to independent runway cratering, parachute retarded bombs, each dropped from an aircraft hard point. Internally, the aircraft was equipped with a twin-barrel GSch-23L cannon. Four pilots from Drewitz took their 'BN's to Luninez Range in Belarus in September 1989, where they excelled in a tactical/weapons exercise, showing that the AS-7, which the Russians considered obsolete and had withdrawn from service some ten years before, remained very effective.

JBG-31's two MiG-23 squadrons were each required to maintain two 'BNs' on 30 minutes readiness and an additional two on two hours stand-by at all times, with weapons loads specified for each 24 hour period, a standard fit being two UB-32 and two UB-16 pods – a total of 96, 57 mm rockets. In 1982, JBG-31 was re-named JBG-37.

Without air-to-air guided missiles, and a limit of 3'G' when practising the limited defensive combat manoeuvres permitted, there was no intention of employing this fighter-bomber in an air defence role, but in extremis, the GSch-23L cannon could have been a defensive weapon of last resort, using the basic ASP optical gunsight. Speed at low level would have been the MiG-23BN's best means of defence against any fighter opposition. Although it had been anticipated that the 'BN' would be able to operate from grass airstrips, it was found that the aircraft's natural tail-down attitude on the ground rendered this impractical. Indeed, early trials on the airfields at Brandenburg and Barth had caused such damage to the grass runways that the 'BN's were confined thereafter to operations from paved surfaces, and JBG-37 was believed to have earmarked the Russian airfields of Finsterwald (MiG-27) and Brand (MiG-27/Su-24M) as deployment bases. The MiG-23BN has been compared to the American F-5 and the British Jaguar, but having spoken to MiG-23BN pilots the author, a Jaguar pilot also acquainted with the F-5, suggests that the similarities are few.

Andreas Dietrich flew the MiG-23BN. He completed his GST on the Z-42 at Neuhausen, Cottbus, in 1977, 80 hours of basic flight training on the L-29 at Primorsko-Achtarsk in Russia in 1981, 50 hours of advanced fighter training on the MiG-21UM and MiG-21bis at Krasnodar, Russia, and 50 hours of dual and solo flying in the MiG-23UB and MiG-23MF at the Soviet base of Lugowaja. Returning to Germany in 1983, he carried out his operational training with JBG-37 at Drewitz, and remained with the wing until it disbanded in September 1990. During this time he accumulated a total of 750 hours on the MiG-23, qualifying for his LK.III certificate in 1984, LK.II in 1985 and LK.I in 1987; he became a local air traffic supervisor in 1985 and a pre/post maintenance flight test pilot in 1987.

Andreas was quite happy flying the 'BN', but some of his fellow pilots were less charitable, commenting on the need to avoid excessive yaw and any condition conducive to a spin (the aircraft being 'nose light'). The correct landing techniques were also crucial in getting the aircraft to settle firmly on the ground – its aerodynamic qualities, wings spread, earning it the nickname 'jet-glider'. Andreas recalled that most of his 'dumb' bomb training was carried out with concrete 'shapes', but that the S.5 unguided rockets, fitted with operational warheads, had spectacular effects on vehicle targets, while in the air-to-ground mode the BN's cannon, with its sophisticated weapons computer and laser range finder, was easy to operate and very accurate. All the pilots were trained to deliver the AS-7 missile in the flight simulator, but few had a chance to launch the weapon 'live'. In training for war, tasks involving conventional weapons would usually be carried out by pairs of aircraft or 'four-ships', in most cases the low level training flights following the well known, standard routes, terminating at a weapons range. Strike sorties were normally flown by single aircraft. Generally, MiG-23BN pilots were required to complete a 'dry' pass before firing or delivering weapons on the ranges, and were limited to one attack direction.

On a few training missions, the MiG-23BNs were escorted by recce MiG-21s of TAFS-47 (below) but in the air the strike/attack pilots were usually unaware of their presence, or what tactics they employed; perhaps it was envisaged that they would combine their escort duties with pre- and post-attack recce? Accurate route flying at night or in instrument conditions could be expected, given the cross-feed of data between the Radioteknicheskaya Sistema Blizhney Navigatisii (RSBN) radio navigation system (similar to NATO's VOR/DME equipment) and the IKW inertial platform. Andreas recalled one very satisfying night flight in 1987, flown at 300 m (1,000 ft), in very marginal visibility, to the range at Wittstock, via six turning points, for the successful delivery of two parachute retarded bombs at low level, followed by similarly lonely return legs for a flight total of 60 minutes, which gave him his LK.I certificate. The wing expected to play a full part in any Warsaw Pact offensive, but Andreas was not aware of any plans for JBG-37 to move forward to support Warsaw Pact advances westwards into the FRG, or of any pre-planned targets for them in war, and assumed that they were more likely to be called on to react to events as they occurred. They expected FACs to be deployed on the front line to identify and perhaps mark Close Air Support (CAS) targets, and this was practised several times a year during tactical air/ground exercises with the Russians.

Although he had very few technical defects in the air, Andreas does remember the one which earned him the role of functional test pilot on JBG-37. It was in the mid-1980s, while on a high level navigation sortie, that he lost his primary flight instruments and was able to restore them only by disengaging the autopilot. This left him with the difficult task of controlling his aircraft manually on an instrument descent and approach in rapidly deteriorating weather, and without any automatic glide slope information for the runway in use. Another MiG-21BN was sent to 'shepherd' him down, but the turbulence was so bad that the two lost contact and Andreas was forced to abort the descent and climb above the cloud again to consider his options. It was then that the EGAF insistence that its pilots had a thorough technical knowledge of their aircraft paid off, Andreas correctly engaging the autopilot again by switching off the onboard navigation equipment, which was connected to the complex IKW-1 compass system, thereafter depending on distance and altitude information from the NDB and GCA. By this means he recovered the aircraft successfully to Drewitz, to be commended for his knowledge of the aircraft's systems, judgment and sound airmanship, with the result that he became the youngest member to be recruited into the wing's prestigious flight test team, all of which helped him gain a place in the GAF after reunification.

Frank Born, by then an experienced ground-attack pilot on the MiG-17F, recalls acting as a Range Safety Officer (RSO) at a VIP demonstration involving the MiG-17Fs and MiG-23BNs of JBG-37 on the army range at Weisswasser (north of Görlitz) – which did not go quite as planned. The two flights of MiG-23BNs caused mayhem among the spectators when their parachute retarded bombs impacted slightly off the target, showering the carefully prepared banquet with debris, amid a crescendo of noise. Perhaps the collective effects of so many 500 kg (1,100 lb) bombs, and the inexact art of 'dumb bombing' had not been fully appreciated by the organisers, and even Frank was so mesmerised by what he saw that he was barely ready for the follow-up attack by two flights of MiG-17Fs which added to the confusion with salvos of 57 mm rockets. No report is available on the debriefings.

Off duty, JBG-37 seemed to have enjoyed more social contact with their Russian neighbours in the fighter-bomber force in East Germany than was usual between the Soviet and East German fighter wings, exemplified by a special relationship with the Soviet S-24M wing at nearby Brand. In Andreas Dietrich's words: 'this was a normal part of everyday life'. Drewitz does appear to have been a very happy base, with all the pilots interviewed claiming to have enjoyed a 'calm, serene and stressless social climate there, with no excessive parties in the very mixed community', and they felt that the Stasi, although very evident, had little adverse affect on their lives.

JBG-37 lost only four MiG-23s during its 11 years of service, 1979–1990, one with fatal consequences. In December 1985, Olaf Haenschke lost control while simulating a nuclear weapon delivery and recovery; he probably became disorientated after entering cloud, and may have been unable to reach the ejection handles due to the violence of the flat spin which ensued. He was seen to re-emerge from cloud in a steep dive – too low to effect a safe recovery. Andreas, waiting to take off, witnessed his final seconds. In June 1986, a 'BN' pilot was unable to level out following a descent for a night landing, this being attributed to a technical malfunction in his aircraft's control system, and he was forced to eject at 800 km/hr (430 knots), landing safely beside his aircraft. With no welcoming party to meet him, he made his way to the nearest road by foot and 'persuaded' a none too enthusiastic motorist to take him to the nearest air base (Preschen) from where he was taken, dirty, shocked but happy, to his home at Drewitz. A year later, the pilot flying a MiG-23UB from the front seat on take-off, with the aircraft's captain in the back, either triggered the brake parachute release by mistake when seeking to raise the undercarriage, or had a technical malfunction which caused the brake parachute to deploy. In a daytime take-off in reheat, the parachute would have burnt off, but reheat was not used at night, in order to minimise the noise nuisance, so the parachute continued to counteract the thrust and the aircraft failed to get airborne. At this point, the captain decided that they must eject, and used the command ejection system in the rear cockpit for them both to do so. The aircraft broke into three pieces as it slithered to a halt some 300 m (330 yd) further down the runway – but the two pilots landed safely nearby. Considering the nature of the new aircraft and its operations, JBG-37 could claim to have had a very creditable safety record with its MiG-23s. The wing flew its last training sorties from Drewitz on 25 September 1990.

For Andreas this was not the end of his military flying; he was accepted into Führungskommando Ost, within the Bundeswehr, initially to fly a further 20 hours on all variants of the MiG-23, including ferry flights to the US air base at Ramstein and to the Luftwaffe airfields at Manching and Laage. In April 1991 he re-trained on the Alpha Jet, and flew 90 hours on the aircraft with JaBoG49, at Fürstenfeldbruck.

Demands on the few air-to-surface weapons ranges in the GDR were high, and increased greatly as the NVA's offensive forces grew in size and capabilities. For its secondary role of ground-attack, the LSK/LV had, in its first decade, depended solely on space being made available on Russian ranges, with limited use of the facilities at Gadow Rossow (Wittstocker Heide) being one of their few options. The range at Wittstock, measuring 15 km x 15 km, and later to include an overlay of the runway on the US base at Bitburg (West Germany), was quite adequate for all forms of air weapons training in the early days of the Cold War, and also for some of the first guided missiles to come on line later. However, despite every precaution, even the more advanced weapons could go astray, one JBG-37 pilot losing control of his radio guided AS-7 'Kerry', launched from his MiG-23BN, which to everyone's dismay, found its way outside the range – bringing to an end the use of this weapon at Wittstock. Limited use was

also made of other Soviet/NVA army manoeuvre areas such as Letzlinger Heide, close to the IGB, and Lieberose, north of Cottbus.

With a clear need to provide additional range facilities for the EGAF in the GDR, 1.LVD established a range at Jerischke (Döbern), to be known as Bombenwurflandplatz 31 (BLP-31), which was activated in 1972. The targets included redundant military vehicles, which were said to disintegrate with spectacular effect. The range was administered by an officer and range party of some ten men, but during flying operations, RSOs, pilots specifically qualified for the job and approved by the Chief of Fighter Operations, 1.LVD, were detached on rotation from the local fighter, and later fighter-bomber wings, to supervise every aspect of safety on the range. Unlike Qualified Weapons Instructors (QWIs) in the RAF, these pilots had not undergone special courses, but were judged fit to instruct on weapons and undertake supervisory tasks such as RSO, based on their experience and performance with air weapons. They were responsible for clearing the range of mushroom pickers *et al*, before and during flying, and for ensuring that pilots observed the correct airborne procedures (with special attention to safe pull-out heights), and they had the authority to dismiss any who erred from the range. The RSO was also required to give his assessment of the accuracies achieved by the bombs, rockets and cannon fire, but without the assistance of definitive scoring systems available on most NATO ranges; his estimates were based on simple triangulation. At the end of the day, the resident party cleared the range of all the wreckage, unexploded ordnance and spent ammunition. In the 17 years of its use, Jerischke witnessed three accidents in the air, all of which involved MiG-21s of the LSK/LV. One was lost close to the range in June 1973 and another on the range, attributed to loss of control – the pilots killed in both cases. However, the two MiG-21s of JG-1 which were damaged when they collided in the range pattern, in December 1983, were recovered safely to Holzdorf. Much use was also made of the air-to-ground range west of Peenemünde and the semi-submerged ship targets on the sea range nearby, but no accident statistics were available to the author for these or other ranges in the GDR.

Aufklärungsfliegerstaffel 31 (AFS-31)

The need for a tactical reconnaissance force to assist NVA land and sea forces in finding the enemy and monitoring his progress was foreseen in 1974, with the formation at Preschen of AFS-31. AFS-31 was an independent tactical reconnaissance squadron, initially part of JG-3 and made up of MiG-21F-13s and MiG-21Us, with pilots and groundcrew drawn from 3.JS/JG-3 and redundant assets from JAG-15. The squadron built up slowly until, in 1976, it was fully established with four flights, each of four aircraft. The pilots were given an introduction to the role and the basics of visual and photo reconnaissance at Kamenz – thereafter learning 'on the job' in MiG-

21F-13s equipped with an AFA-39 digital camera, manufactured in the GDR and installed in a 'Kameracontainer CLA-87', a detachable pod under the starboard wing. The camera was capable of providing acceptable photography from oblique and vertical stations, between 100 m (330 ft) and 11,000 m (36,000 ft). No conclusive evidence could be found of an in-flight reporting system within the NVA, for the pilots to pass on their visual sightings to ground stations, to enable a rapid reaction, but photo negatives were expected to be ready for viewing on light tables within 15 minutes of 'engines off'. Commanders were quick to realise the value of this asset in war, and in peacetime to demonstrate the capability to VIPs, the archives showing that the GDR's First Secretary, Erich Honecker, was indeed impressed to hear that pilots had reported tracks into a forest and tyre marks leading to a divisional HQ, supposedly camouflaged during a field exercise, and then to see the photographs proving that they had been right. AFS-31 was re-designated AFS-47 in 1982, when it joined the fighter-bombers and attack helicopters within the newly established FAFK. In 1985, the squadron began to exchange its MiG-21F-13s for MiG-21Ms, and in 1986, AFS-47 (now within the FMTFK) was re-named again 'Taktische Aufklärungsfliegerstaffel 47' (TAFS-47), and earned high plaudits from a Warsaw Pact combat ready evaluation team for its contribution to tactical operations. A second recce squadron, TAFS-87, was born at Drewitz in 1988, with 12 MiG-21Ms and 2 MiG-21Us no longer required when JG-7 disbanded

For its secondary air-to-ground role, the MiG-21MF had twin 23 mm cannon internally and could carry a variety of unguided rockets, external tanks or free-fall bombs (shown here).

Author/Cottbus Museum.

In 1980, MiG-17F pilots of 3.JS/JBG-37, on detachment to the reserve airfield at Garz/Heringsdorf, together with MiG-21MF pilots from 3.JS/JG-9 took part in the Warsaw Pact Exercise 'Waffenbrüdershaft '. Their task was to prevent 'enemy forces' which had landed on the Baltic coastline nearby from gaining a foothold, using air-to-ground gunnery, 57 mm unguided rockets and 250 kg bombs.   *Frank Born Collection*

Frank Born flew his first solo in a MiG-17F at Drewitz in 1979.

Frank Born Collection

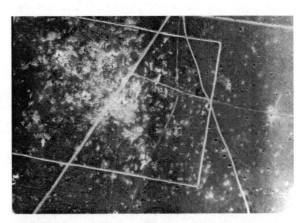

The NVA had occasional use of the Soviet weapons range at Wittstock.   *Frank Born Collection*

MiG-21Ms of TAFS-47, fitted with 490 litre drop tanks on the fuselage pylons.   *Rudolf Müller Collection*

A MiG-17F of JBG-31, the first fast-jet to be dedicated to the air offensive role.   *Rudolf Müller Collection*

This MiG-23UB started its service life with JB-9 at Peenemünde in 1979, but served most of its time on JBG-31 and JBG-37; it is seen here in the Cottbus Museum carrying a Kh-25MR, AS-10 'Karen' air-to-surface missile. *Author/Cottbus Museum*

Three MiG-23BNs of JBG-37. *Andreas Dietrich*

Captain Andreas Dietrich – MiG pilot. *Andreas Dietrich*

Down Time. MiG-23BN pilots from JBG-37, with their Russian comrades, during live firings of their AS-7 air-to-surface missiles at Luninez Range in Belarus. *Andreas Dietrich*

A MiG-21M of TAFS-47 taxies out for a night reconnaissance sortie. *Rudolf Müller Collection*

The JBG-37 MiG23BN weapons' inventory included 'dumb' bombs, UB containers of S-5 unguided rockets, 23 mm cannon pods and the AS-7 guided missiles. *Andreas Dietrich*

MiG-23BNs recovering to Drewitz. *Andreas Dietrich*

there, but both squadrons disbanded in October 1989.

Jagdbombenfliegergeschwader 77 (JBG-77)

The mid-1980s saw a significant increase in the EGAF's offensive firepower with the acquisition of the Russian Sukhoi Su-22 fighter-bomber, an export version of the Soviet Air Force Su-17, which first flew in 1969. The single-seat Su-22M4 'Fitter K', and two-seat Su-22UM3K 'Fitter G' were optimised for offensive operations, but with a limited air defence capability. Powered by a Lyulka AL-21F-3 turbojet, which developed 11,000 kg (24,200 lb) of thrust in reheat, the Su-22 had a service ceiling of 14,200 m (46,600 ft), and without external stores could achieve M1.7 at height, 1,400 km/hr (760 knots) in its usual habitat at low level. The single-seat aircraft had a slight edge in performance over the two-seat trainer, which was a little heavier, but the latter retained a similar operational capability, albeit with one rather than two cannon. Visually, the 'UM3K' could be identified from the 'M4' by its two-seat tandem cockpit, four pairs of chaff and KDS-23 IR flare ejectors astride the rear fuselage (whereas the 'M4' had only two), smaller air intakes either side of the nose with another at the base of its fin, and a periscope to improve the forward view from the rear seat. The comprehensive navigation and weapon delivery suites were 'state of the art' in both aircraft, consisting of a sophisticated inertial platform to feed the navigation equipment and artificial horizon

(with a back-up gyro), a Doppler radar, Radio Systema Dalncj Navigazii (RSDN), similar to LORAN C (with base stations in Prague and Kiev), RSBN, ILS and ADF equipments. A radar altimeter, coupled to the autopilot, provided a limited terrain following capability down to 50 m (160 ft), at maximum speed, but this detected only those obstacles within a very narrow forward scan and most pilots felt that it was reliable only over the sea or flat terrain. The aircraft had an IFF SRO-2 transponder, a SPO-15LE radar warning receiver and an SO-69 active transponder, another popular feature being the K-36D ejection seat, which enabled safe ejections from ground level at speeds above 75 km/hr (40 knots).

The fixed armament for the 'M4' consisted of two, 30 mm NR-30 cannon, one in each wing root, while the 'UM3K' had one only – mounted in the starboard wing root, and the aircraft was equipped with a KLEN-45 laser range-finder. An innovative twin-barrel 23 mm cannon, carried in a detachable SPPU-22–1 pod and slaved to the pilot's ASP-178C gunsight, could be preset to fire forward or rearwards (at any gunners following an overflight). Operating in the forward hemisphere the twin barrels could traverse to 30 deg below the horizontal, the pilot locking the target into an ingenious sighting system, which triggered the weapon automatically when the target came within optimum range, while in the rear-facing configuration the guns would be preset to 16 deg below the horizontal, again to fire automatically as the target passed through the computed position. Eight hardpoints could carry 4,000 kg (9,000 lb) of mixed stores externally, ranging from 100 kg–1,000 kg 'dumb' bombs, parachute retarded or ballistic, with concrete piercing or anti-armour heads, AR, radio command, TV, optical or laser-guided weapons, including the AS-10 'Karen', AS-12 'Kegler', AS-14 'Kedge' and AS-11 'Kilter', ECM pods or fuel tanks. Within the cockpit there was space, at the top right-hand side of the forward consol, for a TV missile monitor or AR missile control panel, numerous banks of switches and indicators underlining the aircraft's versatility, but the author found the overall layout and cockpit ergonomics wholly acceptable. There was also provision for the carriage of nuclear stores.

For diverse reconnaissance tasks, at high or low level, day or night, a KKR-1 multi-sensor recce pod could contain a thermal imaging system, Sideways Looking Airborne Radar (SLAR), up to 152 illuminating flares for 'wet film' oblique, pan or vertical photography, but a full working day was needed to re-configure the pod and attach it to special mounting points below the fuselage. The chaff, flares and two R-60/R-60M IRH missiles, gave the Su-22 a limited self-defence capability – the aircraft's cannon considered ineffective for this role.

In 2008 the author examined, in some detail, the potentially airworthy, ex-NVA Su-22M4, then resident with Hawker Hunter Aviation at RAF Scampton, and spoke there to the team of experienced aircraft engineers, led by Michael Elliot, responsible for maintaining the aircraft. They had not encountered any particular problem with the aircraft, but they did suggest that the use of high torque, rather than quick-release fasteners on many panels, and open-line rather than pressure refuelling, must have been detrimental to fast OTRs.

Forty-eight Su-22M4s and eight Su-22UM3Ks were destined for Flugplatz Laage, the NVA's new airbase, some 16 miles south of the Baltic port of Rostock, where 75 aircraft could be protected in HAS (land-scaped and turf covered) or blast pen revetments. Much thought had been given to both active and passive defences, with most of the operational and technical support facilities situated well away from the flight line; the wing's headquarters and domestic buildings were located some ten minutes drive from the airfield, and all traffic entering the airfield had to pass through an anti-FOD water pit at the main entrance. Laage had ready access to an alternative operating strip at Kavelstorf, five miles north of the airfield on the Rostock-Berlin autobahn, and another, four minutes flight time away at Warbelow, had a hardened grass airstrip with a servicing pan for ten fighters at the north-east corner of the site. Warbelow was used regularly for rehearsing rapid deployments and limited off-base operations.

In the second half of 1984, pending the completion of facilities at Laage, the first two 'UM3Ks' and eight 'M4s' were delivered to Flugplatz Rothenburg in crates aboard Russian An-22 and Il-76 transports, to be assembled by Soviet engineers and flight tested by Russian pilots. Meanwhile, from May-July 1984, eight experienced MiG-21 pilots underwent training on the Su-22 with Russian instructors at Krasnodar, thereafter building up their experience on the aircraft at Rothenburg and preparing to instruct the next intake of German pilots to man the first of two NVA Su-22 wings at Laage, within the FMTFK.

By the end of 1984, 12 Su-22M4s and 2 Su-22UM3Ks, with their LSK pilots, had moved to Laage, where the training resumed on a more formal basis. There was no Su-22 flight simulator in the GDR at that time, and during this formative period the number of conversion sorties programmed depended on each candidate's experience and progress on the aircraft. Much of the instruction was carried out in the two-seat aircraft, but on some solo sorties students were 'chased' by an instructor in a second Su-22M4.

Oberst Manfred Janichen was the wing's first commander, and he was supported by a deputy responsible for all flying operations, a political officer, navigation leader and a tactical/weapons officer, all experienced MiG-21 pilots in their mid-30s, and by an engineering officer – a total of six executives.

On 1 December 1985, the first of JBG-77's two squadrons was declared 'operational', and in February 1987, the wing was granted the name *Gebhard Leberecht von Blücher*, after the Prussian general who excelled in the war against Napoleon.

The German pilots soon found the big aircraft, 62 ft long and 22 ft high, to which they gave the endearing name of 'Humpback', to be a formidable fighter-bomber. They relished the aircraft's high performance, one recalling that the awesome power of the aircraft in reheat (when it consumed some 25 lb of fuel/sec) allowed a take-off to be continued if, by mistake, the pilot attempted to do so with the wings fully swept back. The aircraft could lift-off at 310 km/hr (170 knots), depending on its fuel and weapons load, and accelerate very rapidly to high and sustainable speeds to give a very steady ride and stable weapons platform at low level. The pilots, comfortable in the roomy cockpit, were equally complimentary about the aircraft's very effective and reliable avionics system, and with this confidence in the aircraft, and all its strengths, JBG-77 always did well in tactical competitions with other Warsaw Pact air forces.

Hans-Joachim Hartwig was among the first of the LSK/LV pilots to be chosen to fly the Su-22. He had undergone the standard pattern of training, starting with GST in 1972, followed by three years at OHS, with 250 hours of flying instruction on the L-29 in the first two years at Bautzen, and 103 hours on the MiG-21F-13 in the third year at Rothenburg. On graduation, his course of pilots was divided into two streams, one to fly the MiG-17Fs with JBG-31 at Drewitz and the other, which included Hans-Joachim, going to the MiG-21MFs of JG-8 at Marxwalde. There he accumulated 171 flying hours in the next two years and became a pairs leader, before being posted to JG-1 at Cottbus, where he converted to the MiG-21SPS. He moved with the wing to Holzdorf in 1982, where his flying became increasingly demanding – with night interceptions and four v four air combat. In 1984, having then flown some 924 hours, he left JG-1 to begin his conversion to the Su-22 at Rothenburg, moving to Laage at the end of the year to complete his transition to the aircraft, and learn the many different skills for the overland and maritime strike/attack and reconnaissance roles.

When Frank Born joined JBG-77 in 1985, he was able to put all the ground-attack skills he had learned on the MiG-17Fs of JBG-31/37 to good use. Armed with a thorough understanding of the aircraft's electronics fit and navigation system, which he said was 'a dream for us', he had no difficulty converting to the 'comfortable', easy to handle, higher performance Su-22 at Laage, and despite spending four years at the very prestigious Lenin Political Military Academy in Moscow, he flew 350 hours on the aircraft before reunification. This was made possible because, while in Moscow, he returned to Laage every six months for a month's intensive flying (and flight simulator checks) – never finding any difficulty re-acquainting himself with the aircraft. He too was delighted with the potential of the aircraft, its excellent forward view in flight and good handling characteristics, which he found similar to those of the MiG-17F – albeit at the higher speeds. Clarifying the capability of the navigation and weapons system, which drew its inputs from the best of several sources available, Frank explained that the flight computer had the capacity to store six targets or 'way points' and four alternative airfields, with lateral optical sights and laser equipment to simplify any changes to them required in flight. All this enabled the aircraft to deliver bombs 'blind', at night or in instrument flying conditions, and recover the aircraft to base on its 'excellent' autopilot down to 60 m

(200 ft) for landing. He recalled that the accuracy of weapons deliveries was impressive and, in 1989, he was one of Laage's Su-22 pilots fortunate to be selected for training with the laser-guided AS-10 'Karen', at Luninez, Belarus, each of the German pilots firing two missiles in three days. JBG-77 also took part in joint exercises with the Soviet MiG-27s at Lärz, and Su-22s at Neuruppin and Templin, and in 1989 participated, with these wings, in Exercise 'Northern Wind'.

Unlike the air defence pilots with their relatively short range MiG fighters, the fighter-bomber pilots at Laage could expect to fly much longer sorties in their Su-22s, delivering a variety of weapons mounted on up to eight pylons without the need to land and re-arm, or up to four sorties a day with OTRs and short transit times to nearby overland or sea ranges. The EGAF also seemed to have had more (invaluable) experience of flying heavy aircraft with full war loads, than did the RAF in Germany during the author's time there. Frank Born was not aware of any specific, pre-planned tasks for JBG-77 in war, as existed for offensive pilots/crews in 2ATAF's contingency plans, but knew that they could have been called on to carry out counter air, interdiction and CAS tasks in support of Warsaw Pact frontal armies. On a few occasions, CAS training was carried out with live weapons (bombs up to 500 kg, 'firebombs' and rockets), on the Soviet range at Wittstock, with some choice of approach direction at low level, for level deliveries or dive attacks, under FAC control. While not a regular feature of JBG-77's training, Frank confirmed that they did practise recce/attack interface, but only within their wing, sending one or more Su-22s ahead of an attack element, to identify suitable targets and pass the positions back to the strike leader, for him to feed them into his nav/attack computers. Despite the practice of carrying a variety of weapons to the ranges for pre-planned routine and exercise training, to maximise the Su-22's relatively long sortie times and ability to carry heavy loads, it seems that there were no plans to exploit this capability with in-flight tasking or opportunity attacks against high value targets found en route to primary tasks – options which were practised regularly by the RAF in Germany.

JGB-77 put their KKR-1 recce sensors to good use by day and night, high and low level; a continuing task being to fly down the length of the IGB, from the Baltic to Czech border, and return, at 9,000 m (30,000 ft), in all weather conditions, recording the electronic emissions from NATO radars out to a range of 200 km (100+ nm). Underlining the importance attached to the aircraft's recce versatility with the KKR-1, it is believed that the NVA had intended to set up a separate reconnaissance squadron of Su-22s – but that this was overtaken by reunification.

JBG-77's token air defence capability was not neglected in operational training programmes. In addition to having simulated missile launches recorded on film, live deliveries of the R-60M missile took place within LSZ-II, but there was no air-to-air gunnery training.

In common with NATO ground-attack pilots, the Su-22s planned to penetrate hostile airspace in war at high speed and the lowest practical height, and to this end the Su-22's navigation and attack equipment was invaluable, its computers being fed with very precise inputs from the RSBN and RSDN, giving accuracies in the order of 10 m (30 ft). This information could then be data-linked or passed by voice via airborne relays, perhaps provided by another Su-22 or a piston-engine An-2, into the Warsaw Pact's C3I air defence networks for action or information.

In general, the EGAF strike/attack wings followed similar work routines to those in the LSK/LV, with executives getting airborne early on flying days to assess the weather and choose one of the three training options planned on the previous day, while groundcrew towed those aircraft scheduled to fly that day to the flight line, from where they would operate until close of play. JBG-77 was not required to maintain the very high readiness states held by the LSK/LV wings, but a percentage of the wing's aircraft and pilots had to be available, combat ready, within given timeframes, and surprise exercises, sometimes including dispersal to reserve airstrips, could be expected at any time to ensure that these requirements were being met. These somewhat reduced levels of preparedness were less detrimental to the lifestyles of all personnel on the offensive wings, but otherwise the fighter-bomber pilots remained subject to the general rules which applied to all EGAF fast-jet pilots. They too attended communal breakfasts, underwent basic medical examinations at the start of every flying day (with serious consequences if there was any evidence of alcohol), a one hour physical training session every 'non-flying' day, regular parachute, survival and fitness training. Hans-Joachim Hartwig remembers the physical demands well. His final test, after one three week spell of mandatory fitness training, involved a triathlon comprising a 35 km (19 nm) cycle phase, a one kilometre swim and a two kilometre uphill/five kilometre downhill run, with any pilot who failed in the time allowed having to repeat – and pass – this test before being released back to the flight line. All this would have been an anathema to RAF combat pilots; other than the need to curtail their drinking and take an annual medical, the RAF pilots had no such requirements. Periodic attempts to introduce regular physical training sessions on the RAF flight lines rarely lasted for long, but most pilots kept themselves fit with some form of active sport, some squadrons and every RAF station fielding rugby, football, hockey, skiing, athletics, swimming, cricket and tennis teams.

Hans-Joachim Hartwig spent the rest of his military career flying the Su-22, his proficiency in the air underlined by his appointment as unit test pilot on the aircraft. He found this role largely uneventful, with an insignificant number of incidents, and indeed remembered only one major accident involving the aircraft on JBG-77. This occurred on 4 September 1987, when one of its single-seat aircraft crashed during an all-arms weapons demonstration for VIPs on an army exercise area near Kleitz (south of Havelberg). This involved a co-ordinated sequence of strafing, delivery of fire bombs and artillery fire, all of which contributed to the noise, smoke and confusion, which may have obscured the probability that the Su-22, flown by Oltn Frank Nösse, had a weapon 'hang-up', resulting in an asymmetric condition which caused Frank to lose control during the recovery and eject – successfully – on his K-36DM seat. Hans-Joachim Hartwig and Frank Born left the air force when the wing disbanded in 1990, with many happy memories of their flying days in the LSK.

Marinefliegergeschwader 28 (MFG-28)

In 1985, a second Su-22 wing formed at Laage, MFG-28 breaking new ground in becoming the first and only fixed-wing offensive unit to be established in the Volksmarine (NVA Navy), but for its first four years it was manned by air force personnel who retained air force ranks and wore light blue air force uniforms. Only in July 1990 did it become a truly naval wing, with its personnel changing into dark blue uniforms with distinctive bright blue shoulder epaulettes and brass propeller insignia to identify the pilots. Upon formal recognition, MFG-28 adopted the mantle of *Obermaat der Kaiserlichen Wieczorek*, the WW1 revolutionary naval aviator. Mirroring JBG-77 in its organisation, it operated on the opposite side of the runway at Laage.

Hannes Mallwitz was one of 20 carefully chosen fighter pilots, all with LK.I or LK.II qualifications, to form the core of MFG-28.

After three months of ground school, he converted to the Su-22 at Laage and made his first flight in the dual aircraft there on 17 December 1985. In 1987, another group of recently qualified German pilots arrived at Laage, having completed the full, three-year flight school and a brief introduction to the Su-22M4 in Russia. They then returned to Germany to join 2.JS/MFG-28 for their operational training, conducted by experienced leaders on the wing, on a mere handful of single and two-seat Su-22s.

When at steady state, the two Su-22 wings were largely identical in their manning and composition, with aircraft allocated from a centralised servicing pool at Laage. However, they worked independently in the air and on the ground, with separate planning and briefing facilities, the pilots invariably flying only with others in their wing, wing or divisional staffs. While both Su-22 wings were trained to carry out overland and maritime tasks, and operated together in joint air/land/sea exercises, JBG-77 would have expected to be committed primarily overland, MFG-28 to maritime support in the Baltic. Accordingly, MFG-28 worked closely with the Volksmarine and other Warsaw Pact navies, their ships at sea and coastal batteries.

Aware of their vulnerability when closing in on heavily armed ships at sea to deliver 'dumb' bombs or unguided rockets effectively, maritime attack pilots of all nations welcomed the alternative of more accurate, low level, 'stand-off' deliveries, made possible by the advent of guided weapons. In addition, MFG-28 used standard ballistic bombs, given the name: 'Topmastbomben-wurf' when dropped some distance from the target at high speed, say 1,000 km/hr (540 knots), from a height of 10–15 m (30–50 ft), for inertia alone to take them the last 800 m (880 yd) to their objective, skimming just under the surface of the water to penetrate the target below a vessel's waterline. The author recalls no such weapon delivery during his time with the RAF's Buccaneer force in 1972. There appears to have been no laser-guided bombs (LGBs) in the EGAF's arsenal, but the Su-22's combined laser range-finder/designator, buried in the nosecone of the fuselage air intake, was used for delivering the AS-10 'Karen' missile fitted with a laser seeker head, either direct to the target or from a loft manoeuvre to bring the missile down vertically on to the target with greater impact/penetration. Within the EGAF Su-22 force, only MFG-28 had the AS-14 'Kedge' TV-guided missile, specifically for ship targets, the pilot required to illuminate the target until impact, using a well-positioned VDU on top right of the cockpit instrument panel. This was interchangeable with a weapons panel for controlling the AR missiles, the largest of which was the general purpose AS-11, credited with a maximum range of 160 km (86 nm). Attacks against the elusive fast-patrol boats, under way at speed, were practised by pairs of Su-22s, with one lofting flares to illuminate the target for 15 seconds while a second attacked with guns or unguided rockets. The Su-22s of MFG-28 were also equipped with R-60 AAMs.

A handful of selected pilots from JBG-77 and MFG-28, in addition to those in JBG-37 and the LSK/LV wings, were trained in nuclear delivery tactics and techniques, using similar delivery profiles to those adopted by NATO nuclear forces (e.g. 'loft' 'laydown', and 'toss'), initially at the Soviet naval base of Baltisk near Königsberg and later also at Peenemünde. This would have enabled the NVA to contribute to a Warsaw Pact nuclear offensive if ordered to do so, but at wing level the NVA pilots were not thought to have taken any part in any nuclear planning, nor were they aware of any pre-planned targets for them with these weapons. War stocks of conventional and 'dumb' weapons, and most training weapons, were held on the Su-22 wings, but some specialised weapons, such as the Precision Guided Munitions (PGMs) and the nuclear stores, would have had to be shipped in or uplifted from Soviet bases, with Soviet technicians then loading them on to the German aircraft, while the pilots were briefed on their tasks – with Soviet officers supervising. The author found no evidence that the NVA groundcrew were instructed in handling nuclear stores.

As in any other air force which operated sophisticated, high performance aircraft, things could go wrong, but the archives suggest that in its relatively short life MFG-28 lost only one aircraft, on 12 December 1989, when Maj Gen Zimmerman became disorientated, lost control and had to eject. Another pilot is reported to have neglected to lower his undercarriage for landing and to have had a very close shave when he allowed his aircraft to alight on its centreline fuel tank and scrape its flaps. Fortunately, the tank was empty and merely left a groove along the runway as he selected afterburner and took off again to subsequently land normally. Technical problems were few, but there were some cases of magnesium fires breaking out in the wheel units, especially if the brakes were applied harshly when a tyre had burst or was otherwise deflated.

While most of the EGAF pilots interviewed seemed to have had little contact with their Russian counterparts during the Cold War, MFG-28 struck up a professional relationship with their Soviet comrades who shared a common commitment in the Baltic, and in the 1980s this led to token exchanges at a social level. Such mutual interests also resulted in detachments from MFG-28 to the Soviet naval base at Kaliningrad on four occasions. Joint air/land/sea exercises, other professional exchanges and social events were more frequent in NATO, indeed, they formed a central plank of its defensive posture. The author recalls that in the two years he served with one fast-jet squadron in Germany, he was included in several detachments to German, Norwegian, Danish, American, Canadian and Dutch air forces, in some cases joining in routine training and flying in mixed formations with the hosts – and always with a cross-fertilisation of ideas on tactics.

In 1987, at the age of 37, OSL Hannes Mallwitz took command of MFG-28 from Oberst Jürgen Roske; little did he know then what the future held in store for the NVA. Then came October 1989, with its cataclysmic events in Eastern Europe, but while the two wings at Laage awaited their destiny, the pilots continued to hone their operational skills in the skies over Germany,

A KKR-1 reconnaissance pod mounted below the fuselage of this Su-22M4, and an SPS 141 ECM pod carried on a pylon below the port wing. *Author/Cottbus Museum*

Although this Su-22UM3K carries an SPPU-22, twin-23 mm, rearward-firing cannon on a port wing pylon, MFG-28 is believed to have operated this weapon solely from the fuselage pylons on its Su-22s. *Author/Cottbus Museum*

Frank Born landed his Su-22M4 at the Soviet Air Base of Templin during the Warsaw Pact Exercise 'Northern Wind' in 1990.
Frank Born Collection

Weapons visible on this Su-22M4 are the SPPU 23 mm cannon, AS-10 'Karen' and R-60 (AA-8 'Aphid'). *Frank Born Collection*

Frank Born welcomes the deputy wing commander of a Polish Su-22M4 detachment at Laage, for a joint exercise.

Frank Born Collection

'Touch and Go': The rapid reaction of this Su-22 pilot saved him and his aircraft from severe embarrassment or a disastrous accident, when he failed to lower his undercarriage for landing. In the event he was able to overshoot and land normally.

Frank Born

Maritime Targets. Partly submerged shipping, off the Baltic coast, provided an excellent target array for the Laage based Su-22s.

Gert Tönnesen-Hoffman

The German Su-22M4s could carry clusters of 50 kg, 100 kg or 250 kg bombs on four MBDT-U6–68–1 racks, together with R-60 IR, self-defence AAMs.

Hans-Joachim Hartwig

A badge of honour, awarded to those who achieved LK.I, the highest of three flying standards recognised in the LSK/LV.

Hannes Mallwitz

191

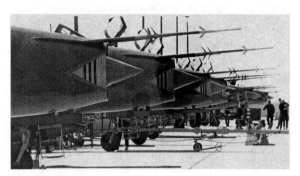

The MFG-28 flight line at Flugplatz Laage.   *Hannes Mallwitz*

An MFG-28 Su-22M4 preparing to leave its dispersal in the south-east corner of Laage, on a reconnaissance sortie with the KKR-1 sensor pod on the fuselage centreline.   *Hannes Mallwitz*

Maj Hannes Mallwitz aboard a Su-22M4 in1985.

Hannes Mallwitz

The cockpit of the Su-22M4 boasts ergonomic tidiness and a good forward view.

Hannes Mallwitz

This display of Su-22 weapons includes (L to R): S-25 ASM; S-24 unguided rocket; UB-32 pod for S.5 unguided rockets; S-8 unguided rockets; GSch-23L, SPPU-22–01 podded cannon; Ch-29T, AS-14 'Kedge' single NR-30 cannon in each wing root (not visible); Kh-25, AS-10 'Karen'; AA-8 'Aphid' AAM; Kh-58, AS-11 'Kilter'; OFAB 500 ChaN (a low level delivery, parachute retarded, 'dumb' bomb). *Hannes Mallwitz*

Maj Hans-Joachim Hartwig, in 'the office'.

Hans-Joachim Hartwig

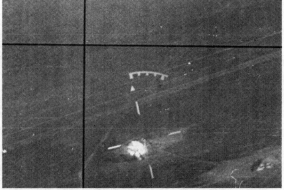

Targets for the Su-22s being towed into position on the sea range. *Hannes Mallwitz*

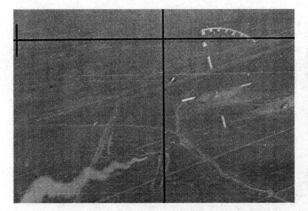

A MFG-28 Su-22 delivers a Kh-25ML laser-guided missile at a target on the Wittstock Rrange. *Hannes Mallwitz Collection*

The Laage Su-22 had plenty of practice against shipping in the Baltic en route, these simulated war targets believed to be from the Eastern Soviet Fleet on exercise in 1987.
Hannes Mallwitz

A pair & a four-ship of Su-22M4 on a training mission from Flugplatz Laage in 1988. *Hannes Mallwitz*

(Above and Below) MFG-28 practises a war dispersal to the grass airstrip at Warbelow, a mere 4 minutes flying time at 16 km (9 nm) from Laage. *Hannes Mallwitz*

Hannes remaining in command of MFG-28, but now with the rank of Fliegerkapitän in the Volksmarine. The Su-22 pilots at Laage made the best of their bitter-sweet final year, visiting old enemies in the West who had become new friends, exchanging information and memories with them and sometimes flying in mixed formations. 'Rolltag', 27 September 1990, was the last full day of flying for the EGAF's Su-22s at Laage, one aircraft from each wing sporting new and very distinctive 'paint jobs' for the sad occasion. On reunification, all the Su-22s were initially absorbed into the Luftwaffe and given new serial numbers, but most were then on borrowed time. The exceptions were the five which were taken on charge by the Wehrtechnische Dienststelle für Luftfahrzeuge 61 (WTD-61), for evaluation at the Aircraft Test Centre, Manching AB in Bavaria; the two which were delivered to the USAF at Ramstein AB, in west Germany, and the one to RAF Scampton, England (reported above), while the Laage's very decorative '798' (25 +44), was given a proud place at the Luftwaffenmuseum Berlin-Gatow.

NVA Attack Helicopters

The development of rotary wing operations in the NVA was both convoluted and protracted, with outsiders perhaps confused by the number of name changes as each component within the force evolved, starting in 1957 with the acquisition of Soviet transport helicopters, some of which were lightly armed. However, this section deals only with the more heavily armed helicopter assault gunships, which had the potential, in particular, to put Allied ground forces and SAM defences along the IGB at risk.

After gaining valuable fixed-wing flying experience in the target-towing force (Chapter Three), Peter Peil began his transition to transport helicopters in 1972, starting with the Mi-4 'Hound' and progressing to the Mi-8 'Hip', on which he later became an instructor with 5.JS/HG-34. In November 1975, he was given command of 1.JS/HG-54, and moved to a base undergoing refurbishment at Basepohl, with four Mi-8T 'Hip C' transport/attack helicopters. The Mi-8T was an armed version of the Mi-8, with a 12.7 mm machine gun in the nose and able to carry up to six pods of S-5 rockets, bombs or anti-tank missiles, mounted on racks either side of the fuselage. When they arrived, Basepohl was 'a sea of mud, with very few facilities', but gradually, with a lot of ingenuity and self-help, conditions improved, to provide a home for the 12 aircraft and 10 pilots of HG-54.

In November 1976, a group of well qualified helicopter pilots, which including Peter Peil, was sent to Kazan, in Tatarstan, to be introduced to the Mi-8TB, which was due to arrive at Basepohl in February 1977 – where a conversion programme was to be conducted by Soviet instructors. The German pilots welcomed the aircraft's ability to carry an impressive war load, and the survivability offered by its armoured cockpit and twin-jet reliability, but found the helicopter very unwieldy and, in some circumstances difficult to handle, especially when heavily loaded. However, it served well to introduce the pilots to the attack role, pending the arrival of the Mi-24D 'Hind'.

In the summer of 1977, Peter Peil was among ten pilots selected to train on the Mi-24, in a programme run by the Russians at Frunze, Kirgistan. This began with a four week ground school, followed by 20 hours flying in the aircraft, with Peter having his first solo flight in a Mi-24 on 4 July 1978. The EGAF Mi-24Ds were ferried to Basepohl by Soviet pilots, and HG-54 was declared 'operational' with the new aircraft in late July, 1978. These heavy lift helicopters were put to good use during the extreme conditions of the winter which followed, flying 144 sorties – including 24 rescue missions – and on 7 October 1979, seven of HG-54's Mi-24s took part in the 'Berlin zum Republik-Geburtstag' (Berlin's Republic's Day). In March 1980, HG-54 was granted the title: *Adolf von Lützo*, and when an additional 18 Mi-24Ds arrived in 1981 the wing was placed on DHS. On 1 December 1981, HG-54 was re-named 'Kampfhub-schraubergeschwader-57' (KHG-57), later KHG-5, within Military District V.

A second helicopter attack wing, KHG-67, came to life at Brandenburg-Briest in 1982, equipped with Mi-8TBs and Mi-24Ds, moving to Cottbus later that year where it came under the command of Military District III, and in 1984 it was granted the name *Ferdinand von Schill*. In addition to their operational squadrons, the two helicopter wings maintained a small force of Mi-2s and Mi-8s for photographic, reconnaissance, communications and liaison duties, and Mi-9s to act as airborne command posts. In 1986 KHG-67 became KHG-3, *inter alia* charged in 1989 with maintaining patrols along the IGB.

The Mi-24 was a quantum jump from the Mi-8 in performance and operational capability. It had entered service with the Soviet Air Force as a multi-role, infantry and armoured support assault transport and gunship, to be used primarily in the CAS role. With a crew of three, the captain sat behind and above the second pilot/weapons operator in the nose, with the crew chief/engineer seated behind them. Armoured cockpits, a titanium rotor head and two (jet) engines improved the aircraft's chance of survival over the battlefield, but losses during the 1980s war in Afghanistan were high, with one result being the retrofitting of all the Mi-24Ds with chaff/flare dispensers below the rear fuselage – and some with IR jammers behind the rotor shaft. As with the Mi-8TB, the Mi-24's main weapons were carried on six stations, above and below stub wings mounted in mid-fuselage. Successive modifications to the aircraft's avionics and weapons systems greatly increased its offensive capability, typically by replacing the wire guided/infra-red AT-2 'Swatter' missile, carried by the Mi-8TB with the more advanced, laser guided AT-6 'Spiral' anti-tank missile, but the helicopter was still able to carry a platoon of troops. A typical war load in the anti-tank role might comprise six AT-6 and two UB-32 rocket pods, adding to the firepower from its twin-barrel, 30 mm cannon mounted in the nose. The Mi-24P 'Hind F', which joined the NVA in the final months of the Cold War, was equipped with an additional twin-barrel, 30 mm cannon on the starboard side of the nose. The crews were proud of their proficiency in weapons delivery, but one admitted that radio controlled missiles could be severely affected by radio interference, deliberate or incidental, this being proved when several of the weapons went astray during one exercise on the Peenemünde Range. While this 'maid of all work' was capable of 368 km/hr (200 knots), and could carry an impressive load of weapons and troops, its high IR signature, lack of agility and armour, rendered it vulnerable to contemporary battlefield air defence systems, and a poor adversary for the American AH-64 attack helicopter with which it was so often compared. A suggestion that the Mi-24 pilots should increase their personal protection by wearing what was effectively a suit of armour, was rejected on the grounds that, at 30 kg (65 lb) it was too cumbersome.

Despite their role being predominantly that of supporting the Warsaw Pact's land forces, the attack helicopter units were placed initially under the command of the two air defence divisions within the LSK/LV, albeit with some of their operational pilots joining army comrades on the ground during joint exercises to ensure their optimum utilisation. Understandably, the NVA army, the 'Landstreitkräfte' (LaSK) argued that the attack helicopters could be used more efficiently and effectively under its command – and this argument prevailed. The helicopters were transferred to the FAFK in 1981, and to the FMTFK in 1984, within an 'Armeefliegerkräfte' (Army Aviation) force, with its headquarters units 'Hubschrauberstaffel der Führung und Aufklärung' (HSFA) and helicopters wings at Cottbus (HSFA-3 and KHG-3) and Basepohl (HSFA-5 and KHG-5). However, to ensure a

smooth handover, and best use of the force, a small number of specialists in helicopter operations from the LSK/LV, including engineers, were transferred to the army staff. Moreover, with their role and the original training and operating procedures unchanged, other than taking on the additional duties of DHS, the two wings retained their own servicing teams and the 'army airmen' continued to wear their air force uniforms.

The *modus operandi* for the NVA Mi-24s, observed during the Cold War (typically by BRIXMIS) and verified thereafter in contributions to this text, revealed the manner in which these helicopters might be employed, with two to twelve aircraft flying several types of formation for penetration and egress, with and without escorts or ECM cover. Unofficial extracts from the NVA's manual for attack helicopter operations outlined four basic, but adaptable and flexible attack profiles, for horizontal approach, dive, pop-up and hover attacks, each catering for particular target arrays, terrain, weapons, weather conditions, the defence environment – and the results to be achieved.

Compared with many of their fixed-wing colleagues, the airmen within the NVA helicopter force tended to have more contact with their Soviet counterparts, frequently taking part in joint exercises which generated a degree of unofficial competition, and Peter Peil remembers one of them well. Both nations had committed their Mi-24s to a joint air/land exercise in the Letzlinger Heide training area, when the weather fell below official limits and the helicopters should have ceased flying but,

The Mi-8TB attack helicopter could be heavily armed with UB-32, S-5 unguided rockets, AT-2 anti-tank missiles and a forward-firing 12.7 mm machine gun, but this made the helicopter very unwieldy in flight.   *Author/Cottbus Museum*

An Mi-8 of 1.JS/HG-54 at Basepohl, in 1978.   *Peter Peil*

This Mi-24 'Hind' is fitted with two canisters of 20 x S-8 unguided rockets inboard, two launcher rails for Malcusta anti-tank missiles outboard, and a target illuminator between the two stores; it could also carry eight fully-armed troops. The cockpit ergonomics were good, with map displays for the two pilots seated one above the other in tandem to give excellent visibility ahead for both. Both had weapon aiming devices, while a 'chin' under the nose contained a TV recorder, for weapon analysis. Late models of the Hind had two, 30 mm cannon attached to the starboard side of the nose.   *Author/Cottbus Museum*

Mi-8s prepare for the 30th anniversary celebration of the GDR, at Müncheberg on 5 October 1979.   *Peter Peil*

An Mi-24 of HG-54 over Flugplatz Peenemünde in 1980.
                                                        Peter Peil

A Mi-24D of KHG-3 at Basepohl.   *Cottbus Museum*

Peter Peil , with his crew, on the occasion of his last flight in a Mi-24 of 1.JS/KHG-67 at Cottbus, on 6 September 1984.
                                                        Peter Peil

acting independently, the Germans launched a weather check which reported that the conditions were 'acceptable', and resumed flying to accomplish their assigned tasks successfully. Not to be outdone, the Soviets retaliated with an impressive firepower demonstration using a much larger force of helicopters, in the same place and the same conditions. Peter Peil ended his career in the NVA as director of air tactics/aerial gunnery at the FO FAFK, while continuing to fly as an instructor pilot on the Mi-24; he transferred to the reserve in 1984.

A number of the NVA's attack helicopters were lost during their service, in a mix of technical, aircraft handling and airmanship accidents. Particularly worrying was the first accident to a Mi-24 of HG-54 in August 1980, all three aboard being killed when 'flexing and waving' of the main rotors caused them to strike the tail rotor when the aircraft pulled up very sharply after a steep descent. Two years later, on 3 June 1982, another Mi-24 drifted into trees in hot, windy weather, and crashed into the Havel, killing the aircraft's captain.

The NVA had invested heavily in armed helicopters, supported by a strong force of airborne C3I, transport and communications helicopters, all working in conjunction with similar assets fielded by the Soviet forces. Whatever their shortcomings, NORTHAG and 2ATAF had no equivalent.

RAFG Strike/Attack and Reconnaissance

As for the offensive component of the RAF in Germany, the Cold War began with obsolescent piston-engine aircraft, progressively replaced by jet-powered de Havilland Vampire and Venom fighter-bombers and Canberra light bombers, the latter with a nuclear capability, while the air defence Sabres and Hunters (Chapter Three) also had ground-attack as a secondary role. The fighter/fighter-bomber force was reduced to four squadrons of Hunters from 1957, but with an increase in the number of Canberra strike/attack bombers, all of which were accommodated on the four new stations in the 'Clutch' (Laarbruch, Brüggen, Wildenrath and Geilenkirchen). In the strike/attack role, four squadrons of Phantom FGR.2s at Brüggen, and two squadrons of Buccaneer S.2s at Laarbruch, took over from the Canberras in the early 1970s, while three squadrons of VSTOL Harriers were based at Wildenrath but spent much of their time in the field supporting NORTHAG in the CAS role, armed with cannon, bombs, CBUs and unguided SNEB rockets. A few years later they were moved to Gütersloh, to be closer to the front line, until the base closed, when they were re-located to Laarbruch, where they remained for the rest of the Cold War. In the mid-1970s, strike/attack Jaguar GR.1s, equipped with cannon, nuclear and conventional bombs, CBUs and LGBs, took over from the Phantoms, which were then re-roled to air defence and transferred to Wildenrath, they too remaining in Germany until the end of the Cold War. Finally, Tornado bombers, equipped with cannon, conventional and nuclear weapons, LGBs and JP.233 runway cratering and airfield denial bomblets, replaced the Jaguars in the mid-1980s.

While remaining in the UK, or at sea

aboard Royal Navy (RN) aircraft carriers, additional Buccaneers might have been involved in strike/attack operations in the Baltic, or use this route to Warsaw Pact targets overland, as might the RAF's V-bomber strike/attack force, again all based in the UK, so these aircraft too would have been of interest to the EGAF. The RAF's Buccaneer S.2 force evolved from 1969, although the RN had been flying the carrier-borne S.1 and S.2 variants at sea since 1961. In its early days the force was armed only with unguided rockets and 'dumb' bombs, the latter employed in co-ordinated attacks using a mix of toss, dive and low-level delivery profiles, exploiting the Buccaneer's ability to carry eight 1000 lb (450 kg) bombs; four in an internal bomb bay, and two on each wing. In extremis, nuclear stores were also available, for use at sea or overland. However, by 1974 the RAF had taken over the maritime strike/attack role from the RN, its Buccaneers equipped with the Anglo-French 'Martel', using either passive radar homing or video guidance. The missile, with a 350 lb (160 kg) warhead, was launched from the relatively safe stand-off distance of 15 nm (28 km) and height of 100 ft (30 m), at a speed of 500 knots (930 km/hr), climbing to and cruising at 2,000 ft (670 m) until it acquired the target, when it descended to low level. A TV monitor and control column in the Buccaneer's rear seat enabled the operator to steer the missile vertically and laterally, initially to assist in target acquisition and then to direct it to a vulnerable part of the target. In the 1980s, the Buccaneer's Martel was replaced by the more powerful 'fire and forget' 'Sea Eagle', a sea-skimming anti-ship missile, powered by a turbo-jet, which had a range of 60 nm (110 km) and a warhead of 510 lb (230 kg). The author operated with a Buccaneer squadron in 1972, and by the time he flew in the aircraft again at the 1982 'Red Flag' in Nevada, USA, the force was enjoying great success with the podded 'Pavespike' laser designator, coupled with the 'Paveway' LGB, the Buccaneer either designating and delivering LGBs itself, or designating the target for other bombers (typically RAF Germany Jaguars and Tornados). While the 'back-seater' operated the designator and helped carry out many of the operational procedures associated with weapons delivery and countermeasures, the pilot could concentrate on (very) low flying, look-out and general flight management – a luxury not enjoyed by the single-seat Su-22 pilot. The Buccaneers were now fitted with self-defence AIM-9B 'Sidewinder' missiles and AN/ALQ 101-8 noise and repeater jammers, which gave high measures of protection. The tactics used by the Buccaneers against fast patrol boats largely mirrored those employed by the Su-22s, with one lofting Lepus flares ahead of another attacking with 2-inch or SNEB rockets, an unenviable task which put the attacking aircraft at great risk from a ship's defence. That said, the Buccaneer was one of the RAF's most potent weapons systems operating in the area during the Cold War.

Discussions with EGAF MiG-21, MiG-23 and Su-22 strike/attack pilots revealed that their modes of attack, for the delivery of conventional and nuclear stores, were similar to those adopted by NATO squadrons during the Cold War. Accordingly, the author has plagiarised a section from 'Air-To-Ground Operations', published in 1987 by the highly respected RAF Jaguar ground-attack pilot, the then Air Vice-Marshal (AVM) John Walker, and what follows is an abbreviated and simplified outline of dive, laydown, loft/toss and stand-off delivery profiles featured therein.

Dive Deliveries. Given clear weather, high angle dive-bombing, when carried out by the relatively slow piston-engine aircraft of WW2 (vide the Ju-87 'Stuka'), was a very attractive choice in terms of target acquisition, weapons' accuracy and penetration, but lost favour with the introduction of high-speed jets, and their vulnerability to increasingly sophisticated SAM and radar-laid AAA defences.

Laydown. In this new air defence environment, laydown offered an attacking aircraft, inbound at, say, 150 ft (50 m), a far greater chance of survival. True, it might have to get closer to identify the target and deliver weapon(s), thus prolonging its run through local defences and perhaps acquiring the target too late, but, given modern navigation and weapons aiming systems, this mode of attack could be very accurate. Strike/attack pilots were trained to use the laydown technique to deliver parachute retarded nuclear or conventional weapons, at high speed and low level, escaping on the same heading to avoid the bomb blast and debris hemisphere, and indeed this was considered to be one of the most accurate of the unguided delivery options – but this mode would not provide an 'air-burst'. Fast and low was also the means of 'sowing' runway cratering and

airfield denial munitions from the RAF's JP-233 and GAF MW-1 containers.

Loft and Toss. In another means of escaping fratricide from the immediate effects of their tactical weapons (including nuclear bombs), and to avoid heavy defences around their targets, 'loft' (release without 'G' applied) and the 'toss' (release under 'G' conditions), manoeuvres were developed, both of which could also provide an air-burst. However, the time of flight (say, 25 sec) and thus wind effect, was much greater than that with laydown deliveries, so less accuracy had to be expected. Also, the pull-up point, say 4 nm (7.5 km) from the target (identified either from a map or by electronic means) was crucial to accuracy. However, the author believes that toss-bombing could have several useful applications, for instance, in the suppression of enemy air defences (SEAD), surrounding heavily defended targets, including shipping underway, as part of a co-ordinated attack sequence.

Stand-Off. The advent of guided missiles, with a variety of active and passive guidance systems, fired out of range of a target's local defences (but subject to diverse counter-measures), added a new dimension to strike/attack operations, with too many scenarios to describe in this work. The author's experience with the first generation Pavespike Laser Designator and Paveway LGB, on the RAF Buccaneer and Jaguar respectively, during Red Flag exercises in the 1980s, showed the way to unprecedented accuracies and high survivability. While modern avionics greatly improve the accuracy of 'dumb bombing', one hit by a

1,000 lb (500 kg) bomb, from a stick of four, might not inflict crucial damage to a pier of a bridge, whereas the synergistic effect of four Paveway bombs, striking almost the same point simultaneously, could be decisive.

Tactical Reconnaissance in RAF Germany

All purpose reconnaissance had been practised by the RAF since WW1, proving invaluable in many conflicts and circumstances since. At the start of the Cold War, the RAF had two Meteor FR.9 squadrons based in Germany, committed to low level, day only tac recce, these obsolescent jets being replaced in the mid-1950s by the Swift FR.5s, the first RAF fast-jet on the front line with reheat. The FR.5 was armed with two 30 mm Aden cannon, internally, and equipped with three F-95 high speed, strip-aperture cameras, in port, starboard and nose-facing stations, for oblique photography at high speeds and very low levels. The aircraft was capable of 600 knots (1,100 km/hr) at low level, and was a great success in the armed reconnaissance role – a winner in several national and international tac recce competitions. One Meteor PR.10 provided high level recce, as did four squadrons of long range Canberra PR.3/PR.7s, able to operate day and night, at high and low level. The Swift was replaced by the Hunter FR.10, which was also fitted with three F-95 oblique cameras but had double the firepower with four 30 mm cannon; it was as fast as the Swift but far more manoeuvrable at all levels, and could compete in combat with most contemporary fighters; it too was a regular competition winner. The Canberras began to

leave Germany at the end of the 1960s, and one squadron of two-seat, day/night recce Phantom FGR.2s replaced the two Hunter FR.10 squadrons in 1970 – single-seat Jaguar GR.1s then taking over from the FGR.2s in 1976. Both of the latter aircraft had reconnaissance sensors packaged within pods slung below the fuselage, an anathema to the author for their added weight and drag, but the Infra Red Linescan (IRLS) and SLAR they carried added a welcome capability. In 1979, the recce Jaguars were replaced by Tornado GR.1s, carrying pods of more advanced reconnaissance sensors, and shortly thereafter this squadron returned to the UK – leaving only a token, day only, low level recce capability with a small number of Harriers configured with F.95 oblique cameras. Two pairs of eyes in the RAF Canberras, Phantoms and Tornados, were a great asset in visual recce, and simplified the rapid reporting of visual sightings, but with repetitive training, the pilots of the single-seat Swifts, Hunters and Jaguars also proved able to provide very helpful visual reports, via a well rehearsed in-flight reporting system. The RAFG recce aircraft also joined forces with suitably armed attack squadrons in 'recce/attack interface' operations, training to find and attack such fleeting military targets as bridging parties, helicopter sites and nuclear convoys, before they had time to disperse. In-flight tasking, or re-tasking, was another option practised by the RAF in Germany. For instance, in the mid-1960s, it was not unusual for a squadron operations cell at RAF Gütersloh to re-task its armed Hunters, already airborne at low level on pre-planned sorties, on to higher priority targets, for reconnaissance or attack, using a communications 'air bridge', perhaps a simple, piston-driven liaison aircraft flying at high level in friendly airspace, to re-transmit new tasks and in-flight reports. Plotting new tasks in the air was no easy matter for the pilot of a single-seat aircraft flying at very low level and high speed, often in the perennially poor weather over Germany, but with practice it too could be highly successful, enabling very rapid reaction between tasking and mission execution, in such short timeframes as to obviate the need for secure communications. Here again, two-man crews had a great advantage, as did those pilots flying single-seat fast-jets with state-of-the art avionics able to accept details of an in-flight task.

RAFG Offensive Summary

All combat-ready RAF recce/strike/attack pilots/crews in Germany were required to pre-plan their assigned war missions in great detail, and to learn every aspect by heart, ready for the frequent tests by national and NATO evaluation teams – and war. RAF aircraft were equipped with British nuclear bombs, stored on each RAF strike station in Germany and the UK, whereas all other NATO nations had American weapons, cared for and released by US custodians resident on each strike base. In war, nuclear stores could only be released from storage and up-loaded with very specific authority from the highest levels in NATO.

While more NATO air-to-ground ranges were available to RAF fighter-bombers based in Germany, than there were for the LSK, most involved long flights, some at high level with very little productive flying *en route*. The major exception was RAF Nordhorn, a multi-purpose strike/attack bombing, rocketing and strafing range, with a long, low level approach from the north to the strike target. Nordhorn lay just inside north Germany on the Dutch border; it was open for use by all NATO aircraft, day and night, with a resident range party and RSOs operating accurate scoring systems. In addition, the Dutch offered the use of ranges on the Friesland Islands, the Belgians in the north-east of the country at Helchteren, and the Germans at Grafenwöhr in Bavaria. Early in the Cold War the RAF ran an air-to-ground range on the German island of Sylt, and later RAFG aircraft flew long distances to several ranges off the coasts of England and Scotland, especially for loft and toss bombing training, had regular detachments to Decimomannu, Sardinia, and took every opportunity to deliver live weapons during exercises in the UK and North America.

The EGAF and RAFG offensive assets, albeit with their different strengths and capabilities, were forces to be reckoned with – now gone but not forgotten.

In the late 1950s, Canberra tactical bombers, gun-armed night interdictors and reconnaissance aircraft joined the RAF 2TAF in North-West Germany.   *RAF Brüggen*

A Hunter FR.10, of No.2 Squadron, on an armed reconnaissance sortie over the Sauerland.   *Hugh Cracroft*

The Swift had a poor reputation as a high level fighter, but the FR.5 was an excellent platform for its F-95 cameras and two 30 mm cannon at very low level and high speed 600 knots (1,100 km/hr). Here, Flt Lt 'Harv' Harvie showed that, with its powerful reheat and huge flaps-cum- air brake, a 'clean' FR.5 could be a spectacular low level aerobatic aircraft.

Author's Collection

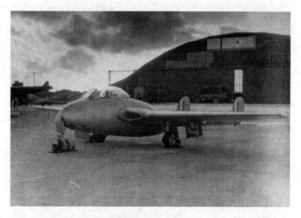

At the start of the Cold War, the RAF jet fighter-bomber contribution to the defence of West Germany consisted of a small force of first generation de Havilland Vampires.   *Dennis Caldwell*

Single-seat Jaguars replaced all the RAFG Phantoms in the ground-attack and recce roles in the mid-1970s. While this Jaguar models AIM-9 AAMs underwing, in the operational fit the missiles were mounted overwing.   *RAF News*

(Left and Above) Four squadrons of McDonnell FGR.2 Phantoms started replacing the RAFG Canberras in 1970, for strike/attack and tac recce, the strike/attack force reinforced by V-bombers from the UK, as required. From the 1960s, all these aircraft trained at low level. *RAF Brüggen*

Three Hawker Harrier VSTOL fighter-bomber squadrons (one with a low level reconnaissance capability) joined RAFG in 1970. Based initially at RAF Wildenrath and later forward at Gütersloh, they spent much of their time in the field (under camouflage and without concrete runways) supporting NORTHAG armies. *12 (Air Sp) Engr Gp*

This flypast to represent the 'teeth arms' of RAFG's contribution to 2ATAF in the early 1970s, comprised three FGR.2 Phantoms in the lead, followed by a Lightning air defence fighter flanked by two Buccaneers, and a Harrier bringing up the rear. *RAF Brüggen*

Two RAFG squadrons operated the formidable, strike/attack Buccaneer at Laarbruch from 1971; the aircraft could be equipped with four 1,000 lb (500 kg) bombs internally, additional stores on wing pylons, and later, AIM-9 'Sidewinder' missiles for self-defence. *Graham Pitchfork*

No.16 (Buccaneer) Squadron, at Nellis AFB, Nevada, USA, acting as 'strike force' in Exercise Red Flag. *Graham Pitchfork*

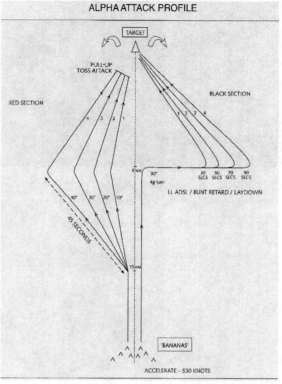

ALPHA ATTACK PROFILE

All the Jaguars and Buccaneers would leave Germany in the early/mid 1980s, to be replaced by eight squadrons of Tornados at Laarbruch and Brüggen; the Brüggen Strike Wing of four squadrons shown here on Runway '28'. *Brüggen Circuit*

One of several 'eight ship' co-ordinated attack options practised by the RAF's Buccaneer force in the 1970s and 1980s. *Graham Pitchfork*

The author (second from right) commanded No.II (AC) squadron, 1964–67, seen here on detachment to the Canadian F-104 Starfighter base at Marville, France. *Frank Mitchell*

RAF Buccaneer over the Baltic, carrying Martel anti-ship missiles. *Graham Pitchfork*

On his final flight on II(AC) Squadron, May 1967, the author led a four v four combat training sortie at high level, and finished with a flypast at RAF Gütersloh. *Jim Diamond*

A No. 237 OCU Buccaneer, equipped with a Pavespike laser designator pod, leading two Royal Navy Sea Harriers, carrying Paveway LGBs to the weapons range. *Graham Pitchfork*

Four Paveway LGBs, launched simultaneously from one Buccaneer and designated by another equipped with Pavespike, about to hit the target. *Graham Pitchfork*

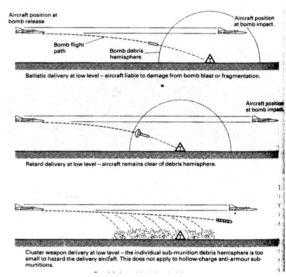

Weapons delivery options. *John Walker*

Bridging parties (Left) and important military units found in the open (Right), would be typical 'opportunity targets' which RAF tac recce pilots might be authorised or use their discretion to attack *Peter Riley & Sandy Burns*

Chapter Seven

Peace Restored

Eternal peace lasts only until the next war

Russian Proverb

After the 'Peaceful Revolution' in the GDR, the fall of the Berlin Wall in 1989 and the first free elections in East Germany in March 1990, came the strong desire among the German people for a unified, democratic Germany – and the restoration of full sovereignty. This was recognised by the former occupying powers in the 'Treaty on the Final Settlement with Respect to Germany' (the 'Two Plus Four Agreement'), signed by the four Allied Powers, the FRG and GDR, in Moscow on 12 September 1990, in which the Allies relinquished all their residual rights in the two Germanies, with reunification to be formalised on 3 October 1990 and the one Germany to become a sovereign state on 15 March 1991. All Soviet forces were to withdraw from the country by the end of 1994, after which the former GDR was to become a 'Nuclear-Weapon-Free-Zone', with the new, single nation confirming its adherence to the Nuclear Non-Proliferation Treaty and renouncing the possession of NBC weapons. The new state also agreed to limit its combined armed forces (Bundeswehr) to a ceiling of 370,000 personnel.

Then came the mammoth task of repatriating 380,000 Soviet troops of the GSFG, with 6,000 main battle tanks and an air army of 2,000 aircraft, together with all the associated equipment and 200,000 dependents. By far the largest Soviet force outside the USSR, the GSFG had occupied 7,000 military sites, 36,000 buildings and hundreds and thousands of hectares of now contaminated training areas, and all these facilities had to be vacated in the very tight timeframe of four years, despite there being insufficient accommodation for a force of this size back in its homeland. Anxious to ensure that this target date be met, Germany offered to provide all reasonable help and to build 36,000 apartments in Russia. In August 1994, a grand parade in Berlin marked the end of a Soviet presence in Germany.

Meanwhile, the NVA faced a traumatic time; any hope of it remaining as a separate entity in the unified German military faded rapidly, with West Germany demanding its complete disbandment but accepting a number of carefully chosen NVA personnel into the Bundeswehr. As a first step, all NVA generals, many senior colonels and officers over the age of 55 were retired at once, while 360 others were retained to join 240 officers and NCOs from the West to head 'Bundeswehrkommando Ost' (Bundeswehr Eastern Command), working from the former East German MOD at Strausberg. The final selection of former NVA personnel applying to continue their military service in the Luftwaffe got underway immediately, during a major re-organisation of the Bundeswehr. Seventy percent of the 26,000 officers and NCOs who were offered probationary periods of two years, while their credentials were checked and their performance evaluated, were finally accepted. The successful candidates were then given a three month transition course to acquaint them with the disciplines and protocols which differed from those with which they had been accustomed in the NVA, and some had to accept a lower rank because of their relatively young age. Of those rejected while on probation, some were found to have belonged to the Stasi, and were now *persona non grata,* while others could not acclimatise to the different culture, mentalities and leadership styles in the West, or give their full co-operation. Writing in the British Journal of the Forces Pension Society 'Pennant', Bundeswehr Brigadier General Victor Wilcken spoke of the success of Bundeswehrkommando Ost in bringing two great armies together in an enduring harmony. This was not an occupation by the Bundeswehr, nor a victory by one army over the other; it was a result of the political will of the majority of the East German people who voted with a clear majority for the reunification in the free elections of May 1990.

In addition to its responsibilities for the residual NVA, the Bundeswehr Eastern Command was charged with assisting the departure of the GSFG and the disposal of all surplus equipment from the NVA, including aircraft and major weapons systems from all three military arms. Of the 390 fighter aircraft in the NVA, only the two squadrons of the recently acquired MiG-29s, which had served briefly with JG-3 (Chapter Four), were retained for use operationally, moving from Preschen to join JG-73 'Steinhoff' at Laage in 1993, while several of the more advanced fighters, typically MiG-23s, were taken to the West for evaluation – and a number of transport helicopters remained in use with the Luftwaffe.

With the collapse of the Warsaw Pact, the RAF began withdrawing its part of NATO's defensive shield in Germany. In 1993, RAF Gütersloh was the first operational base to go, its Harriers and transport helicopters falling back first to Laarbruch, its Tornado squadrons leaving for the UK or disbanding, before that station too – and RAF Wildenrath – closed. RAF Brüggen was the last to go, bringing to an end a major RAF presence in Germany since 1945, a presence which contributed to a successful conclusion to the Cold War.

Together Again. East German pilots, formally of JG-1, dine with their new comrades of JaBoG36, at Hopsten AB in West Germany; Jürgen Gruhl and his opposite number at Hopsten exchanging tokens of mutual respect. *Jürgen Gruhl*

Klaus Schmiedel's last flight in a GAF MiG-29; 24 March 1993. *Klaus Schmiedel*

In common with other LSK wings, this Su-22M4 of JBG-77 was suitably dressed for the Wing's disbandment.

Hans-Joachim Hartwig

Sqn Ldr Gary Thomas was the host for this visit to RAF Brawdy, UK, by L-39 operational trainers and a MiG-23ML of the Czech Air Force in 1991. *Geoff Lee via Gary Thomas*

This MiG-21UM of JG-8 was still going strong when the wing disbanded in 1990. Author's Collection

Lieutenant Colonel Rudolf Mullër, now in the Bundeswehr, presented with a certificate to mark his first flight in a MiG-29 at Laage in 1998. *Rudolf Mullër*

Ready for its brief life in the Bundeswehr, this MiG-21 of JG-1 now bears the GAF cross and serial number. *Jürgen Gruhl*

Hannes Mallwitz led two Su-22M4s and one Su-22UM3K to their new, albeit temporary home at Manching.
Hannes Mallwitz Collection

Change of Allegiance: the formidable MiG-29 and infamous East German Trabant car. *Rudolf Müller Collection*

(Right and Below) In the final year, the Su-22 pilots of Laage enjoyed their flying, including joint sorties with the old friends and new allies.
Hannes Mallwitz Collection

An RAF Tornado, from one of the four bomber squadrons at RAF Brüggen, taxies in front of a visiting Czech Air Force MiG-29 in 1994. *Brüggen Circuit*

New Tricks: Commander of the Budapest Air Defence Region, Col Attila Kositzki (Left) welcomes Sqn Ldr Archie Liggat, OC 234 Squadron RAF, from a ground breaking dissimilar air combat training sortie: Hawk v MiG-21, with Lt Col Sando Gal, Head of Flight Safety, Hungarian Air Force, on 12 August 1993. *Archie Liggat*

Listen Up: No.234 Squadron pilots learn to operate in Hungarian airspace. *Archie Liggat*

This MiG-23ML, seen at Laage in January 1991, remains well decorated for its farewell to JG-9, with the new serial 20–26, but with the unified Luftwaffe's distinctive cross yet to be added. *Andreas Dietrich*

In 1993, Frank Born met an old friend from their time together at the Lenin Air Force Academy in Moscow, Soviet Lt Col Hermann Gaedke, commander of an Su-24MR reconnaissance wing at Welzow, in the former GDR, shortly before that wing deployed to Chechnya. *Frank Born Collection*

Post-reunification, this ex-EGAF Su-22, carrying the anti-radar missile AS-11 'Kilter', was evaluated by the Luftwaffe at Manching, Bavaria. *Frank Born Collection*

Chapter Eight

Military Realities

For the first time I have seen 'History' at close quarters, and I know that its actual process is very different from what is presented to Posterity

General Max Hoffman

Ten years of research, comparing archive material with personal testimonies from combat pilots who served with the EGAF and RAF in north Germany, has questioned a number of the precepts which conditioned Cold War thinking in the respective camps, and on which the Warsaw Pact and NATO may have based some of their defence strategies and tactics in exercise scenarios. The author now returns to some of these conventional wisdoms, to test their validity against what now seem to be the military realities of the day. In this he has drawn again on the invaluable help of Oberst Gert Overhoff, a former GAF fighter and fighter-bomber pilot and Oberst Hans-J Barakling, another retired GAF officer who offered some personal views on the Russian military psyche, gained in his final years of military service as the West German Air Attaché in Moscow. At the outset Hans made the point that, despite Soviet dominance within the Warsaw Pact, its thinking, military structures and practices may not have been replicated to the letter throughout the alliance, with some member nations retaining aspects of their military traditions – provided these did not run counter to the central political dogma. Above all, Hans warned that the Soviet leaders should not have been underestimated; at least until the early 1980s the top military leaders had WW2 combat experience, and remained driven by the historical threats to their homeland – memories of the German invasion in WW2 continuing to haunt them. Accordingly, they had deployed strong military forces throughout the GDR, within striking distance of the IGB, in effect creating a buffer state against any aggressive move from the West. With no overarching political determinate, NATO's defensive posture, while led by the Americans, was based largely on consensus, but both alliances purported to fear a pre-emptive attack, hence the rationale for the EGAF's DHS and NATO's QRA (Chapters Three and Six) – but what was the likelihood of such attacks?

It is hard to believe that those at the helm in the Warsaw Pact, with easy access to their many informants imbedded in Western Europe (some covertly) watching every NATO military activity, and many other intelligence sources, believed that a surprise attack on them was likely, or even possible, so why such high states of readiness? To a man, the EGAF officers interviewed had been persuaded that their homeland was seriously threatened by NATO, with the West bent on destroying communism in the GDR and reunifying Germany – an anathema to the GDR's leaders and their Soviet overlords. They pointed to the very large number of strike/attack fighter-bombers and light bombers based in Germany as an earnest of NATO's aggressive intentions. The author did not dispute the numbers, but argued that this was simply because NATO viewed offensive action in the air as one of the best means of offsetting the numerical superiority of the combined Warsaw Pact forces, on the ground and in the air, in the Central Region of Europe. Given that air defence could never be fully effective, and that NATO ground forces, in place, could have had great difficulty countering a surprise attack by the Warsaw Pact, the UK had taken a political decision to reduce the number of its air defence fighters in Germany from 283 in 1957, to 24 in 1965, and to increase its strike/attack contribution to 2ATAF. The addition of strike/attack and reconnaissance Canberras, either assigned or earmarked to SACEUR, and their subsequent replacement by multi-role fighter-bombers, did not imply a 'first use' option; this was essentially a deterrent or retaliatory force. Deterrence was also the name of the game during the Cuban crisis of October 1962, when the Allies placed its forces, including large numbers of strategic and tactical nuclear bombers, on high alert,

and had pilots in the cockpits of fighters at the end of runways – all thinking the unthinkable.

Having been responsible, at his level, for conventional and nuclear offensive operations in 2ATAF, and thus privy to some highly classified NATO defence plans, the author has no hesitation in firmly refuting any suggestion that NATO had plans to cross the IGB into the GDR, on the ground, in strength. True, NATO air power could, and almost certainly would have been used in war, of necessity, in reconnaissance and strike/attack missions across the IGB, in attempts to reduce the impact of Warsaw Pact air power, and slow any advance by their ground forces into the FRG. Again, however, this would have been no more than the use of offensive means for defensive purposes. Incidentally, on one exercise to demonstrate the adaptability and flexibility of its air power, 2ATAF used all the aircraft within its inventory, with even a token air-to-air weapons capability, in the air defence role, to help counter a simulated attack on the FRG by a Warsaw Pact fighter-bomber force. They proved able to integrate seamlessly into the overall air defence system, with its dedicated air defence fighters, SAM belts and point defences, in a scenario which also tested the de-confliction of their respective operations to avoid fratricide. So the reality was that NATO had no intention of mounting a pre-emptive attack on the GDR, and it may be that the perception instilled there, of a threat from the West, was as much a political expedient as a military contingency, seeking to ensure the collective loyalty within the Pact and to spur the NVA on to ever greater efforts? Whatever the real reason, it certainly seemed that the EGAF, at least, was convinced that their homeland was at risk – and they prepared as best they could for the worst.

Did the Warsaw Pact have any intention of invading the FRG? None of the EGAF officers interviewed admitted knowing of any plans to do so, or spoke of any practice deployments by their squadrons to bases in the west of the GDR, where they would have been better able to follow up and support such an offensive. However, Hans Barakling believed that the strong Soviet political and military presence in the forward areas of the GDR had more than an ideological dimension in expressing an enduring conviction that, if a third world war could not be avoided, the Warsaw Pact strategy must be to take the fight to the West, and exercise plans were found to that end. Despite comforting and convenient assurances from the NATO intelligence community, that they would have been able to give adequate warning of any impending attack by the Warsaw Pact, there were those in NORTHAG and 2ATAF who remained unconvinced, given the formidable array of military might facing them – and too close for comfort. From the evidence available it seems that, with little or no warning, a combined Soviet and NVA force could mount an attack on a relatively weak sector of NORTHAG's front line, with some chance of success – and NATO would have been unwise to ignore the possibility.

It is no secret that, whether for offence or defence, the Warsaw Pact sought over-whelming superiority in numbers of men and machines, the GSFG alone comprising some 24 divisions of 340,000 men in five land armies and an air army, mainly concentrated in the Brandenburg region, between Berlin and the IGB. At one time they were equipped with up to 4,000 tanks, 8,000 other armoured vehicles, 3,000 guns and 1,400 aircraft (of which 700 were helicopters), based on 47 airfields spread throughout the GDR. To this could be added the NVA land, sea and air forces of 170,000 personnel, equipped in 1990 with 760 aircraft, 200 ships, 2,700 tanks and 2,200 guns. In the 1980s, in north-east Germany, the NVA, Soviet 2nd Guards Tank Army and the 3rd Shock Army had twelve divisions within easy reach of the IGB, some estimates at the time giving the Soviet/NVA ground and air armies a superiority of 2.5:1 in tanks, 3:1 in artillery pieces, 4:1 in APCs and 9:5 in combat aircraft. As if this imbalance was not daunting enough, it could have been greater in the event of a surprise attack, when the NATO forces might not all have been in position or at full strength. In particular, the front lines in the northern and southern corps areas of NORTHAG, for which the Dutch and the Belgians were responsible, respectively, were undermanned in peace-time, their corps being heavily reliant in on strong reinforcements from their own countries and sufficient warning for them to take up their defensive positions. While the German and British Corps might have been up to strength, a number of units were garrisoned some distance from their assigned defensive positions, and in the 1980s, one of the UK's four divisions returned to the UK, where it was held at readiness to return to Germany if needed. Likewise, a very strong III (US) Corps, earmarked to reinforce NORTHAG, while ready to move at very short notice from its Fort Hood base in Texas, with all its personal equipment, had to be flown to airfields around the Ruhr to pick up their heavy weapons and transport from 'POMCUS' (Pre-positioning of Material Con-figured in Unit Sets), sites before moving to the front line. This plan was rehearsed in annual 'Reforger' exercises, in which the author, who was responsible for providing offensive air support, witnessed this huge US force (three divisions scheduled to arrive in the first week) thunder across Germany to their pre-planned positions on the IGB. In addition, hundreds of RAF and US combat aircraft would move to airfields on the Continent, helping to redress the numerical superiority of in-place Warsaw Pact air assets. Typically, three USAF A-10 'tank buster' squadrons of the 81st Tactical Fighter Wing, based at Bentwaters/Woodbridge in the UK, were expected to deploy rapidly to prepared sites in north Germany. Again, however, ample warning time was crucial if NORTHAG/2ATAF was to respond in time, and with sufficient assets, to arrest a heavy Warsaw Pact armoured thrust into the North German Plain, perhaps using nuclear weapons – an option which they are now known to have rehearsed.

The 4 July 1994 edition of 'Time International' carried an article entitled 'The Plan For World War III', written by James Jackson in Brussels, the central hub of NATO; which was based on plans found at the NVA headquarters at Strausberg, supported by detailed maps, postulating a surprise attack by Warsaw Pact ground and air forces on Western Europe. These plans and other archive material suggest that half a million Warsaw Pact troops were held at readiness in the GDR for this purpose, throughout the Cold War. Conscripts formed a high proportion of this manpower, spending much of their time on exercise or confined to barracks, in frugal conditions and on strict physical training regimes which deterred heavy drinking or fraternization with the local people – a far cry from the freedoms enjoyed by their opposite numbers in NATO. General Jorg Schönbohm, the first com-mander of Bundeswehr Eastern Command, post-reunification, revealed that new traffic signs had been prepared to help speed the Pact's advance westwards, while 3,000 com-munist officials had been earmarked to administer the newly occupied FRG, once the dust had settled, and that a new currency, *Besatzungsgeld,* had been printed to replace the *Deutschmark.* Other raid plans, left behind by the Soviet Air Force when it departed from the GDR, underlined their numerical superiority in aircraft, with the possible use of very large numbers of aircraft to attack NATO airfields. For example, one plan suggested that 47 Su-25s were ear-marked to attack the GAF base at Oldenburg, when it was home to the Alpha-Jets of FBW-43.

Further evidence that the Warsaw Pact had seriously considered the option of advancing westwards was found by NATO officers who gained early access to head-quarters and units from which the Soviets and NVA had operated. Among their more interesting discoveries was a sophisticated, computerised synthetic training facility, 'Operative Ausbildungszentrale' (OAZ). This once top secret and highly secure building, located within the compound of the East German MOD in Strausberg, consisted of a huge, three-dimensional floor plan, displayed in a four feet deep basin, measuring 33 ft by 50 ft (10 m x 15 m), overlooked by tiered balconies for high-ranking players (generals and politicians), distaff and observers. For eighteen months after reunification, the whole facility became the home of the German Liaison Detachment with the Soviet Forces, later the 'Western Group of Forces' in Germany, who named the map basin the 'Swimming Pool'. Topographical details were correct, in a three dimensional model to illustrate any difficulties in surface transit and to show where terrain masking could give aircraft an extra degree of security. Warsaw Pact and NATO force levels and dispositions were brought up-to-date on a daily basis, and Soviet 'advisers' were present throughout all exercises. Significantly, the floor plan stretched from the Polish border on the Oder/Neisse west to the Channel ports, and from Italy north to Scandinavia – clearly suggesting that this would be the battleground. There was no cover east of the GDR. The facility was used primarily for training senior NVA officers from the three armed services and to give high level political representatives an insight into battle management. None of EGAF officers interviewed admitted knowing about the 'Swimming Pool' – but it was a reality.

Within the Warsaw Pact, military activity in the field was grounded on an extensive programme of academic, political and specialist training at the OHS, similar to that at the RAF College, Cranwell, in the early decades of the Cold War – but without the politics. Hans Barakling also noted a heavy investment by the Soviets, and by example the NVA, in additional staff training for its few 'chosen men'. These 'politically suitable' men could expect intensive training in staff work, 'leadership' and politics, at academic establishments in Russia and the GDR. Frank Born was one; he spent four of his five final years of military service on JBG-77 at the prestigious Lenin Political Academy in Moscow, albeit with intensive refresher flying on the Su-22 at six monthly intervals (Chapter Six). Political instruction also remained high on the agenda throughout an average front line pilot's career in the EGAF, but otherwise they concentrated on their specialisations, seemingly with 'need to know' a common theme. By comparison, many more RAF officers received additional staff training at several levels in their careers, and were encouraged to expand their interests in all aspects of their profession – and well beyond into all military and international affairs. There was also a marked difference between the RAF and EGAF in the training of specialists in the air, the RAF providing special courses for QFIs, IREs, QWIs *et al*, while the EGAF selected the best pilots from within the wings for these instructional roles. In war, the relative value of these two approaches to the training of combat pilots could not, of course, be tested in isolation of myriad other factors.

Good flying and ground training in peacetime would amount to little in war if it were not related directly to – or indeed driven by – a realistic appreciation of the true threat. Chapters Three and Four leave little doubt that the EGAF fighter pilots were very capable of getting the best out of their equipment, particularly when intercepting subsonic and supersonic targets in the middle and upper airspace – but in reality there was little chance of them finding NATO targets at those heights in war. In the 1960s, the widespread introduction of SAM, new AAA systems and improved radars, required the strike/attack forces on both sides of the Iron Curtain to approach, attack and egress their targets at low level – thereby greatly increasing the problems for air defence forces. The war in Vietnam (1964–1975), in which the same or similar weapons were used to those deployed in Europe at that time, albeit with different procedures for that environment and with other operatives, showed that while the upper airspace had become a very dangerous place, 'low level' was no panacea to safe and effective air operations. General principles applied in both cases, with fighter aircraft complemented by SAM in the upper airspace and advanced AAA, of all calibres, posing great risk to low flying aircraft. Indeed, all the author's friends lost from his RF-101 'Voodoo' wing when it went to war in SEA, fell to the guns. NATO pilots respected the American experience in SEA, and learned from it, their offensive planning and training avoiding repetitive use of otherwise attractive routes, a 'gate'

mentality and regular, predictable flying schedules. Where possible, tactics were varied, large attack packages rejected in favour of small, well co-ordinated elements, using separate routes to common targets. To their advantage, they enjoyed a great deal more low flying practice than did the LSK in the GDR, being able to operate at 500 ft (150 m) over much of West Germany and 250 ft (75 m) in specific areas, while in parts of the UK and North America they could be authorised down 50 ft (15 m). While none of this could guarantee their safety, the RAF remained convinced that, pending significant improvement in navigation equipments and more comprehensive ECM support, they had no sensible alternative but to operate their offensive aircraft at low level in Europe. For their low flying, other than for specific exercises, the EGAF offensive aircraft were generally restricted to 300 m (1,000 ft) agl on a number of routes in the GDR, routes with which the pilots became all too familiar and were therefore of limited training value. However, BRIXMIS and NVA sources reported seeing Soviet and NVA aircraft flying in other areas, well below that height and in poor weather, as they would have been expected to in war.

Earlier chapters have stressed the difficulty, given the physical problems inherent in contemporary, ground based radars, of detecting low flying aircraft in time to effect successful interceptions. Soviet fighter pilots in the GDR were thought to have trained with their AWACS aircraft, starting with a modified An-26 'Curl' and later the A-50 'Mainstay', but no evidence was found that this training was made available to the NVA. So, at least pending the use of AEW, AWACS and the introduction of effective 'look-down/shoot-down' weapon systems, other means were sought to provide early warning of incoming intruders, and in the GDR it is said that these included a network of visual observers sited near likely NATO penetration routes, typically in the Harz mountains and on the island of Rügen. With some knowledge of the routes, the author noted the accuracy of these predictions, and wondered whether this was a result of good covert intelligence, astute professional analysis or 'guesswork'? Equipped with simple but effective communications, these observers were required to pass visual sightings of low level intruders into the C3 network, to supplement any sporadic radar traces, in the same way as communist spotters contributed successfully to the air war over North Vietnam. There were also reports that both the Soviet Air Force and the EGAF planned to employ CAPs on these suspected routes, and that they practised these procedures using the NVA's L-39s to simulate NATO fighter-bombers. While an expensive tactic in aircraft utilisation, with little hope of high success rates, anything which might distract a strike/attack pilot from his well-laid plans, especially during weapons delivery, could have been worthwhile. Despite these measures, the author's team concluded that the LSK/LV may not have given the predominant low level threat a sufficiently high priority in on-going pilot training, the exception perhaps being JG-9 at Peenemünde, which guarded the Baltic approaches with the MiG-23MF/ML, and

when the MiG-29 joined JG-3, to make use of their 'look-down/shoot-down' capability. As for the RAF in Germany, their air defence squadrons continued to adapt their CAP and 'Rat and Terrier' procedures throughout the Cold War, with each development in radar systems and fighter aircraft (Chapter Three), again emphasising the need to integrate and de-conflict the three defensive systems (fighters, SAM and AAA) to avoid fratricide.

Chapter Three outlined the EGAF's extraordinarily meticulous and highly supervised planning for every training sortie, each of which had very clear objectives and underwent exacting post-flight analysis, to extract maximum value from the relatively few flying hours available, and ensure that little or no time was wasted in the air. Also, the final choice of the best of the three tasks planned the previous day was left to the wing executive flying the morning weather check, with the result that very few sorties were aborted because of unsuitable weather conditions, while spare aircraft were invariably available to replace those which went unserviceable on start-up. Much has been made of the relative paucity of flying by EGAF fast-jet pilots, to wit half the number of hours recorded by their NATO contemporaries, but Chapter Three suggests that it would be wise to look closely at the content of these totals, what was achieved and how the times were recorded. To conclude that 'a NATO pilot must have been twice as well trained as one in the EGAF' could be a calumny.

Critics like to point to a possible loss of individual initiative inherent within the

LSK's rigid plans and the strictly regulated system, but the author's team heard anecdotal evidence from the German MiG pilots, some of which is recorded in Chapters Four and Six, which tends to refute this. Assuming that the time consuming practice of such detailed planning in the LSK would have succumbed to the pressures for immediate air support in war, would the pilots have been up to the challenge? The RAF in Germany always assumed that there would be little time for planning, and on two of the author's front line squadrons it was usual to allow a single-seat pilot 30 minutes only to plan an armed recce sortie, to cover three targets on unrehearsed low level routes out to a radius of 180 nm from base. With 'flexibility' their *sine qua non,* they were also trained to accept airborne re-tasking and many possible eventualities in the air, improvising as they skirted around unacceptable weather and reverting to alternative or reversionary modes of navigation and weapons delivery when primary systems failed.

Also crucial to operational effectiveness on both sides would have been good C3I systems and facilities, and above all battle managers at every level with the right experience (preferably on the front line), training, personal qualities and an ability to respond to the unexpected. Centralisation of authority at high level may have been a guiding principle in the Warsaw Pact, but Hans Barakling thought it unwise to assume, as did some in NATO, that delegation of authority, leadership and individual initiatives would be lacking at the lower levels of command and in the air within the NVA. In peacetime, both sides rehearsed their C3I procedures and operational tasks regularly in 'live' and synthetic exercises, the scenarios attempting to simulate all possible contingencies. Radar and R/T would be jammed, key personnel and C3 nodes 'eliminated', all players, airfields and barracks subjected to incessant NBC and conventional weapons attacks, incurring large number of realistic casualties. While these events sought to stretch all personnel to the full, reveal shortcomings and prompt remedies, the extent to which this was achieved in the NVA could not be verified.

Many western pundits were inclined to believe that the very comprehensive Soviet-style command and control system was too cumbersome and inflexible to maximise the potential of the considerable assets it had to hand. Accordingly, Chapter Five examined this issue in some detail. Immediately evident was the enormous redundancy within the total Soviet and NVA fighter control network across the GDR, compared with that within 2ATAF. Even in the early 1950s, pilots of high flying RF-100 Super Sabre reconnaissance fighters, which sped across the GDR at supersonic speeds, expressed their astonishment at the number of radar spokes picked up by their Radar Warning Receivers (RWR), in a network which continued to develop rapidly thereafter with regular up-dates in the Soviet equipments. Moreover, in theory at least, all these radars were mobile, making them difficult to target, whereas the Pact would have had no difficulty acquiring the four well known and very visible NATO

Tp.80/Tp.13 static radar sites in 2ATAF – which must have been primary targets in the Warsaw Pact's initial offensive counter-air plans. It was the profusion of radars in the GDR which led some in NATO to foresee misunderstandings and confusion in war, and the author, who had been part of the Fighter Command Taceval team evaluating the UK air defence radar system in the UK in the 1960s, put this allegation to the former LSK/LV fighter controllers at the sites he visited. They were at pains to point to the very clear guidance established to avoid this possibility, guidance which had been tested rigorously in periodic exercises and evaluations. They also stressed that all the controllers and future commanders of the LSK/LV had cleared many hurdles in their initial training for their roles, beginning at the OHS and continuing with demanding on-the-job training and testing on operational equipment at dedicated C3I nodes.

Flight safety also impinges on overall military effectiveness, in that injury, damage or loss directly affect the number of aircraft and pilots/crews available for combat, and it would be wrong to believe that the Warsaw Pact accepted losses due to aircraft accidents as 'operational hazards', any more than did NATO or the RAF. Indeed, their peacetime flight safety measures were stringent, to a degree that might be thought to have hampered realistic operational training, although their pilots could have been expected in war to pursue their military objectives with great determination, stubbornness and courage, persisting until they achieved the results required –

history has proved as much. Hans Barakling referred the author to a paper published by the MOD in Moscow in 1976, which called for a balanced approach to flight safety, with realistic operational training to simulate, as far as possible, the risks and hazards of tactical flying at extreme low levels and very high speeds – and in all weather. The paper went on to describe the loads imposed on a pilot within these operating parameters, upon his cardiovascular system, typically manifest in early fatigue, weakening vision and emotional stress, resulting from the demands of aircraft control and orientation, target detection and weapons aiming – compounded by the need to monitor cockpit instruments, radar warnings etc. It claimed that more than two seconds were needed, at speeds of 1,000 km/hr (540 knots) to transfer attention from the ground ahead to interpret internal instruments correctly, during which time the aircraft could cover ½–1 km (1,000 yd), a detail probably known to few if any RAF pilots who regularly trained at those speeds and heights in (simulated) hostile airspace. Contrary to the conventional wisdom in the West, that the individuality held so dear in the RAF was likely to defer to the primacy of central authority in the Soviet/NVA military, the paper espoused the virtues of courage and encouraged individual initiative – with a readiness to take decisions. Flight safety was also treated very seriously within NATO, albeit with member nations according it different priorities, and this was reflected in live flying exercises, with wide variations in their success rates against the tasks they were set, those partners adhering strictly to the rules perhaps losing the expertise and willingness to circumvent problems.

The primary role of the LSK/LV was to contribute to the overall Soviet/EGAF air defence system. Some of the German pilots spoke of specific tasks for them in protecting the crossings over the Oder/Neisse River (the border with Poland), high value targets in the Dresden area and (together with the Czech Air Force), the airspace over the Erzegebirge mountains. However, the part they would have played, if remaining in situ on their home bases rather than deploying to Soviet airfields in the west of the GDR as the battle moved westwards – as had to be expected – would surely have diminished, and with none rehearsed, there may have been no plans for such a move? As for the two EGAF fighter-bomber wings (JBG-31/37 and JBG-77), they too were likely to have been absorbed into combined Warsaw Pact offensive plans, as part of joint operations with other Pact forces or operating independently, but again the author's team was unable to ascertain exactly how they might have been employed. There was no evidence that the pilots had pre-planned strike/attack tasks or standing options, as did all the NATO offensive pilots/crews, who were involved from the start, responsible for planning their sorties, then memorising their routes and all the associated details. Up-dating the threats they might encounter *en route* and regular map study was indeed a major part of their regular ground training, whereas no MiG or Sukhoi pilot questioned appeared to have had access to

maps of likely operating areas west of the IGB. Some pundits claimed that the Warsaw Pact favoured the commitment of small attack packages against targets such as airfields, but this runs counter to the discovery of Soviet raid plans, believed to have been authentic, which pointed to the use of very large numbers of offensive aircraft and escorting fighters, but whether these would have involved LSK aircraft remains unknown. Several EGAF fighter-bomber pilots believed that they were most likely to have been tasked in the Offensive Air Support (OAS) campaign to support their ground forces, in the Battlefield Air Interdiction (BAI), CAS and recce roles, with many of these sorties controlled by Soviet or NVA FACs, and this was practised in peacetime. In this the German pilots could have encountered a practical problem, with only those who had trained or attended staff courses in the Soviet Union able to react effectively to any complex orders given in Russian – the remainder perhaps knowing little more than the basics. It was very rare for NATO pilots or control agencies to have language difficulties – with the great majority of aircrew speaking good English.

The RAF offensive support pilots in Germany were well aware of their specific duties and the priorities for their employment to make best use of their capabilities, but they also understood that, in extremis, they could have been used in tasks for which they were less well equipped. For instance, a Tornado crew was likely to be committed against counter-air or interdiction targets, and indeed had targets earmarked for them and planned by them, but if enemy armour had broken out on to the North German Plain they could have been diverted to help counter them in OAS roles. Those LFK/LV airfields situated close to the Polish border (Peenemünde, Marxwalde, Drewitz, Preschen and Rothenburg) arguably lay beyond the sensible operational range of most of 2ATAF's fighter-bombers carrying realistic combat fuel and useful war loads which would, in any event, have had higher priority targets in the west of the GDR (eg. Soviet nuclear assets). The Su-22 and MiG-23BN strike/attack bases at Laage and Drewitz, might, however, have been of concern to NATO, and indeed, in exercises, the author recalls tasking a large (for 2ATAF) force of Tornados against Laage.

Chapter Six makes much of the diverse capabilities of the heavily armed Mi-8 transport helicopters and the formidable Mi-24 assault gunships, the latter able to carry up to eight fully-equipped troops and armed with a wide variety of cannon, free-fall bombs, unguided rockets and anti-tank missiles primarily, it is assumed, for use in the OAS tasks. Despite the impressive credentials of these helicopters, and their presence in strength close to the IGB, some in NATO downplayed the threat they posed, citing their lack of manoeuvrability, especially when heavily loaded, their vulnerability to small arms fire (they certainly suffered high attrition rates during the Russian war in Afghanistan), and a notion that they neither flew at ultra low level, nor risked flying in poor weather. This surprised the NVA airmen and some within BRIXMIS

who had seen these Mi-8s and Mi-24s operating tactically at very low levels, in packs of up to 12 aircraft, delivering their weapons effectively in poor weather, and the author's team concluded that the Mi-24s, in particular, were a potential threat to NATO's ground forces, including the anti-aircraft defences (SAM and AAA) on the IGB.

These helicopters, when found in numbers on the ground, made very vulnerable and attractive targets, and at times could have been of such importance as to justify offensive sorties against them as primary targets, and this was rehearsed in both synthetic and live flying NATO exercises. Their home bases, typically Cochstedt, Mahlwinkel and Stendal (Soviet) and Basepohl, Cottbus and Brandenburg-Briest (NVA), were well known, as it is now believed were their Forward Operating Locations (FOLs), but the locations of the FOLs did not percolate down to the tasking cells at NORTHAG/2ATAF during the author's time – and this could have resulted in lost opportunities. More in hope than expectation, NATO fighter-bomber crews, *en route* to and from their primary targets, in addition to those on armed reconnaissance sorties, were required to report any sightings of these helicopters on the ground and, if they had enough fuel and weapons (cannon?) aboard, consider attacking them before they had time to disperse.

'Dumb' bombs, unguided rockets and cannon armament, generally the only 'conventional' air-to-ground weapons available early in the Cold War, could have had little effect against concrete runways, the best constructed HAS or hardened C3I centres, armour, shipping *et al*; so the race was soon on to develop new weapons. The Warsaw Pact tended to concentrate on a wide range of guided missiles, with radio, AR, IR or laser guidance, while in NATO they included special long range unguided rockets (eg. CVR-7), a variety of Precision Guided Munitions (PGMs), such as the 'Paveway' LGB, 'Maverick' and 'Sea Eagle'; together with runway cratering/airfield denial weapons, typically the RAF's JP233. When delivered precisely, the JP233 could render a runway temporarily unusable, while scattering a carpet of time-sensitive bomblets to delay its recovery and impede movements in the local area. Despite its theoretical value, the JP233 was not viewed with great favour by all pilots who had the unenviable task of delivering them along, or at a narrow angle to a runway, at very low level and high speed, probably at night, through a storm of LAA and small arms fire already zeroed in on the obvious approach lanes. This was bad enough in Iraq, but it would have been worse in Eastern Europe. Moreover, measures were soon in place to fill the resulting craters and clear the mines expeditiously from the surrounding area, thereby bringing the aircraft operating surfaces back quickly into use. All this, together with the redundancy of take-off/landing strips on most EGAF MOBs, the availability of reserve airstrips across the GDR and the ability of the MiGs to take off and land on grass – now casts some doubt on the merit of placing very high value NATO air assets at high risk to deliver JB233. Likewise, the wisdom of

targeting a HAS, with a CVR-7 or an expensive LGB, remained arguable, if only because it might be empty. Seeking alternatives to traditional means of attacking airfields, some in NATO turned their minds more to the use of stand-off weapons with warheads for specific purpose, against crucial but more vulnerable targets on MOBs: C3I sites, fuel installations, weapons storage and pilot rest areas, some of the latter known to be in 'soft' buildings just outside the airfield perimeters.

NATO also evaluated the concept of large, mixed force packages, incorporating as many as eight nations, sometimes mounted from several bases (as they would have attempted to do in war), in precisely timed, co-ordinated attacks – essentially against very high value targets. Force elements might include pre- and post-strike reconnaissance, SEAD aircraft, fighter escort with AEW or AWACS support, several strike components using stand-off and more conventional weapons, and airborne tankers. In these exercises, appropriate opposition was provided to simulate Warsaw Pact air and ground forces, and some of these exercises (e.g. Red Flag) were monitored by sophisticated battle assessment equipments. Realistically, their use in war would have depended on the availability of sufficient assets (in a degrading force) enough planning time, adequate communications and suitable weather – all together a tall order. The author was involved in several of these very impressive exercises; he noted their value in joint planning, standardisation, a cross-fertilisation of ideas and in building mutual confidence – but was concerned by some professional assessments of attrition rates and the many problems that were likely to occur when mounting such large operations in war. He concluded that they would rarely have been appropriate or practical in the operating environment which had to be expected. A paucity of resources was likely to add credence to the concept of repetitious, small-scale 'nuisance' raids, to cause some destruction but also continuous disruption, frustration and fatigue.

It follows that, for optimum results, raid plans and air launched weapons had to be matched appropriately against the targets selected, with careful consideration given to force levels, the effectiveness and vulnerability of the delivery profiles, skills which should have been practised frequently by battle management teams. However, it is by no means certain that all NATO partners recognised the imperative of selecting the right men for these teams – hence some disquiet among front line squadrons with the tasks they received from above. Accordingly, one RAF strike/attack wing took the unpopular step of diverting a nucleus of the best qualified, highly capable and current operational pilots from flying duties to monitor these tasks and act as final arbiters – in order to get the best out of the meagre air assets available. The team is unable to comment on the efficacy of the Warsaw Pact tasking and targeting system.

While the Warsaw Pact's dual policy of on-base protection and off-base dispersal in the GDR presented NATO with new problems, it also offered new opportunities. Be it exercise or war, it was common practice in the EGAF to deploy one or more of a wing's squadrons to a reserve airstrip (airfield or autobahn), before or at the outbreak of hostilities, creating lucrative and vulnerable 'soft' targets for all 2ATAF's fighter-bombers, tasked specifically or as targets of opportunity for aircraft on other sorties or armed reconnaissance. They could have achieved heavy damage with bombs, rockets or cannon fire, on grass runways, aircraft or support equipment found in the open but again, despite repeated requests, NORTHAG/2ATAF tasking cells were not made aware of the locations of such well used reserve airstrips as Alteno, Warbelow and Klein Koris (Chapter Three).

Consider a surprise attack by strong Warsaw Pact forces already stationed in the west of the GDR, on a weak sector of the IGB. The first Bundeswehr officers to gain access to Soviet and NVA army units after 3 October 1990, reported finding huge numbers of armoured fighting vehicles in the forward areas, fully fuelled and loaded with operational weapons, the advance units being ready to move out in 45 minutes and the remainder within two hours. Some had little more than 100 km (60 miles) to go to the IGB, while others were much closer, those 'exercising' on the Letzlinger Heide being only 25 miles (40 km) from what may have been a thinly held part of the IGB. The author himself, having served with the British Army, was able to cast a semi-professional eye over the huge Soviet and NVA barracks either side of Route 5, as he drove west out of Berlin in late 1990, and was staggered by the sight of so many of the latest Soviet tanks and other armoured vehicles in that enormous military complex. It has been said that Soviet and NVA units were known to have burst out of barracks, to head west at high speed on both sides of the autobahn, at night using side lights only, in radio silence and with scant regard for any other road traffic – but this has not been verified by a reliable source. Could it be that without 'definitive evidence' of these exercises from signals traffic, such visual warning signs were ignored – even in the knowledge that the Soviets (and hence the NVA) were good at moving at night and in radio silence? Was it conceivable that highly covert preparations could have masked plans to drive a wedge rapidly through a relatively weak sector of the IGB, through which follow-on forces could pour? Many NATO commanders argued at the time (and some still do), that such a suggestion failed to recognise the potential effectiveness of their intelligence organisation and contingency planning within NORTHAG/2ATAF's General Defence Plan (GDP). Perhaps so, but history is littered with the unexpected, and with the Warsaw Pact now known to have rehearsed exercise plans to that end, was the notion of a surprise attack so preposterous? Indeed, one NVA officer overheard a Russian general say, at the height of the Cold War in Strausberg: 'We could reach the coast of France before Tommy (British soldier) could tie his boot laces!' In this event, there is no doubt that all NATO strike/attack aircraft would have been needed urgently, initially using conventional weapons, to help 'put the cork back in the bottle', but would this have been enough, particularly if poor weather

had interfered with flying? Moreover, using all the fighter-bombers, of necessity, in this role could have forfeited their use against Warsaw Pact airfields and reinforcement routes, thereby giving the Pact's aircraft and ground forces more freedom to join the fray.

Taking this hypothetical scenario further, what if Soviet and NVA troops had managed to break through NORTHAG's forward defences and spread out in numbers on to the relatively good tank country of the North German Plain, and the West was unable to arrest their advance with conventional weapons? In the absence of a political solution, would this be the point at which NATO would need to resort to the use of nuclear weapons – or accept an equally unthinkable alternative? It is beyond the remit of this paper to discuss the procedures necessary in NATO to secure authority for the use of low-yield, ground-based nuclear mines, artillery rounds, bombs or tactical missiles, or the conditions which might have allowed such decisions to be delegated to lower levels of command. However, the author was familiar with the time taken in exercises to get authority from alliance members and the North Atlantic Council, for the use of airborne nuclear weapons, and wondered whether this might have come too late to have the effects required. It may be a fair assumption that the Russians, who would provide all their Warsaw Pact partners with tactical nuclear weapons, while retaining full authority, did not have to achieve a consensus on their use.

Taking one final step; what if a Warsaw Pact surprise offensive had started with the use of tactical nuclear weapons? Their armies were known to have rehearsed large scale military movements with all their armoured vehicles 'closed down' and their soldiers wearing full protective clothing – and might they have accepted heavy losses to make significant gains? Indeed, one of the most alarming discoveries from the Warsaw Pact archives and other primary sources, post-reunification, were exercise plans which postulated the use of these weapons at a very early stage, if not at the start of an offensive against the West. The article in Time Magazine draws on NVA documents which refer to an Exercise 'Waffenbruderschaft', in which Soviet and other Pact forces were notionally armed with 840 tactical nuclear weapons, using 320 on the first wave, against nuclear depots, air force and C3I facilities, naval bases and troop concentrations, primarily in West Germany. Marshal Viktor Kulikov, a high level Soviet commander in 1983, is quoted as saying: 'The future war will be conducted without compromise until the enemy is completely crushed, and this may require us to consider using the entire arsenal of weapons of annihilation'. Again, could surprise attacks on key airfields in the West, with nuclear or chemical weapons, have been decisive before authority was received to release, in kind, 2ATAF's retaliatory force? A surprise nuclear onslaught of this type, forward of advancing troops, could certainly have rendered the all-important reinforcement of NATO forces impracticable, if not superfluous. However, the NVA officers interviewed seemed genuinely unaware of any such ruthless intentions.

The disposition and condition of Warsaw Pact forces in the GDR, sight of their detailed exercise plans and the battle management facility at Strausberg, together with bellicose utterings of their military leaders and anecdotal evidence, suggest that the Warsaw Pact was ready, willing and able to mount a surprise attack on the FRG in North Germany, perhaps using nuclear weapons. However, the NATO hierarchy stuck to its guns, confident that there would be ample warning of an attack, and a useful period of conventional warfare to precede any employment of nuclear weapons. Perhaps they were right. Who knows?

Epilogue

God grants liberty only to those who love it and are always ready to defend it.

Daniel Webster

Of the mighty Soviet armies once resident on the front line in the GDR there is now little sign. Anything of practical value that could be moved from their numerous installations has been returned to the Soviet Union, with most of their airfields and buildings left to decay, their runways crumbling, many of the HAS and supporting facilities now almost concealed from the human eye by forestation and the natural growth around them. During this research, the author's team visited most of the major Soviet and NVA establishments, sometimes crawling under the wire and through the undergrowth into forsaken airfields, a somewhat eerie, almost sinister experience, but one which could be very revealing. Old newspapers and the domestic trappings of military life were found in a guardroom at Zerbst, while Soviet armour and military vehicles shared huge hangars at Damgarten with tired old GDR Trabants, and the walls of buildings at Parchim still sported white doves and incongruous messages of peace – in Russian. In many places, however, there are now increasing signs of life, the legacy of a war that never was, with diverse German indus-tries exploiting obvious opportunities, for farming, construction, excavation, storage and leisure (an impressive tropical facility within a huge plastic dome is now a centre-piece on the old airfield at Brand). Others, such as Parchim, Altenburg and Cochstedt are active airports, used by civilian airlines, private flying or gliding clubs.

More use has been made of the EGAF airfields, three of which still remain in military use, Laage for GAF Eurofighter Typhoons, Holzdorf for army helicopters and Neubrandenburg/Trollenhagen a transit and exercise base. Drewitz, Kamenz and Bautzen accommodate flying schools, commercial and club flying or various leisure pursuits, but Preschen lies dormant. Also, the former LSK/LV C3I bunker at Schönwalde, con-structed later than other GFS in the GDR, has been extensively refurbished and modified since reunification, to serve to this day as a CRC, now very well equipped and manned to display the current air situation over a wide area of Germany and to control elements of the air defence forces as required (e.g. QRA), in the unified Germany. Many more ex-military installations are homes to aviation museums, large and small, prominent among them being Gatow (Berlin), Peenemünde, Cottbus, Reclin, Merseberg, Finow, Drewitz, Neubrandenburg, Neuhardenburg, Rothenburg and Kolkwitz, all serving as salutary reminders of the Cold War, maintained and constantly enhanced with loving care by enthusiastic volunteers.

The RAF's significant contribution to 2ATAF in north Germany is remembered in one small museum at the former RAF Laarbruch, Goch, but additional evidence of a long presence on the Continent is also on show at national museums in Germany, Holland and Belgium – and in the United Kingdom.

'Thinking the Unthinkable' is not, and never could have been, an exhaustive, definitive thesis on the Cold War. Notwithstanding the depth of research, many important questions on the operational effectiveness of the EGAF and RAF in Germany remain unanswered. For instance, were the respective preparations for war based on sound perceptions of the threats; could the command and control organisations have survived the stresses and strains of war; were the tactics and training geared sufficiently to the threats; in particular, did low level operations receive the necessary priority in defence? All things considered, how significant was the disparity between the number of hours flown by NATO and Warsaw Pact pilots? Were the aircraft handled to the sensible limits of their performance, or were pilots constrained by over cautious handling restrictions – in the cause of peacetime flight safety? How effective would air weapons have been in the fog of war, launched in an ECM environment, and was sufficient attention given to aircraft survivability? Would many,

relatively simple aircraft, with inherent operating limitations, prevail over fewer, more sophisticated aircraft with greater operational capabilities? All 'Thinking the Unthinkable' can hope to have done is to provide food for thought, based on the memories and views of those who served in middle management and on the flight lines on the two sides of the Iron Curtain – views which may not accord with those within the 'establishments'.

Perhaps it is right to end with the comforting view, generally held, that despite some aggressive rhetoric over the years, the Cold War leaders in the East and the West understood fully the rationale of 'peaceful co-existence', and the dire consequences of an all-out nuclear war. Certainly, the Germans on both sides of the IGB knew that if all else failed WW3 was most likely to be fought in their divided country – a fate which neither side would have wished to contemplate – and that is why 'deterrence' was so important. There were, of course, times when brinkmanship might have got out of hand, especially when the East Germans began building the Berlin Wall in 1961, bringing Soviet and Allied tanks face-to-face across the demarcation line, and again in 1962 during the Cuban missile crisis, but in both cases the two sides sensibly held their fire. Had they not, and no immediate political settlement followed, a short period of conventional warfare might easily have drifted into the selected use of tactical nuclear weapons and an escalation into the full use of strategic weapons of mass destruction – with Armageddon then almost inevitable. But that would be 'thinking the unthinkable'.

Bibliography

Antonov, Vladimir: OKB Sukhoi; Midland Publishing, 1996

Belyakov & Marmain: MiG; Airlife, 1994

Billig, Detief & Meyer, Manfred: Flugzeuge der DDR, Band I – III,

Boyd, Alexander: The Soviet Air Force Since 1918; Purnell Book Services Ltd, 1977

Bußmann, Kleest & Freundt: Katapultieren Sie!; Aerolit2004

Feldmann and Zetsche: Das JaboG 43; AirDOC 2008

Fliegerhorst Trollenhagen; local publication.

Freundt & Büttner: Rote Plätze – Russische Militärflugplätze, Deutschland 1945–1994; Aerolit, 2004

Gent, C J van: East German Air Force, Final Flight Line; Airlife, 1993

Geraghty, Tony: BRIXMIS – The Untold Exploits; Harper Collins, 1996

Gibson: The Last Mission Behind the Iron Curtain; Sutton Publishing Ltd, 1997

Gordon, Yefim & Gunston, Bill: MiG-15,MiG-17, MiG-19, MiG-21 & Su-22; Midland; 2001–2004

Gungston, Bill & Gordon, Yefim: MiG Aircraft Since 1937; Putnam Aeronautical Books, 1998

Gungston, Bill: Encyclopedia of Russian Aircraft, 1875–1995; Osprey, 1995

Hackett, Sir John: The Third World War: A Future History; 1978

Hall, Ian: Tornado Times; 2 Group PRU, 1994

Kopenhagen, Wilfried: Die Andere Deutsche Luftwaffe; Transpress 1992

Kropf, Klaus: Jet-Geschwader im Aufbruch; VDM Heinz Nickel, 2003

Lang and Materna: Der Flugplatz Neuhardenberg-Marxwalde; Willmuth Arenhövel 2004

Lehrgang X In geheimer Mission an der Wolga – Baarß; E S Mittler & Son

Lindsay, Roger: Cold War Shield; Roger Lindsay, 2009

Mikoyan, Stepan; Mikoyan; Airlife Publishing Ltd, 1999

Molloy, Peter: The Lost World of Communism; BBC Books, 2009

Nijhuis, Hans: Final Touchdown; Concord Publications Ltd 962361703–8

Pitchfork, Air Cdre Graham: The Buccaneers; Patrick Stephens Ltd, 2002

Spur, Franz: Militär Transportflieger, Dessau-Dresden; Aerolit, 2002

Suvorov, Viktor: The Liberators, Inside the Soviet Army; Hamish Hamilton,1981

Sweetman, Bill: Soviet Military Aircraft; Hamlyn Publishing, 1981

Taylor, Bill: Royal Air Force Germany since 1945; Midland Publishing, 2003

Time International: July 4, 1994

Walker, AVM John: Air-To-Ground Operations; Brassey's, 1987

Walker, Martin: The Cold War; Fourth Estate Ltd; 1993

Willisch, Jürgen: MiG-21; Aeroflight, 2002

Willmann & Kopatz: Gefechtsbereit!; Militärverlag der DDR, 1984

Index

Lightning Source UK Ltd.
Milton Keynes UK
UKOW021819080712

195673UK00003B/10/P